John Huston's Filmmaking analyzes the career of one of cinema's most versatile artists. Lesley Brill argues that Huston created a body of work far richer than the formulaic stories of masculine failure with which he is often credited. Stylish, superbly scripted, and informed by a wry sense of humor, Huston's films portray characters who attempt to conceive their identities. His work consistently returns to questions of love and mortality; of happiness and home; of society and the individual; and of the connections among what one of his most famous characters called "the Lord or fate or nature."

John Huston's
Filmmaking

Cambridge Studies in Film

General Editors:
William Rothman, University of Miami
Dudley Andrew, University of Iowa

Other Books in the Series

John Huston's Filmmaking

LESLEY BRILL

Wayne State University

CAMBRIDGE
UNIVERSITY PRESS

PUBLISHED BY THE PRESS SYNDICATE OF THE UNIVERSITY OF CAMBRIDGE
The Pitt Building, Trumpington Street, Cambridge CB2 1RP, United Kingdom

CAMBRIDGE UNIVERSITY PRESS
The Edinburgh Building, Cambridge CB2 2RU, United Kingdom
40 West 20th Street, New York, NY 10011–3211, USA
10 Stamford Road, Oakleigh, Melbourne 3166, Australia

First published 1997

Printed in the United States of America

Typeset in Sabon

Library of Congress Cataloging-in-Publication Data
Brill. Lesley, 1943–

John Huston's filmmaking / Lesley Brill.

p.   cm. – (Cambridge studies in film)
Includes bibliographical references and index.
ISBN 0-521-58359-4 (hardcover). – ISBN 0-521-58670-4 (pbk.)
1. Huston, John, 1906– – Criticism and interpretation.
I. Title. II. Series.
PN1998.3.H87B76   1997
791.43'0233'092 – dc21   96-47927
CIP

*A catalog record for this book is available from
the British Library.*

ISBN 0 521 58359 4 hardback
ISBN 0 521 58670 4 paperback

For Megan,
and for Ben and Calista

Contents

Illustrations

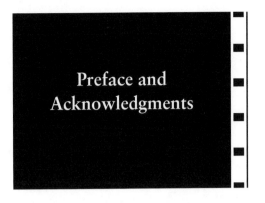

Preface and Acknowledgments

Bergman	Hitchcock	Lang
Dreyer	Huston	Murnau
Eisenstein	Kubrick	Satyajit Ray
Griffith	Kurosawa	Renoir

An alphabetized list of celebrated directors, plausibly someone's favorite dozen on a given day in a certain mood – a list for making conversation at a dull reception after a lecture, in a traffic jam, or for an earnest student. But "one of these things," as they used to sing on "Sesame Street," "doesn't belong": Huston. Few academic film scholars would insert *that* name into such a small pantheon. Those who have made movies themselves might, and those who simply watch them. And I.

Because most of Huston's films have had relatively little extended analysis, the exploration of his authorship that follows is embodied chiefly in essays on a dozen of his movies. I have chosen works that are among Huston's more commonly shown (with a few exceptions). As a result, a number of his most accomplished and interesting films are considered only in passing: *Moulin Rouge, The List of Adrian Messenger, A Walk with Love and Death, The Kremlin Letter, The Life and Times of Judge Roy Bean, Wise Blood, Under the Volcano*. As Huston's work returns to currency, one trusts that these superb movies will get some of the attention they deserve.

Like that of other auteurs of commercial films, Huston's authorship is a complex matter. It extends from his own talents as a writer, visual artist, actor, casting agent, director of actors, and editor to the leadership required for all collaborative undertakings that incorporate the contributions of many people while sustaining a unified objective. Huston's film authorship is affected both by his professional origins in Hollywood and by the fact that he was among the first major filmmakers to move from the great studios to the semi-independent production that became increasingly common in the American film industry. I hope that my discussions of Huston's movies will make clear – perhaps chiefly by implication – that he was a remarkably effective artistic manager as well as a creator of great personal gifts.

Most books are also collaborative enterprises, and this one owes much to many people. Errors of fact, infelicities of expression, and implausibilities of argument are mine alone. Megan Parry commented helpfully upon the entire typescript, as did William Rothman. Various sections were sympathetically read by Stephen Cooper, Marian Keane, James Kincaid, Sue Palmer, James Palmer, Steve Rosen, and George Toles; thanks to all of them for their encouragement. Similar thanks to my amiable colleagues in Film Studies at Wayne State University and to the students with whom I studied Huston's films at Wayne State, the University of Colorado, and the Université de Nantes. James Boyer and Mary Iverson assisted with frame enlargements, and Norman Holland kindly supplied a videotape of the first release version of *Freud*. Lou Ellen Kramer and others at UCLA made available rare prints and videotapes on which Huston worked in a variety of capacities. Sam Gill and Ed Carter at the Margaret Herrick Library of the Academy of Motion Picture Arts and Sciences were energetic in giving me access to a wide range of unique Huston materials. Walter Havighurst was a resourceful copy editor. Leaves and other financial support from Wayne State University provided crucial time and resources for my research. Earlier versions of the discussions of *The Misfits* and *The African Queen* appeared in *Proteus* and *Cinema Journal*. Finally, I am happy to recall three gracious friends and teachers whose memory animates this book and its author: John Hagopian, Claude Richard, and Steve Rosen.

John Huston's
Filmmaking

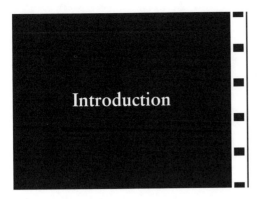

Introduction

I'll be happy to be called what I am and for who I am – nobody's man.

John Huston[1]

A bad job for cinema auteurists, John Huston. A chameleon, taking on the coloration of whatever subject he decided to film, usually someone's novel about some man's screw-up. Nothing more consistent or characteristic, no personal theme beyond masculine failure, no recognizable visual style. A director without direction. Huston himself agreeing with his commentators: no "special message to convey," no aesthetic or philosophic obsessions.[2]

Just enormous talent and secure judgment for telling a lively story, for keeping those high-strung racehorses, movie stars, running the course, for making hits and coming back from duds with more hits. An artistic administrator, steering film companies through the chaos of cinematic production, using whatever it takes – literary talent, personal charm, empathy with horses and other beasts, being mysterious, being male, being lucky.

In sum, the best and least lovable qualities of the American movie industry personified. A corporation in himself of discipline and connections and technical smarts. After hours a pop-press feast of marriages and divorces, seas of alcohol, fist fights, practical jokes, name-brand friends, outspoken social views. And in the neighborhood theaters something easy to sell, something well tailored, sharply pressed, with cleanly turned seams, but maybe as generic and devoid of individuality as most of the Hollywood ready-made wardrobe. Spiritless stuff shaped not by writers, producers, directors, or cinematographers so much as by the publicity departments and stars of gargantuan companies: Warner Bros., MGM, Universal, Columbia, Twentieth Century Fox.

Accounts like this have seemed plausible to most people who think about Huston, or who thought about him for a while and then went on to think about something else during his long, swift-steady gallop through a film career of half a century. But spend a few hundred hours

1

looking again at his thirty-seven feature-length films and the gospel about him begins to ring stupidly inadequate. Obscure movies like *In This Our Life* ('42) and *A Walk with Love and Death* ('69), all-but-forgotten ones like *Moulin Rouge* ('53) and *Heaven Knows, Mr. Allison* ('57), wrenching ones like *The Kremlin Letter* ('70), *Reflections in a Golden Eye* ('67), *Wise Blood* ('79), and *Under the Volcano* ('84), or exuberant, chaotic-looking ones like *Beat the Devil* ('54) and *The Life and Times of Judge Roy Bean* ('72) turn out to be as rich, superbly crafted, and thoughtful as *The Treasure of the Sierra Madre* ('48), *The African Queen* ('51), *The Man Who Would Be King* ('75), or *Prizzi's Honor* ('85), itself a playful recollection of *The Maltese Falcon* ('41). All sharp, strange, and exciting. All with stories, themes, and a style that one begins to recognize as Hustonian.

This book describes significant tendencies in films directed by John Huston. For me, Huston's movies have a coherence-in-diversity, profundity, and artistic energy that place their director among the greatest movie makers. At the same time, I do not believe that the excellence of an artist can be shown directly, and I propose to make no systematic arguments for Huston's aesthetic excellence, social usefulness, political appeal, or genius. Those judgments are matters of taste and, as the old saw has it, not amenable to reasoned dispute.

Identification of the deep consistency of Huston's work is difficult. But once we have managed to penetrate the polished surfaces of his movies and to articulate their stylistic and thematic repetitions, we find in them a rich and coherent artistic configuration. If my sense of Huston's range and versatility is accurate, no single commentary on his work could be comprehensive. I do not make that claim here. My study addresses, mostly through detailed analyses of about one-third of his films, clusters of prevalent themes, images, and techniques. Its delineation of Huston's artistic personality is embodied principally in discussions of specific works. Many of Huston's predilections may also be seen in his early work as a screenwriter, but the movies he directed constitute the main subject of this study. In *An Open Book*, his 1980 autobiography, he wrote, "Always and forever, I'm a director."[3]

As a cinematic administrator and craftsman, Huston's reputation has been beyond dispute. His talent for making critical and box-office hits allowed him as many projects as he had time, inclination, and financial need to undertake. His commercial and artistic résumé – along with a determination forged from early misfortunes with studio executives and intrusive actors – won him considerable artistic freedom in bringing films to conclusion. From the beginning of his career, he was recognized as an eloquent story-teller, an inspired caster of actors, and a director who could induce strong performances from mediocre players and superb performances from good ones. If his films have not been seen as having *a* style, there has never been any doubt about their having style generally, and technical polish, and a vigor that reliably led to profits. Before production, he had a talent for promotion; in a press conference he was capable of upstaging everyone, including his famous actresses and actors.

Given his five-decade career among the first rank of Hollywood filmmakers, the distinction of his collaborators, and his remarkable number of celebrated films, Huston would seem to invite scholarly attention. But though he inspired considerable interest in popular media, his work has been the object of little extended commentary. What there is, moreover, has largely concentrated on his first and fourth films, *The Maltese Falcon* and *The Treasure of the Sierra Madre*. *Freud* ('62) has also attracted explication during the last decade. Meanwhile, *The African Queen*, *The Asphalt Jungle* ('50), *Beat the Devil*, *The Misfits* ('61), *Reflections in a Golden Eye*, *Fat City* ('72), *The Man Who Would Be King*, and a few others hover somewhere between cult films and perennial favorites, maintaining popular visibility if only limited critical or scholarly currency. As for the remaining twenty or twenty-five, they're not quite gone and not quite forgotten but not often the stuff of festival revivals or journal articles, either. In Europe, perhaps, Huston's reputation among film scholars has been somewhat higher, despite his exclusion by most of the *Cahiers du Cinema* auteurists from lists of favored *réalisateurs*. The most illuminating consideration of his films to date is a monograph-length essay by Richard T. Jameson of England; the biographical-critical studies of Robert Benayoun in France should also be counted among the most insightful and careful writings on Huston.[4] Books published in the United States by Kaminsky, Hammen, McCarty, and others have considerable useful information but offer only brief analyses of the films.

As a result of the neglect of Huston's oeuvre, we know little of the sources and main features of his artistic coherence, his thematic and stylistic range as it was inscribed across thirty-seven films. His critical history, to quote Jameson, "derives mainly from the fact that his films have been both celebrated and derided for maddeningly wrong reasons, having more to do with prevailing critical fashion than with the inherent qualities of his art."[5]

There have been recent indications that Huston's reputation may be ready to move from among the penny stocks onto more expensive lists:

an issue of a periodical devoted to his career, a lengthy biography of his family, two collections of essays and documents about Huston and his films.[6] These seem little enough for a director of his range and skill. Moreover, one of the recent collections on Huston – published with the fashionably dreary title of *Reflections in a Male Eye* – rarely makes auteurist gestures toward its subject. To its contemporary contributors, Huston appears less as the author of creative works than as an exemplar of social and economic conditions in Hollywood and beyond. "Huston's films offer a lesson in the economic, ideological, and historically specific contexts that shaped American filmmaking practice."[7] Though this volume reprints older essays and reviews that celebrate the strength and distinctiveness of Huston's art, few of the modern commentators, whose essays constitute the larger part of the collection, appear willing to grant him artistic majority.

Why has Huston's artistic personality gone more or less unremarked for so long? Briefly, his neglect seems to be a consequence partly of the history of taste and fashion among critics and academics in film studies, and partly of a stylistic finish so smooth and self-effacing that it conceals its remarkable art as straightforward, generic story-telling (if such a thing exists). Huston's art looks to us, I suspect, as Shakespeare's did to his contemporaries: like nature itself. Furthermore, the ethnic, national, sexual, and class politics of Huston's films – with a few politically charged exceptions like *We Were Strangers* ('49), *The Roots of Heaven* ('58), and *Under the Volcano* – tend to be implicit and liberal. Neither of those qualities recommends his work to politicized critics. His reputation as a masculinist filmmaker, the purveyor of what Molly Haskell called "The male Huston world-view, bleak and sardonic," has been equally unenticing to such commentators.[8] Whatever the reasons, Huston has been banished, largely by silence, from most film critics' pantheons of directors.

Finally, the dearth of sophisticated commentary on his movies also has to do with a general perception that Huston is a director without consistent themes or a recognizable style, a director without an artistic personality of his own. In interviews, Huston tended to imply that he had few pretensions beyond the commercial virtues of creating visual interest and telling a good story entertainingly.[9] On the other hand, he did acknowledge that his work may have a sort of second-order consistency. When asked, "Do you feel you are trying to say something coherent to mankind?," Huston answered, "There probably is. I am not consciously aware of anything. But even the choice of material indicates a preference, a turn of mind. You could draw a portrait of a mind through that mind's preferences."[10] To Peter S. Greenberg, he spoke somewhat less conditionally: "A deep analysis [of my film career] would probably reveal the real continuity, the deep current of intention. . . . I didn't say *I* know what they are."[11]

The accepted view of Huston's career, however, seems to be that the texture, shape, and thematic content of his movies have been determined by the novels he converted to film. James Agee, in his enormously influential 1950 *Life* magazine portrait, established this understanding: "Each of Huston's pictures has a visual tone and style of its own, dictated to his camera by the story's essential content and spirit."[12] The continuing power of Agee's assessment is symptomatic of the critical neglect of the director's middle and late career. Thirty-five years after the article in *Life*, Scott Hammen still echoes Agee when he writes that "To apply the term *Hustonian* with any consistency even to the films Huston directed is difficult."[13]

There have been notable dissenters from the dominant story of Huston-the-styleless, the authorial cipher. James Naremore declares, "while many people deserve credit for the success of *The Maltese Falcon*, its special quality owes chiefly to John Huston's style, a style so recognizable and individual that it is anything but the sign of a 'competent craftsman.'"[14] He characterizes Huston's method by contrasting it with Dashiell Hammett's: "Hammett's art is minimalist and deadpan, but Huston, contrary to his reputation, is a highly energetic and expressive storyteller who likes to make comments through his images."[15] Jameson agrees with Naremore not only in asserting that there is such a thing as a Hustonian style but also in characterizing some of its particulars. In *Treasure*, he argues, "Huston's realism is in fact covertly, seamlessly expressionistic."[16] More generally, "while he has a genius for truly and faithfully rendering the literary originals in motion-picture form, at the same time his own personality has so pervaded and illuminated the material that the designation 'a film of John Huston' is fully validated."[17]

To my knowledge, at least thirty-four of Huston's thirty-seven feature films derive directly from novels, stories, or plays. He dealt with some literary properties quite freely, but usually he worked with literature for which he had a respect that led him to preserve on screen the virtues he found on the page. Perhaps the most resourceful adapter of complex literary texts in the history of American and British cinema, he began as a director with a film based on a book that accomplished directors had already screened twice, Hammett's *The Maltese Falcon* (1930); but he made it for the first time a critical and box-office success.[18] It is difficult to imagine any other director (with the possible exception of Stanley Kubrick) transforming works so effectively from such a wide variety of writers: B. Traven, Stephen Crane, C. S. Forester, Herman Melville, Tennessee Williams, Flannery O'Connor, Malcolm Lowry, and James Joyce, among others. And it is difficult to imagine anyone else getting certain of his originals on the screen with any success at all. *Wise Blood, Under the Volcano*, and *The Dead* ('87) are bravura adaptations to film of works manifestly resistant to such translation. Kipling's "The Man Who Would Be King" occasioned another conversion of real virtuosity. It is an unusually elliptical, compressed, and nonvisual story, especially for that writer, but Huston successfully expanded and translated it into the medium of motion pictures, while at the same time remaining faithful to most of its details and its precarious tone.

Huston began in the movies as a writer of screenplays. Among his credits are such strong and commercially successful scripts as *Jezebel, Juarez, Dr. Ehrlich's Magic Bullet, High Sierra*, and *Sergeant York*; and he worked with top directors at Warner Bros.: William Wyler, Anatole Litvak, William Dieterle, Raoul Walsh, and Howard Hawks. He has spoken of the intimate connection between writing and directing: "There's really no difference between them, it's an extension, one from the other. Ideally I think the writer should go on and direct the picture. I think of the director as an extension of the writer."[19]

I am not going to argue for the "development" of John Huston from writer to director, or as a director, though I believe that his movies become denser and richer, more assured and fluent, as he matures in his profession. In particular the editing, *mis en scène*, and writing of his films seem to me to become more resonant between *The Maltese Falcon* and, say, *Freud*. But this is a highly subjective judgment and there are undeniable exceptions to it. In any event, Huston was thirty-five when he directed his first film and he had been in and around show business and other arts all his life. When he returned from World War II to pick up the career that he would follow for the next thirty-nine years, he was forty years old. From the start of his directorial career, then, Huston was a relatively mature artist. If he did not spring fully formed from the head of Zeus, most of his parts were in place from his remarkable debut, and virtually all of the main ideas, aesthetic tendencies, and complications of his cinematic world are identifiable in the pictures of his first decade as a director. Thematic emphases change from film to film; genres are taken up, dropped, returned to, parodied; technical opportunities and interests evolve. But Huston's work exhibits most of its multifaceted coherences without fundamental change through time.

"Fashioning human nature," wrote Benayoun, "is Huston's main occupation."[20] Fashioning their own natures is the main occupation of his central characters. In virtually all of his films, Huston chronicles his protagonists' attempts to discover, create, or recover themselves, to conceive and articulate their identities. Their quests for self are often embodied in the most time-honored of metaphoric vehicles, the adventurous journey – films like *The Treasure of the Sierra Madre, Moby Dick* ('56), *A Walk with Love and Death*, or *The Man Who Would Be King*. Implicit in early works like *The Maltese Falcon, In This Our Life*, and *Key Largo* ('48), themes of identity continue to dominate at the end of Huston's career in *Prizzi's Honor* and *The Dead*. Near the center of his forty-six years as a director, he explicitly addresses questions of who we are and how we create ourselves in *Freud*, "an intellectual suspense story."[21] He follows that tightly packed, difficult film with a breezy semi-comic meditation on related themes of self-creation and the revealing lies that we tell each other in *The List of Adrian Messenger* ('63), another suspense/detective story. Very variously, Huston's other movies also incorporate insistent querying of the processes by which humans create their identities. *Moulin Rouge* portrays Toulouse-Lautrec's recovery of himself and his place in society through art; *The Kremlin Letter* and *Under the Volcano* dramatize the pains of self-loss or self-abandonment. Diverse as Huston's pictures are in other respects, they may be seen from perhaps the most comprehensive perspective as returning to fundamental questions of identity and individual integrity.

Huston directly addressed the idea of happiness – both good fortune and abiding pleasure – in his long-suppressed documentary of an Army psychiatric hospital, *Let There Be Light* ('46, released '80). The definition of human fulfillment embodied in it, "the ability to give love and to receive it," occupies the center of fiction movies like *The Misfits* and *The Night of the Iguana* ('64).[22] In some of Huston's films, however, love comes into conflict with personal integrity or with the protagonists' places in their cultures. *The Barbarian and the Geisha* ('58), *Heaven Knows, Mr. Allison*, and *The Unforgiven* ('60) make such conflicts central.

Selfhood, happiness, and love are intimately connected to the idea of home, a congenial place among other people and in the world. Huston seemed to regard "being at home as the full achievement of identity" (as

Hayden White once put it).[23] Quests for homes of one kind or another are nearly as pervasive in Huston's films as quests for identity and love, and they are often portrayed as practically equivalent.

Enlarged and extended through time, a home becomes a group, then a society. Huston's films give emphasis to one of the historically dominant issues of narrative, the relation between individuals and their cultures. As far as Huston is concerned, everyone needs other people; there is no future for the class of individuals to which Ahab assigns Moby Dick, "the great solitaries and hermits." His films are imbued with consciousness of the extent to which culture determines the lives and personalities of individual human beings. The exotic settings of his movies bring together cultures that are partly incomprehensible to each other, a clash underscored by frequently untranslated foreign-language dialogue.

The encompassing subcategories of class, historical moment, and ethnicity (or, rarely, race) also have recurrent importance. Gender, a preoccupation in academia for the past fifteen or twenty years, gets less attention than culture and history. Despite the insistence of commentators and biographers on Huston's masculinity, his films do not often emphasize distinctions between living as a female and as a male. (*The Dead* and *The Life and Times of Judge Roy Bean*, to a greater degree than most of Huston's other movies, differentiate men and women.) Culture, class, and ethnicity, however, frequently obstruct or abridge the capacity of Huston's characters to create their identities and discover their humanity. Whether in the majority of films that have significant female characters or the few that do not, gender rarely plays such a role.

The people that Huston portrays are often as complex as their worlds. With the exceptions of a few films in which the clear moral separations of romance prevail – *The African Queen* or *Annie* ('82), for example – Huston's audience is neither invited to side exclusively with his protagonists nor discouraged from sympathizing with antagonists. Commentators have discovered in the most famous of Huston's heroes, Sam Spade, everything from a spiteful sociopath obsessed with insecurity about his masculinity to a self-sufficient, stylish hero of unimpeachable integrity. (Huston himself has attracted a similar spectrum of characterizations.) One could expect as much disagreement about other Huston figures as about Spade, if they were to receive as much critical attention; for such disputes reflect characters' variegated qualities, which will appear predominant in turn according to the directions from which critics approach.

In most of Huston's films, humanity, the natural world, and divinity are intertwined; what characters can become is determined by all three, which are both within and outside them. To seek one's self in Huston's films is to seek the truth of the world. Dismaying discoveries of vanity, corruption, and weakness are inevitable; strength and courage consist in facing and accepting the profound limitations of human life without despair or resignation.

Responding during a visit to Huston's Irish home to an interviewer's question about "her duty as a writer," Carson McCullers gave an answer that the director found memorable enough to repeat in his autobiography: "Writing, for me, is a search for God."[24] Making films, for Huston, seems to have constituted a similar search for divinity, which he sought in fate, the natural world, and humanity. Several years before McCullers's visit, while working on *The Bible . . . In the Beginning* ('66), Huston remarked, "I believe that all man builds, creates or constructs is religious. . . . The only religion in which I can believe is creation."[25] Huston's films generally show little fondness for institutionalized religion, setting it in opposition to private, personal piety and the godhead to be found in individual human beings. The divinity of self-creation is central to *The Man Who Would Be King*, *The Life and Times of Judge Roy Bean*, *Moby Dick*, and, tragicomically, *Wise Blood*. The aesthetic distance and objectivity that become increasingly distinctive as Huston's career proceeds reflect at once his skepticism and his reverence toward the universe and toward human life.

In any single movie, Huston attempted to subordinate all formal aspects to its particular quest, to what Huston called "the idea" of the film.[26] Across his work as a whole, a solar system of identifiably Hustonian imagery, situations, figures, actions, and attitudes revolves around the central ideas to which he repeatedly returns. We have already noted plots that take the form of quests, exotic settings, and strikingly individualized, complex characters. Add to them a sympathy for the natural world; the capacious symbolism of sky, earth, water, and fire; Huston's inclination to find in the extreme and eccentric the universally human; and an empathy for weakness or futility joined with a deep respect for the pertinacity of anyone who remains upright, who survives. The Hustonian also includes smaller, more particular stylistic and thematic tendencies: the association of mirrors with falsehood or deception, a fondness for opening shots that end by panning down from the sky, a penchant for striking introductory shots of major characters, and so on. Out of such materials, Huston constructs narratives of people who struggle, who occasionally win outright, who manage an unlikely draw (*Vic-*

tory, '81), or who in losing still win. His stories mean the world, as we say, and require the best possible telling. Hence the importance of his meticulousness, the combination of vividness and exactitude that he required of his pictures.

It is possible for a director to make a strong, original film or two without the kind of formal engagement and ingenuity that Huston brought to his art. But few directors have been able to sustain significant careers without absorbing themselves in all the possibilities of their medium. Prolific filmmakers who have created bodies of work at once coherent and varied evolve as artists through their ongoing fascination with the formal qualities of story, camera, sound, light, and editing as much as through recurrent ideas and feelings. Without formal inventiveness, a filmmaker who tells similar stories over and over will seem less an author than an automaton.

Huston's cinematic contemplations of the paradoxes of heroic successes and failures make up one of his central aesthetic (as well as thematic) preoccupations. Most of his other recurrent formal concerns – his interests in color and composition within the frame, for example – are also linked with the thematic content of his stories. Still others belong to a dimension of film that we understand and talk about with difficulty, its momentary patterns and its abstract rhythms of image, movement, and sound.

An accomplished, lifelong painter, sketcher, and art collector, Huston brought to his films a visual resourcefulness and literacy evident from the graphic energy and precision of *The Maltese Falcon* to the casual mastery of the *tableaux vivants* of *The Dead*. Unfortunately, the difficulty of viewing many of Huston's films in the form in which he composed them handicaps our understanding and appreciation of his visual art. Prints that retain the painstaking alterations of the usual palette of Technicolor cinematography in *Moulin Rouge, Moby Dick*, and *Reflections in a Golden Eye* are generally unavailable; indeed, the desaturated color version of the last may survive only in a single reel. Only slightly more accessible are the widescreen versions in which Huston made two-thirds of the films of his last thirty years. Despite this impoverishment of his oeuvre, however, we can still find in the standardized versions of his pictures inventive, systematic use of color and light/darkness. His expressive disposition of figures and other elements within the frame, his consciousness of the implications of characters' movements into and out of the picture and toward or away from each other also remain evident.

Huston handles entrances and exits with a deftness and wit, especially in his earlier films, that testifies to his background in theater. As his instincts increasingly become those of film, editing and camera work supply more of the fluidity and connective tissue for his stories. But the techniques of the stage never wholly disappear from Huston's creative repertoire, and those of cinema are present from the beginning. As early as 1950, Manny Farber was attacking Huston with complaints about the influence of Von Stroheim and Eisenstein and about the hyperactivity of Huston's "vitaminized photographer."[27] Although Farber's attacks are overheated, his observation raises an apposite point: Huston's editing, wherever he learned it, has great importance for the emotional and rhetorical rhythms of his pictures. Whether building a story toward a climax or an anti-climax, treading water or erupting, Huston loads much of the sense and sensuality of his filmmaking into connections between shots. Editing was largely his responsibility; by many accounts, including his own, Huston did most of his editing in the camera during shooting.

And before filming, during the writing and revising of the script. For Huston was always a writer as well as a painter. Whether he took a screenwriting credit or not, it seems certain that he participated extensively in the screenplays of virtually all his films. His writing, like the other formal aspects of his filmmaking, is subordinated to his movies as total entities and has a skill and grace that conceals deftness rather than flaunting it. At moments of greatest intensity and significance, Huston's writing is plainest, least adorned by rhetorical or poetic decoration; it is closest to a transparent medium through which the hearts of his characters can be seen in their ordinary human vulnerability and grandeur.

Qualities of character and outcomes of action approach inseparability. As David Bordwell argues, action as a function of character is a dominant attribute of the classic Hollywood cinema.[28] As a screenwriter at Warner Bros. in 1940, Huston already had a strong conception of the link between fictional personality and narrative consequences. Writing to Hal Wallis about his adaptation of W. R. Burnett's novel for the movie *High Sierra*, he emphasized his desire to retain "the strange sense of inevitability that comes with our deepening understanding of the characters and the forces that motivate them."[29]

Though his literary talents and his experience as a studio writer converge in his classicism, Huston rarely simply refashions old formulae. Improvising on standard generic conventions, he turns them upside down and parodies them as often as he works straightforwardly within them. He is characteristically playful and inventive within the forms of narrative that he inherits from literature and drama, from the writers, directors, and producers of Warner Bros., and from film at large.

The son (and later the father) of a distinguished actor, Huston was on stage at age three and intermittently performed in theater or films for his entire life. Assessments of his acting vary greatly, but his casting and directing of actors are generally accorded praise. Even Andrew Sarris (long Huston's detractor, though he warmed toward him late in both their careers) grudgingly gave him credit for "casting coups."[30] Whatever one may think of John Huston's own acting, he had intimate knowledge of what actors do and need.

As a filmmaker, then, Huston brought a broad and pertinent array of developed talents to his career: writer, painter, theatrical and cinematic actor. All gave him deep understanding of the verbal, visual, choreographic, and gestural aspects of movies. The music tracks seem to me to gradually strengthen and become strong additions to the writing, direction of cast, and visual composition that the director did so well from the beginning.

Huston approached all his films, even the saddest or most ironic, with a sense of humor and playfulness. One is tempted to speak of his instinct for wit, incongruity, and mimicry as leavening the loaves of his art, but that would understate its importance. We may extend to Huston's attitude toward existence the words of his father (as Howard) in *Treasure*: "It's a great joke played on us by the Lord or fate or nature, whatever you prefer." Howard's Olympian laughter proclaims that appreciating the joke liberates us. From the savvy, wry theatricality with which Spade and his adversaries divert each other, the roars of laughter that Howard delivers both upon finding and upon losing a fortune, and the belated adolescent high spirits that Hepburn's Rose and Bogart's Charlie find in love, through the oversized ebullience of Peachy and Danny in *The Man Who Would Be King* and of Judge Roy Bean, the picaresque satire of *Sinful Davey* ('69), the weirdness of *Wise Blood*, and the discrepant mixture of naivete and corruption in the protagonists of *Prizzi's Honor*, Huston's sense of the self-contradictions and vanities of life expresses itself in amusement. Not always, of course, in laughter. Traces of his antic muse vary from the hardly perceptible to the blatant, from the slightest hint of skepticism about stories or characters to the broad parody that makes up the whole of *Beat the Devil*. Huston's sense of humor and play define his apprehension of the universe and of humankind, of the gloriousness and futility of people's desires and creations. It is perfused by what Camus and other existentialists called the absurd, the incongruous discovery of dignity in humiliation, optimism in hopelessness, purpose in a meaningless world. It compendiates truths and the impossibility of finding a transcendent Truth. Above all, Huston's playful amusement with the world, other people, and himself expresses his sense of human community in shared fate.

The end of that shared fate is death, the most pervasive and intricately inflected of Huston's subjects. "One by one," Gabriel muses in *The Dead*, "we are all becoming shades." His words, at the conclusion of the last movie of Huston's career and the end of his life, acknowledge the source of vanity and despair that human consciousness must unavoidably confront. But facing death liberates us, invites us to play our games and multiple roles with all possible spirit, and with the consolation that if nobody escapes our common end, no one faces it singularly.

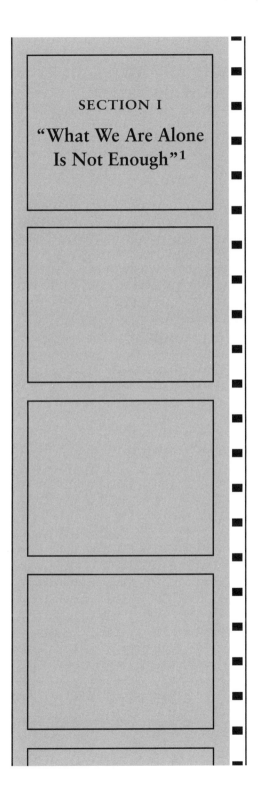

SECTION I

"What We Are Alone Is Not Enough"[1]

*The Treasure of the
Sierra Madre*

*The Man Who Would
Be King*

The African Queen

Opposing outcomes are expressed in The Treasure of the Sierra Madre *through a traditional contrast between the demonic and the innocent.*

Huston's fourth feature movie and the first he directed after World War II, *The Treasure of the Sierra Madre* constructs patterns of story and image that recur across Huston's career. It explores characteristic Hustonian themes about personal choice and the possibilities of living honestly and satisfyingly with other people. At the same time, it scrutinizes the contingencies and limits of freedom and embodies an often ironic meditation on wealth.

Like the boll weevil of Leadbelly's song, most of Huston's protagonists spend themselves, sometimes deviously or unconsciously, looking for a

17

home. In *Treasure*, Howard (Walter Huston) and Curtin (Tim Holt) labor toward that goal quite explicitly. Dobbs (Humphrey Bogart), on the other hand, seeks wealth only for economic power – a reductive understanding of human relationships that leads inevitably to his murder. Cody (Bruce Bennett) leaves his home and family in search of the wrong treasure and, like Dobbs, he pays with his life.

The novel of B. Traven in which Huston found the story of his film announces its central irony with a curiously awkward epigraph: "*The treasure which you think not worth taking trouble and pains to find, this one alone is the real treasure you are longing for all your life. The glittering treasure you are hunting for day and night lies buried on the other side of that hill yonder.*"[1] In the letter Cody's wife writes about family, marriage, and home, Huston's film describes its "real treasure." The letter does not appear in Traven's novel; from Huston's insertion of it we can infer its importance. Howard and Curtin read it aloud just after Cody's death and their own miraculous rescue, a placement that increases its poignancy.

Little Jimmy is fine, but he misses his daddy almost as much as I do. . . . I've never thought any material treasure, no matter how great, is worth the pain of these long separations. . . . The country is especially lovely this year. . . . I do hope you are back for the harvest. . . . remember we've already found life's real treasure. Forever yours, Helen.

Commenting on Huston's adaptation of his novel, Traven urged that

after you have run the credit title you offer the audience the same introduction the book has, that is: The real and genuine treasure you are hunting and also the ideal happiness are always and forever on the other side of the mountain – but if you prefer, offer it in the same wording as you find in the book. . . .[2]

Traven's desire to include the epigraph testifies to his sympathy with Huston's emphasis on the clash of gold with the real treasure of affectionate human relationships. In a subsequent letter, Traven suggested adding the scene in which Curtin hesitates before entering the collapsed mine to rescue Dobbs.[3] This addition, which Huston made, further emphasizes the conflict between gold and emotional commitments.

Communities extend the bonds of families and friendships. In *Treasure*, the Indian village represents an idealized, almost prelapsarian society. When Howard is forced to return to the village to receive its gratitude for reviving an unconscious Indian boy, Huston begins the sequence with a crane shot that he will practically duplicate for the openings of *The African Queen* and *The Barbarian and the Geisha* ('58). The camera tracks through a lush forest canopy then pans to the ground, the site of human activities. In *Treasure*, it comes to rest on Howard, luxuriating in a hammock, a young woman attending him. Behind, children splash in a pond. These archetypal images introduce themes of primitive innocence and human harmony to which Huston will return for the next four decades.

Variants of the shot of playing children in other Huston movies contrast native bathers with outsiders who observe but remain aloof. Such sequences participate in a larger motif of life-giving waters, a motif prominent in *Treasure* and one that Huston uses symbolically throughout his career. Dobbs and Curtin are washing at a fountain when they decide to ask Howard to join them in prospecting. Later, when they become euphoric over a vein of fool's gold, Howard advises his greenhorn partners, "next time you fellas strike it rich holler for me, will you, before you start splashin' water around? Water's precious; sometimes it can be more precious than gold." Similar emotional overtones attach to water when the three miners cluster hopefully around the pan in which Howard is washing gold ore and when Curtin first opens the sluice gate at the mine.

Huston's next movie, *Key Largo*, takes place in a marine environment so important that it practically figures as another protagonist. Like *Treasure*, *Key Largo* is set among Indians who live very differently from the Americans who have disrupted their world. Four more films Huston made in the next ten years, *We Were Strangers*, *Beat the Devil*, *Moby Dick*, and *The Barbarian and the Geisha*, have similar harbor settings associated with exotic cultures. The Ulanga in *The African Queen* is the first in a series of symbolic Hustonian rivers; rivers also figure crucially in *The Red Badge of Courage* ('51), *The Life and Times of Judge Roy Bean*, and *The Man Who Would Be King*. Other images of water have special importance in *Across the Pacific* ('42), *The Roots of Heaven*, and *The Bible . . . In the Beginning*. In *Under the Volcano* and *The Dead*, water occurring as rain or snow is associated with destruction and death. Similar images pervade two of Huston's war documentaries, *Report from the Aleutians* ('43) and *San Pietro* ('44, released '45).

Like Howard among the Indians, Curtin's memory of fruit-picking dramatizes an ideal of community cohesiveness.

Hundreds of people, old and young, whole families workin' together. At night, after a day's work, we used to build big bonfires and sit around an' sing to guitar music, till morning sometimes. You'd go to sleep, an' wake up and sing, go to sleep again. Everybody had a wonderful time.

Curtin's description is too sentimental and the spectacle of Howard among the Indians too comic to take entirely seriously, even in the tall-tale world of *Treasure*. Ironic reservation balances romantic enthusiasm throughout. At the same time, such fantasies oppose equally stylized demonic visions. Somewhere between the two, we may infer, lies ordinary human life.

Adversity catalyzes community. Down and out, Dobbs offers a cigarette to Curtin. Rinsing away the blood of their brawl with Pat McCormick (Barton MacLane), the two impoverished Americans agree to pool resources. Before Gold Hat (Alfonso Bedoya) attacks their camp, the three miners decide to execute Cody rather than allow him to share their find. As they prepare to defend themselves, however, all thought of murder disappears and they invite Cody, called "stranger" before, to eat with them. "Come on down, friend."

Conversely, wealth and power destabilize the bonds of friendship and solidarity. As Howard remarks, "So long as there's no find, the noble brotherhood will last. But when the piles of gold begin to grow, that's when the trouble starts." Neither of the younger men is persuaded by his prophetic observation. Nor will they remember his warning later when their confidence in each other begins to decay. Howard knows how bad such trouble can be, both because he has experienced it and because he understands that all people are always in trouble, whether they realize it or not, and that they are more vulnerable in prosperity than in hardship. With good fortune, they develop illusions of self-sufficiency. In difficulties, they must acknowledge their limited power and need of others.

The most socializing of the main characters, Howard is also the most socialized. He votes to let Cody join the group, and he later offers to finance Curtin's visit to Cody's widow. Among the partners, only he can speak enough Spanish to communicate with the Mexicans and Indians. Barriers of language in Huston's films typically signify empathetic as well as cultural gaps. Foreigners in Mexico, Dobbs and Curtin are isolated by their inability to speak Spanish; Howard moves among Indians, Mexicans, and Americans as easily as he moves between English and Spanish.[4]

But Howard is neither saint nor altruist. Although he has enough money to make up what Curtin and Dobbs are short when they propose to go prospecting, he never offers to invest more than two hundred of his three hundred dollar stake. Later, he is enthusiastic about the profits he can expect from his exalted position among the Indians. Least reassuringly, he accepts the will of the majority when Curtin and Dobbs vote to kill Cody.

Yet his defects and devotion to his self-interest give Howard's fundamental kindness a plausibility that might be less convincing in a more perfect figure. Huston's aversion to implausibly noble characters is explicit in a letter he wrote to Traven.

Let me now mention my chief criticism of the script I have written. It seems to me it's on the black and white side. . . . I would like, if it were possible, to . . . further dramatize the message of your book that all men are subject to certain pulls and temptations and that one man is better than another only in so far as he has the strength to resist.[5]

Howard's weakness allows him to sympathize with others and to help them resist the pull of ordinary human temptation. Such a source of moral authority, in general, is the only secure one in Huston's films. It is also the beginning of hope. As Howard brags, he is truly "a born medicine man."

Wealth creates anger, distrust, and insecurity. The opening sequence of *Treasure* cartoons greed and rage; we see Dobbs compare his lottery number with the posted winners and throw his ticket away in disgust. A few minutes later, he dashes water in the face of a boy (Robert Blake) who is trying to sell him part of another ticket. Other incidents amplify the association of wealth with distemper. The Man in the White Suit, though he responds to Dobbs's appeals, finally becomes irritated and delivers a cranky dismissal. (White Suit is played by Huston himself, perhaps making a private joke about the fact that three of his four feature films at that point – and a film that he wrote, *High Sierra* [Raoul Walsh, '41] – star Humphrey Bogart. Huston may be suggesting that, like Dobbs, Bogart is going to have to diversify the sources of his livelihood.) Later in the mining camp, Dobbs explodes when he thinks that Curtin is calling him a "hog." As the mine prospers, the unity of the small group begins to crumble. Each man begins to take care of his own share of gold. Once the "goods" are divided, so is the group. Suspicion escalates. The expressive sequence in which Dobbs misinterprets Curtin's pursuit of a Gila monster summarizes the rupture between them. Even after he watches Curtin expose and shoot the poisonous reptile, Dobbs refuses to admit that his suspicions were groundless. The Gila monster twitching as it dies on Dobbs's bags of gold provides *Treasure* with an emblem for the dangers of wealth.

Money delivers the power to buy sex and control people, relations as unconducive to affection and trust as outright hostility. After Dobbs spends part of the second peso he gets from White Suit, he looks longingly after a passing prostitute. By the campfire, he imagines using his new wealth to command and humiliate barbers, haberdashers, and waiters. In contrast to the homey reveries of his companions, his ends in a whorehouse.

Pat McCormick fleeces "foreigners and half-baked Americans" and uses his wealth, as Dobbs imagines doing, for fancy clothes and women. As he and Dobbs walk to the ferry that will take them to the job site, Huston deflates the notion that money can buy love. In a store display we see a male and a female manikin in wedding clothes. The love and respectability that are for sale are as lifeless as the manikins and as unreal as McCormick's benevolence.

The final outcomes of Dobbs's prosperity are isolation and death. He tries to persuade the bandits that "oh no, I'm not alone, I've got a couple of friends coming along on horseback." Unconvinced, they kill him. With an irony typical of Huston, the divisive power of Dobbs's possessions outlives their murdered owner. After they kill him, two of the bandits begin scuffling over his boots.

The imbedded moral that human connections are undermined by wealth puts Huston to the left of center as a social thinker. So may the fact, as Naremore argues, that "By selecting Dashiell Hammett and B. Traven as the basis of his first two films [sic], Huston was indirectly declaring his sympathy with the ethos of Popular Front literature in the 1930's. . . ."[6] Yet Huston typically shies from simple dogma, and *Treasure* does not suggest that wealth is irredeemably evil. Curtin's desire to buy an orchard is constructive, as is Howard's gift of money to help him visit Cody's widow. Even Dobbs uses his money for a common good when he shares his lottery winnings.

The movie partly supports Dobbs – despite the fact that he does not apply his wisdom to himself – when he agrees with Curtin that the destructiveness of gold depends "on whether or not the guy who finds it is a right guy." (Typically, Huston complicates the characters and situations of his sources, and here he shifts these words, Curtin's in the novel, to Dobbs.) But Huston's movie has more intricate lessons to teach. "A right guy" does not escape temptation. No one has such an immunity. Goodness comes from acknowledging and overcoming greed and weakness. Dobbs's denial of his own vulnerability to temptation proves lethal because he cannot overcome what he will not face.

The possibilities that wealth may be turned to good or evil, or that it may be refused, lead to a second fundamental theme of *Treasure*, that of choice. How far does the power to choose extend, what should guide it, and when does "the Lord or fate or nature" take over? As the crisis of the story approaches and choice becomes an issue of life and death, Huston inserts images that give form to the idea of alternatives. These images mostly take the shape of forked trees or cacti prominent in the background as the protagonists wrestle with their dilemmas in the foreground. Graphically they suggest a Y, a figurative fork in the road. In some contexts, these Y's also carry overtones of gallows, or of the Cross.[7]

Although there are unemphasized examples earlier, the first prominent Y appears when Dobbs accuses Howard of plotting against him. Throughout the two-shot sequence, a forked tree appears beyond Howard's left shoulder. It suggests – retrospectively, at least – that he faces an important choice: whether to accept the challenge of a half-crazy Dobbs or to ignore it in the interests of peace. Characteristically, Howard chooses peace.

The next emphatic Y appears when Cody arrives. As the partners fret about what to do if the stranger should show up, whether to drive him away or kill him, Cody emerges from behind a large, forked tree. The next morning, Cody himself puts a slightly different choice before them: kill him or take him in as a partner. The alternatives are familiar, but their extremity is new. While the three partners talk, camera placement again conspicuously puts a strongly branched Y, another tree, in the background.

After Howard returns from the village, the Indians reappear to insist that he accompany them once more. The now-familiar Y shapes are again prominent in the background, and Howard – this time under considerable duress – again chooses peaceable fellowship. When he departs, he bifurcates the plot between his sojourn in the village and the violent action that ensues between Curtin and Dobbs. The Y shapes that proliferate during this segment of the film signal not only the choices that characters have to make, but also the contrasting directions of their narratives: Howard to a bucolic community, Curtin and Dobbs to desolation and conflict.

As the latter struggle along without Howard's help, the choice-signaling Y appears frequently when the temptation arises in Dobbs to betray Howard and then, after Curtin refuses, to murder his other partner. The locations are dominated by forked cacti, trees, and brush. The dense imagery of bifurcation during these sequences symbolizes both the choices that the characters face and the tension of the plot. Dobbs hides behind a forked tree when he attempts to ambush the drowsy Curtin; there is a bright Y prominent in the dark background as Dobbs waits for his partner to doze off; another looms over him when he struggles with his conscience after he has taken Curtin into the brush and shot him. Forked brush and trees continue to dominate the scene the next morning as Dobbs tries to decide whether to bury his partner.

While doctoring Curtin, Howard muses that Dobbs is "not a real killer as killers go. . . . The mistake was in leaving you two alone in the depths of the wilderness with more'n a hundred thousand between you. That's a mighty big temptation, believe me, Partner." Framed in the doorway behind Howard and Curtin rises another forked tree. In contrast to the cactus and blasted shrubs, however, it is covered with leaves. As it bodies forth the dialectic between condemnation and compassion, its foliage suggests Howard's understanding and, in effect, forgiveness of Dobbs.

The Y appears prominently twice more, when Gold Hat and two of his band confront Dobbs, and in the last shot of the film. Howard and the Indians ride off in one direction, Curtin in another. As Curtin rides past, the camera pans to the ground and tracks in to a close-up of a small, doubly forked cactus. On it is caught a torn bag, once full of gold dust. Recalling the close-up of the Gila monster, this shot summarizes the tragic and ironic modes of the film. Like the "poor, bare, forked animal" that Shakespeare's King Lear takes to be the essence of man, the small, forked cactus is an image of human dilemmas. If "the Lord, or fate, or nature" takes some choices out of human hands entirely, spheres of action nonetheless remain for decisions that have profound consequences. The outcomes of Howard's time among the Indians, Curtin's hopeful prospects in Dallas, and Dobbs's death underscore that consequences follow the forking paths of choice.

Opposing outcomes are often expressed in *Treasure* through a traditional contrast between the demonic and the innocent. We should expect such dialectic structure in a fairy-tale narrative whose principal action consists of a marvelous adventure leading from city and civilization into an unknown wilderness filled with legendary "mountains [that] rise above the clouds . . . deadly insects and huge snakes . . . and ferocious tigers so big and strong they can climb trees with burros in their mouths." The struggles between the devilish and the innocent or divine, between high and low, good and evil, the Edenic and the fallen, give shape to virtually all romantic adventures, whatever their political agenda. At the same time, an intermittent ironic realism in *Treasure* opposes its marvelous romanticism, and the generic tension between the two modes energizes central thematic conflicts.

Imagery, dialogue, diegetic sound, and music track evoke the demonic during self-interested actions and evoke the innocent in connection with actions oriented toward another person or a community. The innocent occurs less frequently in Huston's mostly descending story of temptation and distrust; it is located either in the Indian village or in rare moments, frequently associated with water, of communal serenity. The demonic is evoked by smoke, fire, imprisonment, and settings of isolation and emptiness.

Shots of the ferry carrying McCormick's laborers introduce images that will be associated with greed, betrayal, and egotism. The boat emits a dismal whistle, gates swing closed, and men disappear into the darkness as if they were crossing to Hades. Between departure and return, a brief sequence of Curtin and Dobbs at work shows them in an infernally hot camp – "It's a hundred and thirty in the shade an' there ain't any shade up there on that derrick." Steam and smoke billow in the background.

Howard's declaration that "gold's a devilish sort of a thing," is confirmed by imagery. After the three protagonists begin to accumulate gold dust, dark, high-contrast, fire-lighted scenes gradually dominate, and *Treasure* starts to look like a wilderness *film noir*. Infernal images of smoke and flames intensify as Dobbs lies by the campfire after shooting Curtin. From behind the campfire, the camera is focused on his grotesquely shadowed, bearded, dirty face. His self-consuming anxiety mounts, and the expressionistic flames crackle and fill the screen as if they were part of his psyche.

Dobbs has been associated with smoke and heat since the beginning of the film when he watched with disappointment as an urchin snatched up a still-smoldering cigarette butt. After he shoots Curtin, he swelters in the heat of Hades on earth, staggering alone across the desert. Like Milton's Satan, "within him Hell/ He brings, and round about him. . . ."[8] Only Gold Hat – who shadows Dobbs like a fury throughout the film – attracts equally intense demonic imagery. Like Dobbs, Gold Hat is often shown smoking. In our last view of the bandit, one that recalls the final shot of *The Maltese Falcon*, he glares from behind wooden bars. Through them he spits like a cornered, rabid animal, or like one of the damned.

Another image of the underworld in *Treasure*, the action of digging, is associated equally with gold and with death. In the only sequence in which we see gold ore being taken from the earth, we see the mine collapse on Dobbs – making him figuratively and literally what Gold Hat calls him, "the guy in the hole." Cody tells Curtin how the *federales* force bandits to spend their last minutes digging their own graves; indeed, Gold Hat and his comrades do so. By association, gold mining sometimes suggests preparation for burial. After Cody is killed, Huston dissolves to the miners inspecting the proceeds of a day's work some time later and concluding that the vein is nearing exhaustion. Such editing reinforces connections among digging, gold, and death. The demonic symbolism of digging can also be inferred from its absence. When the protagonists restore the mountain, for example, Huston does not show them at work. By avoiding any shots of them filling in their mine, he also avoids showing the act of digging as constructive or healing.

When the energies of *Treasure* turn downward from the Edenic to the demonic, the restorative associations of water tend to be thwarted or reversed. Such a reversal is predictable, for irony may nearly always be understood as a parody of romantic conventions and outcomes. As Dobbs transforms into a demonic version of himself, the usual symbolic suggestions of water invert. The glass of water he dashes into the face of the lottery boy expresses his disappointment and his inclination toward bullying. After badgering and punching Cody, he will claim that the stranger has "stolen" the miners' water. Cody makes the more normative connection between water and community: "I thought perhaps I was among civilized men. . . ." We might also notice Dobbs's practice of spitting when he drinks, a wasteful habit that expresses his love of power, his pleasure in conspicuous consumption, and his habitual disdain.

Reversal of aquatic symbolism combines with another motif Huston used throughout his career, that of reflections – in general associated with falsehood, egotism, or danger. *In This Our Life* typically reserves its mirror shots for the dishonest, self-centered Stanley (Bette Davis). The one exception occurs during a sequence in which Stanley's sister and opposite, Roy (Olivia de Havilland), stung by betrayal, is photographed in front of a mirror vowing to become hard and selfish. She does not keep the vow, nor is she photographed with a mirror again. In *Key Largo*, mirror shots are devoted to the gangsters. The exception recalls Roy's mirror shot in *In This Our Life*. When Frank McCloud (Humphrey Bogart) refuses to shoot Rocco and explains his inaction, he is photographed in front of a mirror, so that we see him both directly and in reflection. Like the shot of Roy, this one emphasizes moral and psychological division within the doubled figure. Frank proclaims that he no longer believes in altruistic ideals and henceforth is going to devote himself only to self-interest. (But like Roy, his life and personality forbid devotion to selfish individualism.) Other characteristic Huston mirror shots include those in *Beat the Devil*, when Gina Lollobrigida's false declaration of love is photographed in mirror image; in *The Misfits*, when Marilyn Monroe tries to learn a canned speech in front of a mirror; and in *Freud*, in Cecily's falsely remembered dream.

The most striking reflection in *Treasure* comes when Dobbs, near death from thirst, scrambles down to a waterhole. The muddy oasis initially reinforces the association of water with life and civilization, reviving Dobbs and apparently making it possible for him to complete his trip to Durango. When the reflection of the bandit appears on its surface, Dobbs's prospects – and the symbolic import of the setting – are reversed; the water announces his death. Similar reversals occur when Dobbs looks at himself in the mirror after his haircut and when McCormick takes him and Curtin into a bar, presumably for a friendly drink before giving them their money. In the first case, a passing woman brings the newly barbered Dobbs back to the reality of his poverty, his inability to pursue such women. In the second, we realize only when the camera pans from the mirror behind the bar to a direct shot that we have been watching a reflection. As at the waterhole, a hopeful action reverses.

If one of the thematic centers of *Treasure* concerns choosing among alternatives, a complementary idea has to do with fate, forces beyond human power to affect or, most of the time, even to comprehend. Wealth, an allurement to egotism, also becomes an instrument of destiny. Like a playwright's benignant *deus ex machina*, the lottery starts Dobbs and Curtin down the road to riches. But Dobbs's fate, like his fortune, will be evil indeed; and the "lucky" number thirteen, the total of the digits on the ticket, will ultimately prove lethal.

When Howard declares that "Up there, up there's where we got to go . . . up there," the screenplay gives a direction to the cameraman, "CAMERA PANS UP to a high mountain peak, wearing in its majesty a crown of clouds."[9] This image and the accompanying score have a portentous ambiguity. "Up there" may be figuratively heaven, the realization of wealth and a peaceful, abundant life. Or it may be something distant and forbidding, even malign. "Up there" will prove to be all of those and more. And it will do so in ways that are either unaffected by the designs of the miners or contrary to them.

Huston's desire to emphasize the operations of fate is reflected in two memoranda in the Warner Bros. archive. Writing in 1940 about turning W. R. Burnett's novel, *High Sierra*, into a film, the then-screenwriter argued, "Take the spirit out of Burnett, the strange sense of inevitability that comes with our deepening understanding of his characters and the forces that motivate them, and only the conventional husk of a story remains."[10] To Traven, Huston explained, "Now as to the three who attack Dobbs being train bandits, let me tell you my reasons for doing this. For one thing, it was my hope that this also would serve to bring out the fate that pursued Dobbs. . . . their destinies are paired in some mysterious way."[11]

Fate in *Treasure* expresses itself as a perfect chain of causality. Characters' intentions either count for nothing or are reversed. At the waterhole, Dobbs points a revolver at Gold Hat and pulls the trigger, but the gun only clicks. It has no cartridges in its chambers because Curtin removed them after he disarmed Dobbs when Dobbs first tried to kill him. Curtin then returned the gun. But Dobbs later shot Curtin with Curtin's own gun, so why doesn't he shoot Gold Hat the same way? Because, in guilt and revulsion, he threw Curtin's gun at the feet of what he thought to be his partner's corpse. An alert audience will remember all this. In doing so, it will feel what Aristotle identified as a characteristic pleasure of tragedy, a recognition – in this case a recognition by memory and reasoning.[12] Gold Hat's nasty laugh conveys his less comprehensive recognition, his contempt and triumph.

For the audience, however, it is the guffaw of a merciless fate. Dobbs will get precisely what he had coming precisely because of what he did. If we cannot wish it on him, neither can we deny its justice. We do not feel like laughing with Gold Hat, as we later do with Howard and Curtin. But the laughter of Gold Hat, for all its ugliness, echoes our own amazement. We see what inevitably results, despite all he intends to the contrary, from Dobbs's actions.

The wind bloweth as it listeth. In *Treasure*, it signifies the indifference to human aspirations of an ironic fate or nature. It first appears as the howling "norther" that buffets the three prospectors, then rises again after Dobbs is murdered, and intensifies as Howard and Curtin, too late to help Dobbs or to recover their gold, enter the village where Gold Hat and his bandits have just been executed. While dirt is being shoveled over them, the wind scuds the leader's sombrero along the dusty ground. As Howard and Curtin ride to search for their goods, Huston intercuts shots of the wind dispersing the gold dust, which the uncomprehending bandits have dumped from its bags.

When Howard perceives the logic of the action in which he has played his unintentional part, the published screenplay calls for "a roar of Homeric laughter."[13]

Laugh, Curtin, old boy, it's a great joke played on us by the Lord or fate or by nature – whichever you prefer. But whoever or whatever played it certainly has a sense of humor. The gold has gone back to where we got it. Laugh my boy, laugh. It's worth ten months of labor and suffering, this joke is.

In the last sequence, Howard's laughter and explanation encapsulate the complex closure of the movie. He does not deny and cannot repair the losses that he and his partners have experienced. But he looks back without regret at what has happened and ahead to a future. When Howard and Curtin laugh, they complete the journey toward self-understanding and reenrollment in the human community that they began, paradoxically, by venturing into the desert.

Nature, fate, and the Lord in Huston's films for the next forty years are practically indistinguishable. In *Treasure*, the Lord is manifest in what Jameson calls "a mostly uninsistent, earthy religiosity that pervades the film."[14] Uncorrupted religion as it appears in the villages joins nature and fate to maintain order in the universe. It is strongly associated with community and mutuality and contrasted with self-absorption and materialism.

Although Huston ordinarily depicts organized religion with hostility, it can play a constructive role when practiced by a relatively innocent native population or when it is individualized by a character like Deborah Kerr's in *The Night of the Iguana*. In such cases, religious values are usually defined in opposition to accepted doctrine, which appears as a distorted or hypocritical version of spiritual life. *A Walk with Love and Death* similarly exemplifies genuine piety in opposition to institutional versions.

When Howard revives the stunned boy, high shots of assembled villagers suggest an immense cathedral with the child on an altar. The score shifts to reverential choral music, and the sequence ends with men removing their hats and everyone genuflecting. Insofar as it suggests a cross, the tree outside as Howard doctors Curtin further associates religious imagery with healing or resurrection. So does Huston's choice of a ruined convent for the affirmations of the final sequence.

Against healing and fellowship associated with religious imagery, Huston sets destructive or selfish impulses. Dobbs contemptuously dismisses motives other than self-interest as naive. When Curtin and Howard decide to give a fourth of their gold to Cody's widow, Dobbs ridicules them: "You two guys must have been born in a revival meeting." He responds with scorn when Curtin refuses to betray Howard: "Get off your soapbox, you only sound foolish out here in this wilderness."

However the characters of *Treasure* resist or succumb to temptations in the desert, they face resistance to lawlessness and greed when they return to civilization and its churches. Gold Hat's attempts at armed robbery are twice thwarted by federal soldiers and, when he does succeed in robbing and killing Dobbs, the burros run off to a ruined religious sanctuary. A church tower reintroduces civilization when the bandits arrive at the village to sell the stolen hides and pack animals. A white cross is prominent in the background just before they are executed. (This image also perhaps reflects Huston's more common attitude toward religion, suggesting something of the violence and hypocrisy that Huston often attributes to it.) When Howard and Curtin enter the village a little later they are greeted by the sound of the firing squad and the sight of the same church.

The problematic relation between personal ethics and social imperatives recurs in Huston's work from his earliest screenplays. Morality "out here in [the] wilderness" concerns the internal lives of individuals. Beyond the power of social constraints, characters face moral issues that have a clarity unobscured by civilized coercion. Are conventional values simply conveniences that allow people to live together securely? Or are they part of the coherence and wholeness of the people who hold them?

Huston's films suggest the latter. Characters who contravene their best impulses spiral down to catastrophe; those who honor them, often at great emotional or material cost, affirm at the same time their deepest identities. From Spade's refusal of Brigid at the end of *The Maltese Falcon*, none of Huston's movies of the next forty-six years contradicts the proposition that identity is at once personal and social, and that neither aspect can be ignored or distorted without painful consequences. The sanity, happiness, and life itself of Huston's characters requires values that fuse the communal and the individual.

Making a home requires other people and the world; it also requires the creation or rediscovery of identity. There must be someone to be at home. Self-discovery usually occurs as a re-creation of innocence, a reclaiming of idealism. Curtin experiences the corruption of the world and his fallible character, but he eventually returns to his childhood dream of family and fruit-growing. He achieves an acceptance of fate like Howard's: "You know, the worst ain't so bad when it finally happens."

As Howard and Curtin suffer and recover, so they "wound" the mountain and restore it when they close the mine. The decision to retain this detail from the novel reflects Huston's reverence for the land – less fashionable in 1948 than today. The miners' act of restoration, in which even the venal Dobbs willingly participates, combines with the subsequent windstorm to efface all marks they have made during their "ten months of labor and suffering." The imagery at the end of the film derives both from Traven's novel and from another book of which Huston was especially fond, Ecclesiastes. "All are of the dust, and all turn to dust again."

"What profit hath he that hath laboured for the wind?"[15] (John Maddow relates that when he visited Huston's home his host entertained him one evening by reading aloud "the entire *Ecclesiastes*."[16])

But if Howard and Curtin have failed to gain the world, they have the greater prize of their own souls. At the end of *Freud*, Huston's voice-over evokes an older sacramental tradition: "'Know thyself.' Two thousand years ago, these words were carved on the temple of Delphi. 'Know thyself.' They're the beginning of wisdom. In them lies the single hope of victory over man's oldest enemy, his vanity." In finding themselves, Howard and Curtin achieve their places among other people and discover the beginning of wisdom. Dobbs gains what for him is the whole world, but in doing so he loses his own soul, his friendships, and his life.

The closing moments of *Treasure* reclaim it from the nihilistic irony of Dobbs's death. The joke is funny, at least for Howard and Curtin, and the sense of a considerable part of the ending is that of comedy, of a plot that has moved from alienation to community, from conflict to accord. Howard will live out his days "worshipped and fed and treated like a high priest for telling people things they want to hear." In more senses than perhaps even he realizes, he's "all fixed for the rest of [his] natural life." Curtin will go to Dallas to join Cody's widow in the fruit harvest and possibly in sharing "life's real treasure." If wealth "in its ideal forms is power and wisdom," as Northrop Frye writes, then the dialectical outcome of the film gives the first and its outcomes to Dobbs, the second to his partners.[17] From the last perspective offered the audience, however, the obsession with power that led to Dobbs's madness stops mercifully in death and his isolation ends posthumously in the forgiveness of those he betrayed.

Howard and Curtin discover what they have been longing for and seem likely to achieve their desires by understanding and accepting their fate and themselves. Life has much worse to offer, like the material allurements that kill Dobbs, Cody, and Gold Hat and from which Curtin and Howard escape in restorative laughter. They win by losing the "devilish sort of a thing" they sought. Like most of Huston's successful characters, Howard and Curtin achieve control of their lives in comprehending how little control they have. That is the happiest and truest outcome of any action, any life, in most of Huston's movies. It is neither perfect nor perfectly awful. But it is perhaps the best we can manage on this earth, in our human existence.

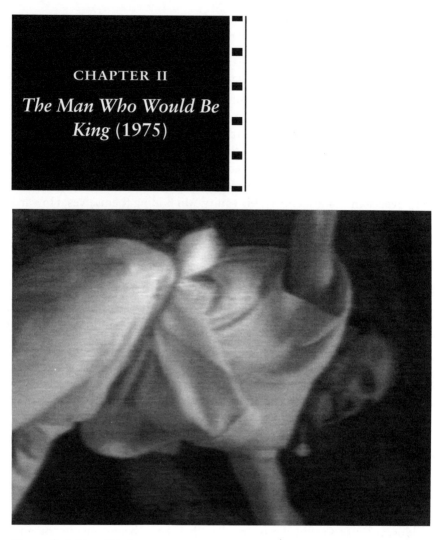

Danny finds himself in loss.

Ironic realism balances the romantic marvelous in *The Treasure of the Sierra Madre*; romance is fully ascendant in *The Man Who Would Be King*. Its larger-than-life heroes, cheerfully implausible adventures, and the death and return of Daniel Dravot (Sean Connery) as a minor deity all push it into the magic world of a quest for a kingdom and a princess. When Danny and Peachy (Michael Caine) set out to become kings of Kafiristan, the movie embraces the expansive fictive physics of *The Thousand and One Nights*, the Grail romances, and the most extravagant of adventure movies. The themes at the center of *The Man Who Would Be King*, nonetheless, remain closely related to those of *Treasure*: the power of human attachments and sustaining communities and the obstacles to both; conflicts between relatively innocent native peoples and intruders from technologically developed societies; interactions between humans and an animated natural world; ambiguities of destiny and choice; the equivocal possibilities of heroism.

"We are going away to another place," Peachy announces, "where a man isn't crowded and can come into his own." Like most of Huston's movies, *The Man Who Would Be King* unfolds a quest for self. Identity is to be discovered in Huston's films both within the protagonists and in the relations among them, with society, and with the natural world. The motive for action is usually a large sum of money, a gold mine, the uncovering of a crime or a secret, or some similar object. But the outcome that matters is the protagonists' realization of selfhood and their discovering or establishing a home. Even in such movies as *The Asphalt Jungle*, *The Kremlin Letter*, and *Wise Blood*, attempts to achieve an identity and a home underlie the action, but the forces of the fictional universe and the dynamics of personality make failure inevitable.

Twenty-seven years and twenty-six feature films after *Treasure*, *The Man Who Would Be King* has more self-consciousness than the earlier movie about its own status as a narrative. Still, most of Huston's works give considerable emphasis to their own textuality and internal storytelling. *The Man Who Would Be King* foregrounds the central figures' creation of their own story and the parallel work of the film. It meditates upon its own performance, and upon the relation of art to a world at once outside it and imitated within it.

Art in Huston films becomes, as Sir Philip Sidney put it, a second Nature, retrieving some of the losses and detoxifying some of the poisons of a corrupt world. That theme occurs most explicitly in Huston's portrayal of Henri de Toulouse-Lautrec in *Moulin Rouge*. Regenerative conceptions of art are also of importance in *Beat the Devil* (as the title of the film suggests), *The List of Adrian Messenger*, and *The Dead*. In *The Man Who Would Be King*, art and ceremony partly lift the heroes above their inclination toward theft and cultural bigotry.

The adventures and suffering of Danny and Peachy are conveyed by a combination of what literary critics call third- and first-person narration. In this regard, the movie departs from Kipling's original, which doubles first-person narrators, an unnamed speaker and Peachy. The film begins with an objective point of view, the camera apparently unconnected to the consciousness of any character. After Peachy enters and identifies himself, the source of the story becomes ambiguous: does the flashback reflect Peachy's consciousness, or Kipling's, or some blend of both? From the point at which Danny and Peachy leave for the Khyber Pass, however, the source of information must be Peachy. At the end of the film, the story returns to the fictional present and the camera to its independent, "third-person" status.

The bulk of the story, then, has a degree of unreliability. It comes from a narrator established in the opening sequences as a thief and liar. But Peachy is a con man of a surprisingly open kind, free in admitting his knaveries. Moreover, he is largely unconscious of auditors' reactions to what he has to tell. As a further brake to his unreliability, his loyalty to Freemasonry usually overrides self-interested motives. At the same time, the correlation of what Peachy says with fictional "facts" beyond his control – the encyclopedia entry about Alexander's conquest of Kafiristan, the explanation of Billy Fish's presence among the Bashgai, and the evidence of Danny's crowned head – assures us that his story has a basis in a reality outside his imagination.

Though Huston portrays Danny and Peachy with affection and sympathy, he treats them at the same time with amusement and condescension – especially when they assume pretensions of control. The information for most of the story comes from Peachy, but the camera nonetheless maintains a point of view separate from his. The "third-person" visual perspective of Huston's film thus puts another frame around both Peachy and Kipling, the character to whom he tells his story. The separation of attitude between that embodied in the film as a whole and that of the narrator-protagonist should warn us against becoming the credulous, unreflective audience that Peachy assumes in a Kipling whom he expects to share his prejudices.[1] If we suppose that the film trusts or endorses Peachy, we will be deaf and blind to its richest ironies and will find in it an apologia for the cultural provincialism and lack of human sympathy that it satirizes in all of its principal figures and most of its secondary ones.

The imagery of *The Man Who Would Be King* recalls that of *Treasure*: water and fire; gold; vast, alternately resistant and cooperative landscapes with looming, personified mountains. The intermittent *film noir* look of the earlier movie is most in evidence during the shadowy narrative framings at the beginning and end, when *The Man Who Would Be King* returns from flashback and Peachy tells his story in the fictional present.

The first two sequences mix native cultures and a transplanted European one. A pre-credit sequence opens with a telephoto shot that compresses a teeming, chaotic bazaar, then anatomizes the scene with images of a forge, grain being weighed, goods being carried through the market, musicians singing and playing, craftsmen exhibiting their trades. As the camera moves through the crowd, the images become more exotic – a mixture of freak show, magic, and religion. A snake charmer serenades his cobra; scorpions dangle from a man's cheek and tongue; another man first drinks, then washes himself in boiling water; a young boy holding two cobras sways in reverie; a procession passes a misty castle as the music shifts from Indian flute and tabla to something liturgical, though of what church or ceremony remains unclear. With the credits, the sound track changes again, to a melody that will be the musical theme of the film. The manifold peoples and trades; the prolixity and mystery of the subcontinent; the mixture of freakishness, fraud, and piety; the imagery of smoke, fire, and water; the sounds and music of diverse tribes – all suggest the collision of cultures that will follow. The flashback that comprises most of the film begins with another heterogeneous crowd, this time at a railway station. In the main story, as in the market, cultural melding leads not to the combination of one group with another but to an unstable suspension, a mixture in which components remain discrete and liable to return to separate homogeneities.

After the credits, shots of bright day are replaced by night, the crowded marketplace by an almost empty street. A solitary figure limps toward a lighted window. Inside, a quill pen scratches English verse across a page, blots a stray drop, and continues: "Boh da Thone was a warrior bold / His sword and rifle were bossed with gold / And the peacock banner his henchman bore / Was stiff with bullion. . . ." (The lines open Rudyard Kipling's "The Ballad of Boh da Thone," a poem that in its mix of satiric comedy and violence, and in the delivery of Boh da Thone's head at its conclusion, has affinities with Huston's film.)[2] The ragged figure enters. It is Peachy Carnahan, who identifies himself to Kipling (Christopher Plummer) as "the same, and not the same, who sat beside you in a first class carriage on the train to Marwar Junction three summers and a thousand years ago." He has transformed from a European in a pith helmet into a filthy, turbaned cripple of no identifiable origin.

In Huston's films collisions between indigenous people and Europeans or Americans expose the cultural assumptions of both. Between the contrasting civilizations in *The Man Who Would Be King*, East is East and West is West. Although the twain meet antagonistically, neither is ro-

manticized. "Different countries, different customs; mustn't be prejudiced." Even though Danny and Peachy could hardly be worse equipped
to truly believe that cliché, the film embodies it. The racist imperialism
of the heroes is emphasized in the movie more than in Kipling's story, but
the predatory violence, internecine hostility, and superstition of the people they encounter hardly constitutes an idyllic alternative.

When Danny and Peachy enter Kafiristan, they view a group of women
and children washing clothes and playing in a stream. The scene recalls
similarly staged moments of innocence in other Huston films, including
the Indian village in *Treasure*. A band of men attacks the bathers, but
Danny and Peachy drive them off, and for a moment it appears that these
Europeans who seek to "loot the country four ways from Sunday" may
become peacemakers and defenders of the helpless despite themselves.
But they do not long play the role of exemplars of civilization "bringing
enlightenment to the dark regions of the earth" – to quote yet another of
Danny's sayings.

Indeed, like the protagonists of *Treasure*, Danny and Peachy scarcely
qualify as representatives of their own culture. They are alienated before
they leave India, "detriments" despised by colonial authorities because
of their free-lance predation of both natives and Europeans. Like Dobbs
and Curtin, they have no true country or real home. Nonetheless, they
retain a ludicrous conviction of their superiority to everyone non-British.
In response to Kipling's incredulity when they propose to conquer a
country unassaulted since Alexander the Great, Peachy simply asserts
that "If a Greek can do it, we can do it."

Their interpreter, Billy Fish (Saeed Joffrey), is similarly deracinated.
He has left behind much of his own culture without fully assimilating a
new one. For him, the British are both well known and comically strange:
"I often tell Ootah about Englishmen, how they give names to dogs, take
off hats to women, and march into battle left right left right with rifles
on shoulders." Billy has a role in *The Man Who Would Be King* somewhat like Howard's in *Treasure*. He connects Danny and Peachy to the
culture in which they dwell but from which they are isolated by language.
At the same time, he remains of their camp, even to the extent of refusing to flee on horseback from the avenging priests of Sikandergul. If he
were to abandon his role as a rifleman subordinate to British soldiers, Billy would lose his adopted cultural identity. His unwillingness to desert
his companions amounts less to loyal suicide than to a refusal to abandon an essential part of himself.

From one perspective, Danny's death is like Billy Fish's. He attempts to fully integrate himself into his new country by marrying Roxanne of Kuwak and founding a line of kings. As a result, he is exposed as human rather than divine, and is executed by his erstwhile subjects. Like Billy, he has adopted his new identity to the extent that there is no going back to his old one, even though to do so would make him one of the richest men in the world.

In most of Huston's films, personal identity and integrity depend upon a sense of placement among other people: a society, as in *The Man Who Would Be King*; a family, as in *The List of Adrian Messenger*; a profession, as in *Reflections in a Golden Eye* or *The Maltese Falcon*; or simply a trusting lover. Surprisingly, because Huston's main figures often appear to be loners, they almost invariably strive to find themselves by forging bonds with others. To gain a home of their own, they must establish a place among other people.

For Danny and Peachy, Freemasonry provides social placement comparable to what religion, trade, and art give indigenous people or British culture gives colonial bureaucrats. When Peachy steals Kipling's watch at the train station, he identifies as little with his own countryman as with the natives. But having discovered that he has robbed a fellow Mason, he takes great pains to undo the theft. As he restores the watch, he claims a bond with his fellow in "the craft." Kipling, in turn, agrees to set aside his plans in order to deliver Peachy's message, "for the sake of the widow's son." To a skeptical official later, Kipling will explain that Freemasonry is "an ancient order dedicated to the brotherhood of man under the all-seeing eye of God. . . . Once a Mason, always a Mason."

Fraternal connections figure heavily in the success that Danny and Peachy find in Kafiristan. "Wish us luck," says Peachy in response to Kipling's entreaties to give up their suicidal mission, "we met upon the level. . . ." ". . . and we're passing on the square. Good luck, indeed," replies Kipling. Reminded of their brotherhood, Kipling gives Danny his Masonic watch-chain token, which will save his life. When the high priest of Sikandergul opens Danny's tunic and prepares to stab him to test his godhead, he exposes Kipling's Masonic talisman, which duplicates the emblem left two millennia ago by Alexander. Danny is thus confirmed as "Sikander's son," and accepted as ruler of the Kafirs and as an immortal. "The craft, Danny, the craft – that's what saved us," exults Peachy.

Their salvation will be temporary, because Freemasonry is failed by Danny and Peachy. "Calm yourself, Brother Kipling," Danny says, "we've never taken advantage of a fellow in the craft." But they do take advantage of the priests of Sikandergul, whom they do not meet "on the level" nor deal with "on the square." They deceive and exploit their distant relations in Kafiristan, and fail to recognize them as part of the fellowship of man. As a result, they crash beneath the all-seeing eye of the highest of the local gods, Imbra – a name that vaguely suggests the brotherhood that Danny and Peachy have betrayed.

As the iconography at the holy city of Sikandergul makes evident, Freemasonry merges smoothly with religion. The incorporation of the Masonic "all-seeing eye" into the statues of Imbra emphasizes the connections. A man feigning divinity, Danny's robing is shown from a striking angle that at first dignifies him but that subsequent cinematography suggests to be an "Imbra's-eye view" of the proceedings. As Billy Fish diffidently proposes later, "Imbra angry because son of man pretend to be a god." At the beginning of their masquerade, Danny prophetically voices doubts about his imposture: "The idea's a bit blasphemous, like."

Increasingly entranced by his status as king and god, Danny tries to invent interpretations of his lies that will transform them into truth. The first indication of his inflating belief in his godhead comes as he is presiding over a supreme court of appeals that he has established in the holy city. Declaring a recess, he takes Peachy aside to request that his partner bow "like everybody else . . . for appearance's sake." Growing more deeply entangled in his own deception, Danny later asserts that "this isn't the first time I've worn a crown" and that he is truly Alexander's son, "in spirit, anyway." What Peachy calls luck, Danny comes to call "destiny."

But he is not willing to trust the idea of destiny so far as to agree, as the distressed priests of Sikandergul urge, that "Imbra decide" about his marrying. This unwillingness to put himself under the jurisdiction of the "highest god" indicts him for bad faith. Insofar as he believes in his own divinity, his refusal to submit to Imbra suggests spiritual presumption, an attempt to usurp the place of the highest god.

Danny's self-deception threatens the integrity of his spirit. His absorption in falsehood separates him from Peachy, his strongest connection to reality and a central part of his own identity. Early in the film, Danny and Peachy operate almost as twins – memorably when they confront the colonial official, dispute his accusations, and march back out in indignant lockstep. While signing the contract, Danny explains to Kipling that "There's no need for the last article, but it's got a ring to it." The article in question specifies mutual commitment: "if one of us gets into trouble, the other will stay by him." It is not needful because the profound trust between Danny and Peachy is self-evident. (At the same time, however, the first phrase of the article pledges "That we conduct ourselves with dignity and discretion," a promise so improbable that its proximity brings into doubt any associated protestations.)

Together Danny and Peachy thrive. As "the mad priest and his servant," when they take the mules from the Afghans, as travelers through the mountains, and as joint commanders of the army and rulers of Kafiristan, they prosper despite the long odds against them. When their mutual equality and commitment begin to crack under the pressure of Danny's delusions of grandeur, their "rare streak of good luck" comes to a halt. Like "Ootah the Terrible," Danny forgets his dependence upon his friends. Like Ootah, he forfeits crown and head – though the latter does not suffer the final indignity of doing service as a polo ball.

When Danny regales his partner with visions of future glory, a suggestive camera set-up underscores his alienation from his friend and alter ego. In head-and-shoulders close-up, Danny fills the left side of the screen. Visually diminished and estranged from his companion, Peachy stands slightly out of focus in the back right. Later, as he pleads with Danny to return with him, their estrangement is indicated by a bead curtain between him and Danny.

"These two men are like the opposite sides of a coin. They are a unit, I wouldn't know how to divide them," said Huston.[3] Without Peachy, Danny is not Danny.[4] When Danny elevates himself, he first loses Peachy and then his life. His motives are not entirely for self-aggrandizement; in part, he wishes to remain as king and to marry in order to benefit the country. But he aspires to become someone else. In Huston's films, such aspirations, however benevolent, nearly always lead to disaster.

Danny is also setting himself up, quite obviously, to mind everyone else's business. Indeed, his ambitions for the country, his flood of royal rulings and decrees, bear suspicious resemblance to the behavior of the bureaucrats he disparaged to Kipling. We encounter here another theme general in Huston's movies: distrust of the impulse to mind other people's affairs, especially for their own good. Such a distrust follows logically from Huston's emphasis on the importance of finding and coming to terms with one's fundamental self. Undertaking the salvation of the world offers an excuse to evade the self-understanding and self-acceptance that make possible identity, courage, and happiness.

Although Danny's pretensions to divinity are fraudulent and dangerous, the religious culture of Kafiristan is not romanticized in contrast. Nor is it portrayed as the spiritually pristine victim of a corrupt Western secularism. As a general rule, Huston's films portray organized religion as neither disinterested nor humane, and *The Man Who Would Be King* is no exception. Like Masonry and like the agreement between Danny and Peachy, the religion of Kafiristan excludes women. It also denies any connection between piety and human error or corruption: the priests who go to collect money walk with their eyes closed, guided by a boy, because "they do not wish to see any badness." For Huston, humans achieve strength by first accepting their weakness.

Similarly, the divinity he conceives as part of human identity is intimately connected with mortality. *The Life and Times of Judge Roy Bean*, a film Huston made three years before *The Man Who Would Be King*, shares its combination of epic sweep, comedy, myth, and the poignant glory of what Huston called "our yearning souls."[5] Roy Bean's (Paul Newman) pronouncement to the Watchbear illuminates Huston's view of humankind: "A man has two loves, an unattainable goddess and a mortal woman. And he loves the mortal woman twice as much for having worshipped Lily Langtry." If Lily (Ava Gardner) is a modern Aphrodite, she is also the expression of human womanhood through whom men can discover the goddess in the mortals they love. Yet in trying to attain both a woman and divinity at once, Roy Bean and Danny stumble in their mortality. Bean loses both the mortal woman and the empire of Vinegarroon when he attempts to see Miss Lily. Danny loses his kingship and his life when he tries to marry Roxanne.

Nearly as xenophobic as Freemasons or the colonial English, the warring cities of Kafiristan and the elitist religion of Sikandergul offer spiritual and cultural choices scarcely more compassionate than materialist imperialism. Indeed, though religion sometimes appears to offer an alternative to warfare, *The Man Who Would Be King* suggests that the two institutions are akin. They share aims of power and dominion. Each rejects sexual love. Tempted by a young Bashgai woman, Peachy exclaims to Danny, "Let's go seek safety in battle"; and Danny's undoing comes about as a result of his desire to wed Roxanne. "For God's sake," says Peachy with a revealing oath, "leave the women alone."

Both religion and the military thrive on ceremony and mystification. The battle masks of the warriors who attack the Bashgai women and children are as appropriate to religious ceremony as to fighting. Danny, puzzled by them, concludes that "[it] must be their Halloween." The Bashgai make a similar mistake, on their part, about the two Englishmen. Billy Fish says, "Oh, Kafir people very ignorant. . . . They [Danny and Peachy] not devils, they British soldiers." After Danny is mistaken for a god, his divine status smoothly replaces his military prowess and he marches triumphantly from city to city on the strength not of his swelling army but of his holiness. In the hymn that serves as a theme song for the movie, religious and military ideas are inseparable, piety and battle synonymous:

> The Son of God goes forth to war,
> A kingly crown to gain.
> His blood-red banner streams afar,
> Who follows in his train?
>
> A glorious band, the chosen few,
> On whom the spirit came.
> While valiant saints that hope they knew,
> And mocked the cross and flame.
>
> He met the tyrant's brandished steel,
> The lion's gory mane;
> He bowed his head his death to feel.
> Who followed in his train?

Danny possesses a religion and culture more benign, truer, and more powerful for him than either the alien one he tries to adopt or the drive for wealth and power of the colonial military. In part, it consists of his Freemasonry, with its commitment to brotherhood, altruism, and reverence. In part, it is the residue of his British Christian background and education. Danny assembles his power – before he becomes a god – as much through mercy and fellow-feeling as through strength. "There'll be no executions of prisoners in this army," he decrees after his first victory, and invites the conquered to join their conquerors as brothers. He and Peachy understand people who feel surrounded by enemies, whether neighboring villagers who steal one's women and piss in one's water supply or bureaucrats who try to drive "detriments" out of India.

"You have to take your hat off to Daniel Dravot," says Peachy, "he dealt out justice as though he wrote the book." His justice comes, more accurately, straight out of childhood primers. It consists of British common sense, clichés, and the golden rule. He and Peachy are emphatically, as Billy Fish says, "not gods, Englishmen." Danny is most himself and most appealing when he is trying to be nothing else: when he exclaims "God's holy trousers"; when he reverses the schemes of a man who has prostituted his wife; when he refuses permission to loot its neighbor to a city whose granary has burned and establishes instead a central grain re-

serve for the entire country; when he recites a banal paean to the virtues
of the cow, "Without cattle, there ain't no meat, nor hides, nor hooves,
nor horns; and without milk, there ain't no butter nor cheese, and the
children's bowls go empty."

Facing death, Danny puts aside his usurped dignity. In the plain eloquence – somewhat formal, mildly comic – typical of Huston's writing at
moments of intense emotion, he acknowledges his fault and asks Peachy's
forgiveness:

> D: Peachy, I'm heartily ashamed for gettin' you killed instead of going home
>   rich, like you deserved to, on account of me being so bleedin' high and
>   bloody mighty. Can you forgive me?
> P: That I can and that I do, Danny, free an' full an' without let or hindrance.
> D: Everything's alright, then.

Never do we see Danny more generous, accepting of his destiny, or sure
of who he is. A few moments later, he walks to the center of the gorge
that as king he had Peachy span with a rope bridge. He stands resolute
and majestic, singing as the cables are cut and he pitches into the abyss.
As he falls, his crown flies from his head, but the Masonic emblem stays
on its chain around his neck.

Danny finds himself in loss. Full acceptance and understanding of his
weakness and humanity make possible the achievement of what he
sought, lasting kingship and divinity. Like the subjects of pastoral elegies,
he is reincarnated as a consoling spirit, a genius of place who transcends
the closure of death. In the end, he recovers both the crown and, in a
sense, his existence. The last moments of *The Man Who Would Be King*
recapitulate Danny's career: his journey, coronation, separation from
Peachy, fall, and elevation into something like a protecting god. For
Peachy, whose return to India he guards, he has been added to the "two
and thirty idols of Kafiristan."

Huston found in Rudyard Kipling a kindred spirit who identified "not
only with people, but with animals and even things, living in a kind of
pantheistic world when trees and rocks had identities. It's this universality in Kipling that I feel close to."[6] The prolonged encounter of Danny
and Peachy with the natural landscape puts them in the midst of beau-
ties and threats as important to their story as the humans they meet. They
give up their camels in order to cross a wild river (just "a little wavy blue
line on the map") into the still wilder landscapes of the high mountains.
Their passage resembles a number of such crossings in Huston's movies
that transfer characters into settings with powerful mythic resonances,

like the land beyond the river that Heron finds in *A Walk with Love and Death* or the wilderness "West of the Pecos" in *Roy Bean*. Across the river, Danny and Peachy enter animated mountains that Peachy describes as characters: "The mountains was tall an' white, like wild rams. They was always fightin'."

After his death, Danny achieves an authority with respect to the land that supersedes his first, illegitimate kingship. The mountains in which he became snow-blind respect Danny's presence during Peachy's journey out. "The mountains they tried to fall on old Peachy. He was quite safe because Daniel walked before him." At the end of the film, Danny has attained his domain in the natural world as well as having regained a crown in the world of humans.

The shape of his transformation is like that of the title figure of *Roy Bean*. Bean is gone for twenty years, then mysteriously reappears to aid his daughter and bring about a redemptive apocalypse. In what amounts to the epilogue of the movie, Bean's surviving cronies have aged, his daughter has married and gone, and Bean himself has long since "cashed in his chips." But the object of his adoration, Miss Lily, remains in an eternal prime, ageless. And the Judge, whose memory presides over the desert as Danny presides in death over the mountains, leaves Miss Langtry a letter expressing his expectation that "sometime in this life or afterward, I may yet stand in your light." Miss Langtry's immortality is directly connected to the Judge's worship, his faith has divined the goddess within her and brought it into full realization. Bean's own immortality thus resides not only in the perpetuation of his memory but in Lily Langtry's deification.

But Peachy does not achieve the timelessness of Lily Langtry nor the poetically triumphant career of Danny. The narrative of *The Man Who Would Be King* commences when he emerges from shadow to announce, "I've come back," and it concludes when he departs again to attend to "urgent business in the South." Unlike Danny, he has not returned permanently; nor does he have full possession of himself. On the contrary, he urges Kipling to "keep looking at me. It helps me to keep myself from flying off." Though he was crucified, he did not ascend from death to divinity. Peachy's destiny, unlike Danny's, is not yet accomplished; he still needs to find himself and his place. What the narrator says in the first paragraph of Kipling's story applies to Peachy in Huston's picture: "to-day, I greatly fear that my King is dead, and if I want a crown I must go hunt it for myself."[7] At the end of the film, Peachy shuffles off "to meet a man at Marwar Junction." His story will begin again where it began the first time, when he sent Kipling with a message for Danny to the same place.

Because the plot of *The Man Who Would Be King* traces the rise, fall, and death of a ruler, we might expect it to take the form of tragedy, and highly conventional tragedy at that. Stuart Kaminsky sees the film as telling a classic tragic story: "Daniel, like Dobbs, becomes obsessed with gold and power and suffers for it."[8] Huston's own description sounds like a recapitulation of classical criteria for tragedy.

"The story has a trajectory. . . . once you attain the place you seek there is the danger of becoming high and mighty, of falling victim to the disease of power that most of those who live in a rarefied atmosphere are assailed with, once you begin to believe that you yourself are indeed the supreme being, issuing the orders and making all the decisions. It has that sweep to it, and an underlying deep truth. . . ."[9]

Yet *The Man Who Would Be King* bends conventional tragic and epic materials into comedy. It redeems its reprobate characters. To miss its wit is to misapprehend it fundamentally. In part, its comedy comes from continuous incidental humor originating in the performances of Michael Caine and Sean Connery; in part, from Huston's playfulness and sense of amusement; in part, as a result of the vote it casts for the ascendance of the commonplace over the rare and majestic. Tragic heroes are grand and noble; comic ones are like us, small and humble. Such characterization of comic protagonists allows us to laugh – in Huston's film, affectionately – at figures toward whom we feel equality or superiority. Finally, the plot of *The Man Who Would Be King* traces a comic movement toward reconciliation and amity and away from social or personal disintegration.

The first half-hour emphatically establishes the humor of the film. The introductions of main characters and the elaboration of Danny's and Peachy's attempt to blackmail the Raja of Degumber are given thoroughly comic treatment. Kipling, who functions as a guide for the audience's responses, finds Danny and Peachy as entertaining as they are improbable, "a pair of lunatics." About the character of Kipling in the film, Huston said, "He tells the audience what to think about those two men and they are coached into seeing them through his eyes."[10]

Small incidents in the opening receive a light touch: Kipling's chauffeur's warning about "a naughty house of disreputation, where he will take you and kill you and murder you and cut your throat and rob the money from your pocket source"; Danny's pride in his performance as "the mad priest" and his miffed, "Alright then, some other time perhaps" when Kipling declines his offer to "froth at the mouth something horrid"; the elaborate, amateurish ceremony of executing the "contrack." Even the unceremonious expulsion of the Indian scribe from the moving train is rendered largely comic by the victim's repulsive habit of spitting watermelon seeds and pulp on the compartment floor, the fact that the train is "not making five miles an hour," and by his abject "Thank you, Sirrrr" as Peachy throws him out. We notice that the heroes of the story are scoundrels; but *The Man Who Would Be King* establishes that fact as entirely obvious and then encourages us to suspend our tendency to moralize about it.

Comedy holds destruction and pain at bay. During the first battle in Kafiristan, Danny leads the Bashgai in a premature charge. The camera work and editing are conventional: fast pans and rapid cutting, a mixture of blurry close-ups and middle shots. After early casualties, the Bashgai forces seem to be prevailing. Then comes a middle shot of Danny on his horse, followed by a brief close-up of a bow and arrow being tensioned and released, then back to Danny being struck by the arrow on the left side of his chest – in the heart, we might suppose. That image gives way to a swaying point of view shot from Danny's horse looking down at his surrounding enemies. Back to a medium close-up of Danny, still slashing with his sabre but appearing to reel in the saddle. Conventionally, he should pitch to the ground or slump onto the neck of his horse at this moment. During the shots just described, moreover, the music modulates into ambiguous chords that fade in volume as the sound of battle comes up. By cinematography, editing, and manipulations of the sound track, we are prepared for the worst.

But Danny remains on the back of his horse and continues fighting, the music returns to its martial exuberance, and the battle ends in triumph. Danny's apparent invulnerability (the arrow stuck in a concealed bandolier) has convinced his opponents that he is a god, the son of Alexander the Great. The sequence raises the threat of catastrophe only to banish it. A comic spirit presides over *The Man Who Would Be King*, protecting its heroes and guiding its plot to outcomes as glorious as they would be, in a realistic fiction, implausible.

Paradoxically, *The Man Who Would Be King* ends happily. As Scott Hammen asserts, it "is not a failed quest at all; it is a gloriously exciting successful one."[11] Peachy's bald conclusion has more authority than may first appear: "Well, he [Danny] became the King of Kafiristan, with a crown on 'is head, and that's all there is to tell." It oversimplifies Huston's retelling of Kipling's equivocal story to call its conclusion an unalloyed victory – given that Danny does, after all, die and that Peachy is hobbled by the ordeal he has undergone. Nonetheless, the dominant tone of the film and the sense of its conclusion remain comic; its conflicts are by and large resolved. The triumph of *The Man Who Would Be King* resembles that of *Moulin Rouge*, about which Huston wrote, "The music of the can-can starts and Lautrec breathes his last. It would be a truly happy ending."[12]

Their sense of humor serves Danny and Peachy as protective armor. So long as they can laugh at themselves, they "will be aided and abetted" – as Huston said.[13] Two episodes, the first when Danny and Peachy face freezing to death and the second when Danny begins to take himself seriously, epitomize the crucial importance of the protagonists' comic sense. Cut off from retreat or advance by impassable mountain crevasses, Danny and Peachy appear doomed. As their campfire burns down, Danny turns to his partner:

> D: Peachy, in your opinion, have our lives been misspent?
> P: Well, that depends on how you look at it. I wouldn't say the world's a better place for our having lived in it.
> D: Hardly that.
> P: Nobody's going to weep their eyes out at our demise.
> D: Who'd want them to, anyway?
> P: An' we haven't many good deeds to our credit.
> D: (after pausing) None. None to brag about.
> P: But 'ow many men have been where we've been, and seen what we've seen?

They go on to remember a ludicrous incident when their mercenary Scottish officer had his moneybag shot off during a retreat and won the Victoria Cross because his troops followed when he turned to retrieve it. We see Danny and Peachy here as they take themselves, without self-pity or self-importance. If they are not conventionally admirable, neither are they mean or bitter.

What happens next confirms the saving importance of their capacity for amusement. As Danny and Peachy roar over Pot Major McCrinnon's accidental valor, the echoing mountains answer, the frozen peaks loosen, and an avalanche fills the chasm barring them from Kafiristan. The laughter of Danny and Peachy thus rescues them; their refusal to take themselves too seriously disarms the world. Their guffaws in the face of death recall Howard's "Homeric laugh" at the end of *Treasure*. In both films, gales of laughter express the characters' acceptance of their fate and their refusal to interpret it as defeat.

Coincidence spins the wobbly wheels of comedy; inexorable logic drives the engines of tragedy. Danny loses his invulnerability when he begins to take himself for a king and god and rejects Peachy's urgings that they cash in the proceeds of their "rare streak of good luck." "More than chance has been at work here," Danny declares in grandiose cliché, "more than mere chance. . . . You call it luck; I call it destiny." Danny and Peachy have held death at bay with their amusement and refusal to regret their lives. When Danny embraces the high seriousness of divine majesty, he unwittingly turns his story in the tragic direction that befalls those afflicted with "the disease of power." The cure that Peachy offers his high and mighty friend is laughter. But Danny is beyond being amused; he turns his royal power against his partner. "I'm a king and you're a subject. So don't you provoke me, Mr. Carnahan."

Even at this pivotal moment, however, the dialogue remains comic: "You have our permission to bugger off!" Though Danny loses his humility and good humor and temporarily detours his story from comic to tragic, Huston's movie does not lose its sense of fun or change its genre. The tragedy is limited; comedy prevails and Danny's quest and its outcome attain the status of myth, a story about a god, however minor.

In order for his immortality to be achieved, Danny's story must be told. This necessary condition accounts for Kipling's importance as a character in Huston's movie. In the literary original, the artist-narrator is rudimentary, nor does Danny attain the mythic elevation that he does in the film. By adding emphasis to the character of Kipling, Huston assures us that Peachy's narrative will be sympathetically understood, preserved, and transmitted. When Huston's other mythic hero, Roy Bean, confronts the realization that "man can't live forever, man is mortal," he grieves not at the prospect of dying but for the disappearance of his story, for a future in which "people'll pass by and never know what it took to make all this, never know about the Bear, never know about me."

Peachy leaves the bag containing Danny's crowned head with Kipling – a detail that might seem inconsistent, given that he has carried it with him for the two years of his journey back to India. But the end of Danny's journey can be accomplished only when his story is known. Danny says to Peachy, "One more thing is needful for my destiny to be fulfilled, that I take her [Roxanne] to wife . . . a queen to breed a king's son for the king." He is only partly wrong. He will be immortalized not in a royal succession but in Peachy's account, Kipling's story, and Huston's movie. Thus his head and crown remain with Kipling while Peachy moves on, his last duty to his friend discharged.

The comic resolution of *The Man Who Would Be King* returns Danny via Peachy to Kipling and Huston, and thence to his community and culture as a memorialized king and spirit of place. Danny's triumph, death, disappearance, and return lead to his small apotheosis, however, only through reunion with Peachy and then through the art of Kipling and Huston. His immortality is intimately bound up with the succession of stories and audiences that sustain him – much as Lily Langtry's ageless beauty depends upon Roy Bean's devotion and legacy. The anecdote that concludes the chapter on the making of *The Man Who Would Be King* in *An Open Book* emphasizes the theme of immortality. Toward the end of filming, Huston showed the sequences in which they appear to the three ancient natives he cast as Kafu Selim and his two subordinates. The men had never before seen a motion picture. Through a translator, the director asked them about what they saw. Their reply was very much in the spirit of Huston's film: "Kafu Selim answered for them: 'We will never die.'"[14]

CHAPTER III

Hustonian Themes in an Atypical Genre: *The African Queen* (1951)

We witness the increasingly intimate partnership of the distant, constrained woman and the rude mechanic.

Trapped in the stifling maze of a tropical delta, Charlie Allnutt (Humphrey Bogart) and Rose Sayre (Katharine Hepburn) confront the end of their attempt to run the Ulanga River, reach the lake into which it flows, and sink the *Louisa*, a German steamship that controls access to central Africa at the beginning of World War I. More important from the point of view of the audience, they also face the end of their lives and their brief time together as lovers. "We're finished," Charlie declares. "I know it," replies Rose. A few moments later, a downward-looking camera cranes up and pans away from the boat to reveal the goal of their journey, the

lake, no more than fifty yards away. From the perspective of the protagonists, however, it is out of sight and out of reach; the camera's revelation thus appears to the viewer as sadly ironic. The exhausted voyagers
lie down and the shot fades out.

As I have already argued, however, water in Huston's films is more
likely to bring a renewal of life than death. Though nature is not uniformly regenerative in *The African Queen*, its water imagery is symbolically congruent with that of other Huston films. The next shot fades in
on gathering clouds. Thunder rumbles. A shower patters on lilies, then
swells into a deluge that seems to drench all Africa. It pours on the river
and the jungle, on flamingoes, ducks, giraffes, hippos, lions, and a herd
of startled antelope. The river becomes a foaming cataract carrying
whole trees in its rush. Like an aquatic *deus ex machina*, it lifts the
grounded *African Queen* across the mud and reeds onto the nearby lake.
This heavenly boost will allow the intrepid travelers both to sink the
Louisa and, still more improbably, to marry. The film thereby concludes
with the wildly unlikely success of its two main actions.

These sequences of despair and renewed hope exemplify much of what
I wish to discuss about *The African Queen*: its concentration of Hustonian shots, themes, and dialogue; the rhythms of its editing and action;
and its construction as a fantastic adventure, the kind of traditional narrative known as romance. The last is atypical of Huston's body of work.
Indeed, as an adventure and love story, *The African Queen* is almost
uniquely uncomplicated among its director's films.[1] Looking at his
movies before and after *The African Queen*, one is struck by Huston's
persistent tendency to complicate the psychology of his characters and to
pry open the closure toward which they are striving. With some notable
exceptions, the endings of Huston's films signal the beginnings of new actions that we will not witness but that promise to be as arduous and problematic as those we have just seen.

The straightforward romance and comedy of *The African Queen* sup-
press such complexity. If its relative simplicity makes the film atypical for
Huston, it also reveals with special clarity the outlines of some of his preoccupations as a filmmaker. As in *The Treasure of the Sierra Madre*, *The
Misfits*, and *The Night of the Iguana*, its adventures and its quest mod-
ulate from the external toward the internal; in pursuing a goal in the
world beyond themselves, Rose and Charlie come gradually to pursue
the familiar Hustonian goals of self-knowledge, love, and the sort of
home that two people make together for each other. At the end of the
saving rainstorm, the world is cleansed as at the end of Noah's story in

The Bible. Such clean slates are not possible in most of Huston's other films, but they are nonetheless persistently dreamed of and sought. Thinking about why such resolution cannot be fully achieved, moreover, constitutes one of the chief subjects of Huston's lifelong filmic musings about the human condition and the possibilities of heroism.

By the time Rose and Charlie arrive at their cul-de-sac, the imagery of water has been strongly associated with revival and rescue. The unlikely lovers began their adventures by fleeing from the threat of German soldiers to the sanctuary of the river. There, in the lee of a sheltering island, they undress to bathe. Their immersion is the first break in the sweat, chaos, and violence that has occupied the opening ten minutes of the film. It is also the first sign that life may yet hold some pleasures for them. Rose's appealing ungainliness when she tries to get back into the boat draws our attention to the fact that she actually has a body under her preposterous, stifling clothes. Later, the association of their love with the Ulanga will be acknowledged explicitly when Charlie remarks that he and Rose are "goin' down the river like Anthony and Cleopatra on their barge."

Fire tends to be associated with the imagery of water. When the protagonists pass the fortress at Shona, the sun reflects from the surface of the water and blinds the German officer just as he prepares to shoot Charlie. At the end of the movie, the lake and the explosions and fire that follow the *Louisa*'s collision with the *African Queen* combine to preserve the hero and heroine. In general, the intimacy of the protagonists with fire and water in multiple forms makes possible both their remarkable military coup and their love. The combination of those images will recur throughout Huston's career, sometimes in the service of goodness and happiness, as in *The African Queen*; often with ambivalent associations, as in *Moby Dick*, *The List of Adrian Messenger*, and *A Walk with Love and Death*; and sometimes horrifically, as in gunfire by the lake in *The Roots of Heaven*, the burning mixture of lime and water with which Hazel Motes blinds himself near the end of *Wise Blood*, and the terrible rain during the catastrophe of *Under the Volcano*.

Besides pervasive water and fire, *The African Queen* contains other images and dialogue characteristic of Huston's films. The opening tracking shots of the film end with Huston's favored descending pan. The credits are displayed against a long track through the crown of the rain forest against the sky, a shot that blends by an inconspicuous fade into another, shorter track and pan down from the sky past a cross on a steeple.[2] Like the closely related shots that open *The Night of the Igua-*

na and *The Barbarian and the Geisha* and that introduce the Indian village in *The Treasure of the Sierra Madre*, the opening of *The African Queen* invokes a heaven above while at the same time suggesting that human actions take place in a more complicated, imperfect world below. The descending crane shots of *The Night of the Iguana* have particular affinities with the first shot of *The African Queen*; in each, the camera descends past a cross and steeple to stop on a church in which we discover something quite different from the tranquil Christian rituals we might expect.

An early exchange between Charlie and Rose stitches the dialogue to the implications of the visual imagery. Charlie calls the isolated village "this god forsaken place." "God has not forsaken this place, Mr. Allnutt," Rose corrects him punctiliously, "as my Brother's presence here bears witness." The ensuing story will present a world that heaven seems sometimes to have abandoned but that it still favors with an occasional, crucial, intervention.

Within Huston's cinematic vocabulary, the pan down from the heavenly to the earthly also works expressively in reverse. At the end of *A Walk with Love and Death* the image fades from a downward-looking medium close-up of the two lovers awaiting death to a very high shot among the clouds that pans up from a sun-spangled sea. In voice-over Heron (Assaf Dayan) speaks from a heaven-haven beyond death and sorrow. At the end of *The Misfits*, as Roslyn and Gaylord look forward to returning home together and to having a child, Huston alternates medium close-ups of the lovers with shots of the starry night sky. The second image promises both direction and – participating in a tradition that extends far back in literary cosmology – a transcending of the impermanence of existence in fleeting time.

The African Queen frequently echoes *The Treasure of the Sierra Madre*, a film that it resembles in story and setting. Like Dobbs and Curtin on the trail, Charlie and Rose argue about the wisdom of continuing their journey when only two hours of daylight remain. Another echo of the earlier film comes when Rose asks Charlie how much farther they have to go to the lake. He replies almost exactly as Curtin does to a similar question: "Oh, not so many miles as the crow flies; no tellin' how many days."[3] When the *African Queen* reaches Shona, the upward-angled long shot of the German fortress conveys the same sense of magnitude and threat as the first shot of the gold-bearing mountain in *The Treasure of the Sierra Madre*.

That film is echoed, and *Heaven Knows, Mr. Allison* anticipated, when

Charlie turns his eyes toward the camera just after he has first kissed Rose. Like Walter Huston in the Indian village and Robert Mitchum uncorking his bottle of sake, Bogart registers a mixture of skepticism and unexpected delight. He also conveys a self-consciousness that implies some kind of audience: the camera, or the spectators in the theater, or perhaps a more circumspect, distanced self watching the one caught up in the action.

Such instances of narrative self-consciousness are relatively infrequent in Huston's movies, but recurrent. They signal moments of great importance. The spastic final pans of *Reflections in a Golden Eye*, the closing of *The Dead* as the camera surveys an Ireland throughout which "snow is general," the visit to the abandoned homestead in *Wise Blood*, and the slow motion sequences near the end of *Victory* – at each of these moments the film seems suddenly aware of itself. At the same time, the audience is reminded of the constructed, artificial quality of what it is watching. The realistic illusion is for a moment disrupted.

Such disruption does not undermine the plausibility of the work but signals the centrality of the moment in which it occurs. Relatively rare in Huston's movies, the frequency and significance of highly stylized shots are greatest in romances like *The Treasure of the Sierra Madre*, *Heaven Knows, Mr. Allison*, *The Life and Times of Judge Roy Bean*, and *The Man Who Would Be King*. In more self-conscious and self-parodic ways, *Beat the Devil* and *Prizzi's Honor* also emphasize both their artificiality and the deep truth of their artistic lies.

By romance I understand not films that focus on the story of a courtship – though a love story tends to be at the center of such movies – but adventurous narratives full of hair's-breadth escapes, terrifying descents and reascents, and clearly differentiated good and evil characters who tend to be somewhat larger than life. Such stories embrace symbolic, archetypal, and animistic modes of representation. When Huston (or anyone else) makes movies that have a high affinity to romance, episodes of conspicuous artfulness and internal implausibility serve not to remind us that what we are seeing is "unreal" and therefore of diminished meaning, but the opposite. They occur at junctures of centrality and climax, and they both indicate the kind of story they are part of and signal at the same time a concentration of significance. We can expect to find technically dazzling movie making at the ends of romantic films or at other moments of crucial consequence, that is, at turning points.

At the other end of Huston's artistic spectrum, irony, cynicism, and inevitable death dominate innocence and hope. Among Huston's ironic works *The Kremlin Letter* and *Under the Volcano* are the most unwavering; elements of antiromantic grimness also occur in less univocal films like *The Asphalt Jungle* and the substandard *Phobia* ('80, released only in Canada and for television). In contrast to more romantic narratives, moments of cinematic artificiality or obvious implausibility in ironic films signal not heightened significance but deception and hollowness. Promises of illumination are rendered false by their contexts or by the continuing development of the narrative. Such lies, whether internal to the action or external as a part of the representation, have no truth. They are nothing, and nothing is the outcome of everything in worlds the principal action of which is decay. Thus Dix (Sterling Hayden) in *The Asphalt Jungle* manages to return to his home in the horse country only to die; Weldon Pemberton (Marlon Brando) in *Reflections in a Golden Eye*, Hazel Motes in *Wise Blood*, and Geoffrey Firmin (Albert Finney) in *Under the Volcano* all struggle to evade their weaknesses but are finally overrun by them. At the end of *The Kremlin Letter*, Rone (Patrick O'Neal) belatedly achieves a degree of the self-knowledge that is usually saving for Huston's heroes, but the world of the film is so profoundly corrupt that he has no power to change it. He ends the film alone and trapped in a dilemma as impossible to face as it is impossible to escape. "'When I read *The Kremlin Letter*,' he [Huston] said, 'I was shocked at the cynicism we have all come to take for granted in everyday life today. The depravity and immorality expressed in the story hold up a reducing mirror to . . . the world we live in.'"[4]

The majority of Huston's films portray human existence as falling somewhere between the extremes of a happy fairy tale and a bleak, ironic tragedy. Within the narratives themselves, the capacity of his characters to cope with the blended textures of success, failure, and change constitutes the critical test of their strength. At their most successful, his protagonists accept disappointment and defeat without losing faith in the consolations of human companionship and the possibility for solutions, however provisional, to dilemmas posed by the existence of other people and by their own mortality. We see successes in Howard and Curtin in *The Treasure of the Sierra Madre*, Gay and Roslyn in *The Misfits*, and Hannah, Shannon, and Maxine in *The Night of the Iguana*. Characters in the same films who fail in various ways to come to terms with themselves and make accommodations with the world include Dobbs, Guido, and Miss Fellowes.

Among Huston's other films, only *Annie* achieves the same cheerful simplicity as *The African Queen*. It too ends with a miraculous rescue

followed by the promise of an endless "tomorrow" embodied in the founding of a family. The conclusion of *The African Queen* anticipates those of *Annie* and *The Misfits*. "I'm all twisted around, Charlie," says Rose after the *Louisa* has sunk, "Which way is the east shore?" "The way we're swimmin', old girl," Charlie cheerfully assures her. The music comes up on the soundtrack and the two swim out of the frame, leaving the typically reassuring (for Huston) image of the lapping waters of the lake. At the end of *The Misfits*, the woman's question and the man's answer substantially duplicate the last lines of dialogue between Rose and Charlie, just as "Roslyn" echoes "Rose." "How do you find your way home in the dark?" asks Roslyn. "Just head for that big star straight on," answers Gay. "The highway's under it. It'll take us right home."

Home in *The African Queen* is something less problematic than in *The Misfits* and most other Huston movies. In the simplicity of its action, thought, and characterization, *The African Queen* is akin to the sort of Hollywood adventure film typified by *Star Wars* and *The Empire Strikes Back*, *King Solomon's Mines*, or *King Kong*. Like those movies, it has the clear relation to popular narrative and story-telling that Harold Schechter points to when he argues that Hollywood movies are essentially a form of folklore.[5] Even the titles of such films, with their frequent emphasis on royalty, evoke the world of the fairy tale. Atypical of its director's work as a whole, *The African Queen* nonetheless sets off the romantic, pop-culture side of Huston's filmmaking with special clarity. That side, however diminished or ironized, recurs in most of Huston's movies.

With *The African Queen*, however, Huston dishes up romantic adventure unadulterated. His collaboration with James Agee on the screenplay may well have something to do with its relative purity of genre. One recalls the insistently archetypal quality of Agee's screenplay for *Night of the Hunter* (Charles Laughton, 1955), another film with a dangerous river journey and insistent turning to the resonant formulae of folk culture.

In Agee's collaboration with Huston, the conventions of the romantic quest control the narrative and the characterization of central figures. Good and evil characters are clearly separated; we are not invited to have much sympathy, for example, for anyone or anything German. The voyage down the Ulanga has the allegorical quality that we associate with such journeys along innumerable rivers, roads, and paths of life, while the setting repeatedly suggests the animism, the participation of nature in human affairs, characteristic of folk tales. Indeed, the jungle, the sky, and the river all operate at critical moments quite as purposefully as the protagonists. Rose, like innumerable storied sisters, has a name that associates her with flowers and through them, with the Proserpine myth that Northrop Frye identifies as the paradigmatic story for romance.[6] Like many other romantic heroines, she is strongly associated with flowers at several important moments in the narrative. The story unwinds with a profusion of incident that gives it an episodic "and then, and then" structure typical of popular romantic narratives like the Sinbad stories or cinematic versions like Michael Powell's *The Thief of Baghdad* and Huston's own *Roy Bean*.

With the exception of *Annie*, a film of which his authorship may have been more limited than usual, Huston never entirely returned to the straightforward comic romance of *The African Queen*. His view of the world and of relations between men and women was perhaps more qualified than such a genre usually allows. His playful, inquisitive interest in the aesthetic and philosophical issues of his narrative art, moreover, tended to lead him to more complicated aesthetic structures. Intricate thematics of politics, religion, existentialism, power, and cultural conflict combine to produce filmic narratives that are energized by generic tension and conflict, as well as by the contentions of protagonists and antagonists. In most of Huston's films, characterization, too, tends to complicate the relatively sharp moral stratification of romance.

Yet Huston did not abandon the generic elements that appear so clearly in *The African Queen*. Indeed, *Heaven Knows, Mr. Allison* can be seen as a sort of artistic self-reply to *The African Queen*, and *The Life and Times of Judge Roy Bean* stands as Huston's most profound and exuberant exploration of the kinds of meanings available to cinematic romance. So if *The African Queen* cannot be claimed as typical Huston, it can perhaps be claimed as one of the generic poles of his art. It stands as an aesthetically unified comic romance opposite which we may see, like a demonic reflection, an equally atypical film at the other generic extreme, the radically ironic *The Kremlin Letter*.

Before putting aside the issue of the genre of *The African Queen*, two further observations may be useful. The first has to do with courtship and the second with the related issue of comedy. In romances generally, love arrives suddenly and improbably, though its consummation or final accomplishment may well be long and arduous. It is mutual and it is essential to curing the human ills and recovering the lost optimism or completing the identities of the protagonists. As we have seen, for Huston an adult innocence must include knowledge and acceptance of self and the world. Innocence for Huston is not the lack of knowledge but its undaunted possession.

Like much of the crucial action of *The African Queen*, the courtship of Rose and Charlie is associated with the revitalizing imagery of water – an association that goes beyond the fact that the film takes place almost entirely on a river and a lake. As we have seen, the first pleasure the heroine and hero have together comes when they bathe in the river after fleeing the devastated village. That night, as Charlie sleeps in the bow of the boat and Rose in the stern under a canopy, a drenching rain falls. Soaked, Charlie is driven to the shelter. His arrival startles Rose, who seems to think he is making advances and sends him back into the weather. When she realizes his motives for coming to her makeshift bedroom, however, she admits him and even opens an umbrella over him where he is still exposed to the rain. This small scene begins the progression of the two central figures toward mutual trust and intimacy. It also typifies the decency and kindness that will characterize their love. Their relationship will humanize and enlarge them both, making Charlie more civilized and responsive while Rose becomes less repressed and dejected.

As the concluding marriage of Rose and Charlie suggests, *The African Queen* develops along comic lines as well as romantic ones. (Romance need not be comic.) Generally speaking, comedy in narrative is established on two fundamental principles. Aristotle identified the first: a story is comic to the extent that it excludes serious pain, prolonged suffering, and irrecoverable destruction.[7] Pratfalls are not funny if they end in, or even plausibly threaten, broken backs or pools of blood. Northrop Frye enunciated the second principle in "The Argument of Comedy": comic plots move characters and societies from isolation, fragmentation, and conflict to integration and harmony.[8] Both as an emblem of this narrative movement and as a practical means of achieving it, marriage or its promise serves as the most usual comic closure.

As with its romance, *The African Queen* serves its comedy almost pure. Among Huston's films, such sunny, unequivocal comedy occurs rarely. The first sequences of *The African Queen* (retrospectively, as must always be the case) evince the clarity of the implicit comic contract Huston offers to its audience, and the last ones exemplify the fidelity with which he honors it. The opening establishes a reassuringly humorous tone that considerably defuses the succeeding violence and fright, allowing the audience to respond to the raid of the German soldiers at least partly as the beginning of an adventure rather than exclusively as an episode of outrage and loss. The scenes preceding the attack convey genial amusement: the aural chaos of the hymn, the sign that incongruously announces the straw hut as the "1st Methodist Church / Kung Du," close-ups of the uncomprehending faces of native singers, a perspiring, hard-pedaling Katharine Hepburn pumping the organ and trying to sing through the cacophony. (This first sequence probably recalls Huston's apprenticeship as a screenwriter. In tone and content, it closely resembles the hymn and much-interrupted sermon of Walter Brennan that begins *Sergeant York* [1941], a film of Howard Hawks for which Huston was one of the writers.) Such scenes promise that we will see life portrayed mostly from an emotional viewpoint of amiable detachment.

The ardor of the natives for Charlie's discarded cigar continues the comedy. It may also serve as an authorial signature, a reference to the cast-off cigarette at the opening of *The Treasure of the Sierra Madre*. More importantly, it embodies a theme that will run through the film, the clash of spiritual and carnal needs, the competing claims of nature and appetite on the one hand, and the human desire to rise above them on the other. As in *The Night of the Iguana*, that conflict will be central to *The African Queen*. The theme continues into the next sequence, a stuffy tea during which Mr. Allnutt's noisy stomach embarrasses the attempt at a decorous, European social moment.

Potential distress caused by the death of Rose's brother (Robert Morley) is diminished by the reduction of his character to a stereotype of an inflexible, self-important middle-class English colonialist. The audience is likely to be further alienated from him by his disingenuous mean-spiritedness about the promotion of a former classmate and his cruel, self-interested appraisal of Rose. In the delirium of his fever, he reveals only too clearly his feelings: "Not comely among the maidens, but she too can be a servant in the House of the Lord. Even for such as she, God has a goodly purpose." Rose overhears this utterance with the same enthusiasm she later accords Charlie's denunciation of her as a "crazy, psalm-singin', skinny old maid." The death of Rose's brother is not shown and immediate pathos is thereby avoided. Furthermore, we are assured by his delusions that he dies without suffering or terror.

As Rose and Charlie stand on the deck of the *Louisa* with ropes around their necks, the implied comic promises of the filmmaker and his penchant for rescuing his protagonists with implausible miracles are reasserted shamelessly. Even before the ceremony of execution begins, Huston and Agee give the German captain a line to reassure the audience that neither it nor the protagonists will suffer unduly. Charlie obviously lies about Rose, and the captain irritably mutters, "I shall hang you twice, I think." A conspicuously arranged waterline shot of the capsized *African Queen* in the foreground with its torpedoes lifted toward the approaching battleship further supports the comedy of this moment. Appropriate to both comedy and romance, the delay that saves the hero and heroine comes about because Charlie asks the German captain to marry Rose and him before hanging them. "By the authority vested in me by Kaiser Wilhelm, I pronounce you man and wife. Proceed with the execution." But only the most untrusting of viewers will by this time be unable to enjoy the luxurious anxiety that precedes the protagonists' last-second escape. The comic muse of *The African Queen* will not allow the tragic spirit of death to share the stage at the finale.

A similar movement concludes *Sinful Davey*. Davey (John Hurt) has a noose around his neck and a hood over his head as he faces his end. Like Charlie, he manages to be remarkably calm in the face of death, devoting his "final words" to a plug for his memoirs, soon "to be sold to the public at a most reasonable price." Rescued just after what appears to be the nick of time, his story ends, like that of Charlie and Rose, with the prospect of life as a married, presumably reformed man, saved by the love of a good woman. It also ends with music and dance, as does the paradoxically triumphant death of Toulouse-Lautrec at the end of *Moulin Rouge*.

The characterization of the protagonists of *The African Queen* reflects the clarity and simplicity of the narrative. Both Rose and Charlie are guileless, untroubled by devious motives or psychological complications beyond ordinary human needs to grow up, to find a mate, and to establish a family. Huston is perhaps more interested in Rose. Charlie, for all that he is an engaging figure played with droll sympathy by Bogart, is drawn with less detail and texture than his feminine counterpart. From a director supposed to be absorbed in male character and interaction, the greater depth of the heroine may be unexpected. In part, Huston's reputation as a maker of masculinist art is overstated; in part, the genre of *The African Queen* accounts for Rose's prominence. Romance often centralizes female figures, for the heroine's literal or figurative return from the underworld brings with it salvation.

Rose blooms. Like the metaphorically floral heroines of a host of folk tales, her character does not so much transform into something else as realize what it already is; she develops into the person that prior circumstances have suppressed. We see this character development repeatedly in Huston's movies, usually in more realistic forms. The link between the quest for an external object or goal and the concurrent, generally less conscious quest for self are especially clear with Rose, but the same structure unfolds in most of Huston's films.

At first, Rose is anonymous and dependent; we do not know even her name for ten minutes, only that she is overdressed, overheated, overwhelmed. Though later developments make early hints of toughness and determination clearer, our first impressions are of her tremulous mouth and timorousness. Huston's conception of her character is memorably recorded by Katharine Hepburn, an account worth quoting at length, both for what it reveals about Huston's view of Rosie and for the glimpse it provides of Huston's direction.

> It was during this pause that John came one morning to my hut.
> "May I have a cup of coffee?"
> "Yes, of course – what?"
> "Well – I don't want to influence you. But incidentally . . . that was great, that scene, burying Robert. And of course you had to look solemn – serious. . . . Yes, of course – you were burying your brother. You were sad. But, you know, this is an odd tale – I mean, Rosie is almost always facing what is for her a serious situation. And she's a pretty serious-minded lady. And I wondered – well – let me put it this way – have you by any chance seen any movies of – you know – newsreels – of Mrs. Roosevelt – those newsreels where she visited the soldiers in the hospitals?"
> "Yes, John – yes – I saw one. Yes."
> "Do you remember, Katie dear, that lovely smile – ?"
> "Yes, John – yes – I do."
> "Well, I was wondering. You know, thinking ahead of our story. And thinking of your skinny little face – a lovely little face, dear. But skinny. And those famous hollow cheeks. And that turned-down mouth. You know – when you look serious – you do look rather – well, serious. And it just occurred to me – now, take Rosie – you know – you are a very religious – serious-minded – frustrated woman. Your brother just dead. Well, now, Katie – you're going to go through this whole adventure before the falls and before love raises its . . . Well, you know what I mean – solemn.
>
> "Then I thought of how to remedy that. She's used to handling strangers as her brother's hostess. And you 'put on' a smile. Whatever the situation. Like Mrs. Roosevelt – she felt she was ugly – she thought she looked better smiling – so she . . . Chin up. The best is yet to come – onward ever onward. . . . The society smile."
>
> A long pause.
> "You mean – yes – I see. When I pour out the gin I – yes – yes – when I . . . "
> "Well," he said, getting up to go. He'd planted the seed. "Think it over. . . . Perhaps it might be a useful . . . "
> He was gone.
> I sat there.
> This is the goddamnedest best piece of direction I have ever heard. Now, let's see. . . .
> Well, he's just told me exactly how to play this part. Oh-h-h-h-h, lovely thought. Such fun. I was his from there on in.[9]

By the end of the film, Rose has shed her timidity along with her excess clothing. The strength and feminine appeal that remain express what she was in potential at the beginning. The catalyst that effectuates her transformation is love. It is almost an axiom of romantic comedy that at the initiation of the action its protagonists will be overdue for each other. Both are likely to have arrived at adulthood, and both are often impeded by the psychic chains of a blocking figure who will not abandon outdated claims to control. The heroine, in particular, may be literally captive or somehow otherwise prevented from pursuing an autonomous adult life. She frequently languishes in the oppressive embrace of an older man, a parent or parent-figure who is usurping the place that belongs to a younger male with whom she should be establishing her own family. Although the hero is occasionally found in similar circumstances, he is more likely to be out and about. But like Gay in *The Misfits*, he is at loose ends and often unable to find, or even comprehend, what he needs.

The eccentric courtship of Charlie and Rose is as central to the film as their mission to sink the *Louisa*. Indeed, the two actions take place all but inseparably. Though the form of her oppression is transformed from the captivity in the lair of a dragon, wizard, or wicked step parent into something more realistic, Rose remains, like the romantic heroines that are her forebears, trapped with an older, repressive male. Her brother has judged her insignificant and taken her to Africa as his servant. The frustration she cannot acknowledge to herself leaks out in the quavering of her mouth and the restlessness of her hands. These gestures suggest both a sexual energy that has been almost but not quite extinguished and, more generally, the repression of her entire personality. They will disappear in the excitement of the mission and in her love for Charlie.

The death of Rose's brother removes the source of her oppression. The first time she and Charlie shoot the rapids, Rose responds with a passion wholly unexpected by her companion. "I never dreamed," she exclaims, "a mere physical experience could be so stimulating!" Then she adds revealingly, "I've only known such excitement a few times before, a few times in my dear brother's sermons when the spirit was really upon him!" With the delicate translation of Forester's novel typical of the Huston-Agee script, these lines suggest that Rose is more than ready for such stimulation, and that her exciting companion in future will be Charlie, not her brother.[10] At the same time, the dominant comedy of the moment muffles any possible coarseness. The scene gives less emphasis to Rose's awakening than to Charlie's discomfiture at her enthusiasm for continuing a mission that he is convinced can end only in catastrophe.

Like Rose, Charlie is also somewhat emotionally retarded. Although he thinks that "Out here, I'm my own boss," his frequent invocations of "poor old Mother" suggest the belated dependence on a parental figure often seen in the protagonists of romantic narratives. His "poor old Mum" would say that Rose is no lady; his mother used to read him stories out of the Bible. He is more than ready for a mate, but like Rose he is still emotionally somewhat infantile and dependent. When he tries to make up with Rose after losing his temper, he acts like a little boy, internalizing and reciting the parental discipline he has been made to regret defying: "Ah, it's a great thing to have a lady aboard with clean habits. Sets a man a good example. Man alone, he gets to livin' like a hog. Then too with me it's always put things off – never do today what you can put off to tomorrow."

But Charlie can no more go back to the bosom of his mother than Rose can retrieve her brother. The shot that opens the sequence after Charlie's binge repeats exactly the shot of jungle foliage with which the film commenced. More than two-fifths through the movie, a new day and a new story begin. It will be the story of Rose and Charlie growing up and coming together as they chug down the Ulanga toward the *Louisa* and their marriage.

After Rose triumphs by ostracizing the recalcitrant Charlie and he agrees to resume their mission, Huston repeats another motif important in the beginning of the film. "Alright, Miss, you win . . . as the crocodiles will be glad to hear. Down the river we go." While he speaks, a cross gleams on the boiler to his left. It is the newly polished relief valve, cleaned as part of Charlie's peace offering, and it recalls the cross at Kung-Du. This inconspicuous image reinforces our sense that Charlie and his boat have replaced Rose's brother and his church in the heroine's life.

For the rest of the film, Rose and Charlie overcome the physical obstacles that stand between them and the *Louisa* and the psychological ones that stand between them and their marriage. Of the two narrative actions, the love story will probably be of more ultimate interest to the audience than the sinking of the German ship. As John McCarty writes, "The film's theme is not about carrying out a mission – this, as in virtually all of Huston's work, is merely a motif. . . . The *Louisa* is not the prize Charlie and Rosie are after. The real prize is each other."[11]

Both actions are developed with the richness of detail and remarkable sense of narrative rhythm that are among Huston's most consistent and distinctive artistic virtues. Few story-tellers in any medium have ever possessed a more secure sense of how to build and vary the rhythms of a story than John Huston.[12] Even in a film as thin as *Victory*, Huston is able to sustain a climax of a length and intensity that only a small number of directors could dare to attempt. His skill with the rhythms of story-telling is even more crucial in *Under the Volcano* and *The Dead*, two much richer films that derive from books so short on action in the popular sense that they seem almost perverse as sources of narrative films.

The dominant rhythm of *The African Queen*, as in most of Huston's movies, derives from alternations of crisis and relaxation. The peaceful forest canopy of the opening shot gives way to the din and sweat of the hymn singing, which itself is broken off when the *African Queen* arrives. The subsequent tea is followed by the attack of the German soldiers. The high tension of Samuel Sayre's death and the flight of Rose and Charlie is relaxed on the river. Reversing the emotional tone again, their sleep is interrupted by storm. The violent rush through rapids is followed by the more tranquil interlude of forging a new propeller blade. The relief of an evening tie-up is abruptly breached by swarms of mosquitoes as, a little later, the relief of Charlie's return to the boat is destroyed by his horror at finding himself covered with leeches. The tranquillity of still water itself eventually becomes nearly fatal in the delta. But that cul-de-sac, as we have seen, is removed by a storm. The excitement of the attack on the *Louisa* and the sinking of the *African Queen* is followed by the comparative stasis of Charlie's interrogation; and so on. The steadily increasing intensity of the protagonists' marvelous adventures alternates with a series of pauses in the action that lets them – and the audience – gather themselves for the next emotional peak, usually a little higher than the last.

The rhythmic structure of *The African Queen* mimics the gradual increase in tension of courtship and lovemaking. It too culminates in resolution and release. Lillian Ross, who wrote a series of articles on the making of Huston's *The Red Badge of Courage* for *The New Yorker*, witnessed a revealing moment in the collaboration of Agee and Huston.

Agee was saying, as Huston paced in small circles, that the trip the river captain, Humphrey Bogart, and the missionary's sister, Katharine Hepburn, would make together down the river on the captain's boat in "The African Queen" could symbolize the act of love.

"Oh, Christ, Jim," Huston said. "Tell me something I can understand. This isn't like a novel. This is a screenplay. You've got to demonstrate everything, Jim. People on the screen are gods and goddesses. We know all about them. Their habits. Their caprices. But we can't touch them. They're not real. They stand for something. They're symbols. You can't have symbolism within symbolism, Jim."[13]

Agee seems in the outcome to have had the better of the argument: the

association of "the act of love" with the trip down the river occasionally approaches the explicit. When Charlie shows Rose the right pace for
bailing the boat, his instruction becomes a barely concealed embrace and
the rhythm of the pumping evokes the rhythm of lovemaking.

Huston develops a variety within the dominant emotional and narrative alternations of his story that saves the abstract design from mechanical (or biological) predictability and gives rhetorical emphasis to
especially critical moments. After Charlie and Rose escape the fusillade
at Shona, the audience is ready for an expected relaxation of tension. No
sooner does Charlie manage the makeshift repair of the steam pipe that
takes them out of range, however, when the river turns into a cataract
through which the *African Queen* tumbles like a toy boat under a tub
spigot. The extraordinary prolongation of suspense and excitement during these sequences has an important function. As Rose and Charlie steer
into quiet water, they embrace in relief and exultation. A new musical
motif, lyrical and carried by strings, replaces stirring horns and cymbals.
As the action that passed was of unprecedented length and intensity, so
will be the remission. By morning Rose and Charlie will be lovers.

Two turbulent adventures, the run past Shona and the rush down the
rapids, are followed by two episodes of quiet: recovery and falling in love
in the anchorage and the domesticity of the next morning. When Rose
and Charlie embrace in the evening, Huston avails himself of a transi-
tional device that is rare for *The African Queen*, a fade-out followed by
a fade-in. The lovemaking of Charlie and Rose is sheltered in the modest darkness of the interval that the fades delineate. The usual succession
of anxiety and relief is broken by a second interval of domestic tranquillity, followed by romantic shots of flowers and hillsides and adolescent
play as Charlie mimics hippos and baboons – to Rose's doting amusement. The high adventure, deep disappointment, loving tenderness, and
threats of death that make up the remarkably paced final sequences continue to vary the rhythms of the action to brilliant effect.

The progress of the mission to sink the *Louisa* parallels the growing love
of Rose and Charlie. The love story eventually assumes a rhetorical and
emotional ascendency over the political one, and the attempt to sink the
Louisa becomes something of an emblem or pledge, an occasion for the love
of the protagonists rather than an action of equal, independent status. Rose's
affection gives Charlie courage and self-esteem. The morning after their run
past Shona and subsequent lovemaking, he manifests a new enthusiasm for
their mission. "Then you think we can do it?" Rose asks dubiously. Charlie's response is not what we have learned to expect from him: "Do it? Of
course we can do it! Nothin' a man can't do if he believes in himself. Nev-

er say die, that's my motto." Rose admits to having had "a moment or two of weakness," but finally sighs, "thank heaven for your strength."

This reversal of usual roles signals a new equality between the protagonists, a partnership that will support them for the rest of the film. At their darkest moment, as they face what appears to be certain death in the delta, their mutuality holds. "Rosie, I'm not one bit sorry I came," declares a worn out Charlie. "What I mean is, it was worth it." As he falls asleep, Rosie prays with the directness and plain eloquence that we have seen to be characteristic of Huston's screenwriting at its moments of greatest emotional intensity: "Dear Lord, we've come to the end of our journey. In a little while, we'll stand before you. I pray for you to be merciful; judge us not for our weakness but for our love, and open the doors of heaven for Charlie and me." The selflessness of the love between Rosie and Charlie is again evident when each tries to persuade the other to leave the *African Queen* during the attack on the *Louisa* and they have what Rose winds up sentimentally cherishing as their "first argument."

Collaboration and mutual healing characterize their relationship after they pass Shona and the rapids. A critical moment in their progress toward intimacy arrives when Rose kneels before Charlie to remove a thorn from his foot. Later Charlie will cover Rose with the canvas canopy and pole the *African Queen* away from a terrifying cloud of mosquitoes that has descended upon them. Later still, Rose will remove from Charlie the leeches that are equally horrifying to him. The profoundest benefits Charlie and Rose offer each other have to do with the self-discovery their love makes possible, their belated maturation, and the new family they will create together. "What a time we've had, Rosie, what a time!" Charlie exclaims. "Ah, we'll never lack for stories to tell our grandchildren."

The romanticism that Huston and Agee assign to the love of Rose and Charlie represents a considerable change from Forester's ironic characterization. In the novel, Charlie is very much dominated by Rose, who serves as both a parent and a lover: "Allnutt was very happy too. Whatever he might do in the heat of passion, his need was just as much for a mother as for a mistress."[14] A little later, Forester continues in the same vein.

He [Charlie] was a man simply made to be henpecked. What with the success they had met under Rose's command up to now, and with the events of the night, Rose's ascendancy over him was complete. He was quite happy to cast all the responsibility onto her shoulders and to await philosophically wherever destiny might send.[15]

In the novel, only Rose grows into adulthood; Charlie remains an overage adolescent, still dependent upon maternal direction.

As the film ends, Rose and Charlie – who happily characterizes himself as "an old married man" – swim off to a future that will presumably include the grandchildren whom he has looked forward to. At the close of the novel, however, the future of the lovers is emphatically uncertain; their return to civilization raises a multiplicity of threats. Rose proposes marriage to Charlie and he accepts her, but that development fails to promise lasting security. Nor does it shed a rosy glow over the character of Charlie or his motives for marriage. Forester's ending is remarkably downbeat, suggesting that the equivocal love between his protagonists on the river is unlikely to survive when they return to the complications of European social and political life.

> Allnutt was a little dazed and stupid. This unlooked-for transfer to the West Coast of Africa, this taken-for-granted enlistment in the South African forces, and now this new proposal left him with hardly a word to say. He thought of Rose's moderate superiority in social status. He thought about money; presumably he would receive pay in the South African army. He thought about the girl he had married twelve years ago when he was eighteen. She had probably been through half a dozen men's hands by now, but there had never been a divorce and presumably he was still married to her. Oh well, South Africa and England were a long way apart, and she couldn't trouble him much.
> "Righto, Rosie," he said, "let's."
> So they left the Lakes and began the long journey to Matadi and marriage. Whether or not they lived happily ever after is not easily decided.[16]

According to Huston, "C. S. Forester had told me that he had never been satisfied with the way *The African Queen* ended. He had written two different endings for the novel; one was used in the American edition, the other in the English. Neither one, he felt, was satisfactory."[17] James Fultz's fuller account supports the point that Huston and Peter Viertel – who joined the director after Agee had several heart attacks – did not use either of Forester's endings.[18] They did not fit the comic tall tale into which Forester's novel had been transformed.

If the ironic end of Forester's novel did not suit the purposes of Huston and Agee, much of its thematic content did. The movie amplifies Forester's unenthusiastic portrayal of organized religion, specifically Samuel Sayre's joyless rendition of it. That bias, we have observed already, is consonant with Huston's career-long aversion to institutionalized Christianity, which he usually portrays as hypocritical. The film opens with a church service and tea that do not exist in Forester's novel. Most conventionally religious characters in Huston's films use their piety as a pretext for self-interest, as an excuse for avoiding their duty to other people, or as an evasion of painful self-knowledge. Huston's inserted sequence in *The African Queen* slightly varies that formula; it characterizes religion as a source of class snobbery and provincialism. Religion is also associated with the parental figures who have retarded the full maturity of the two protagonists.

At its best, Christianity in *The African Queen* derives what glow it has from the radiance of the heroine. When Rose prays that "the doors of heaven" be opened she asks that God judge Charlie and her "not for our weakness but for our love." It is again characteristic of Huston's art, however, that the film presents their "weakness" and their love as inextricably connected. Any God who requires an apology for the most affecting aspect of Rose and Charlie is not likely to prove attractive to the audience.

The screenplay that Agee wrote for Charles Laughton's *Night of the Hunter* reprises much more violently the contrast – characteristic of Huston's films and clearly marked in *The African Queen* – between a benign personal religiousness and the destructive, self-serving uses of conventional, socialized Christianity. In this temperamental predilection, as in others, Huston and Agee appear to have been well matched.

Beginning with his Army films, especially *San Pietro* and *Let There Be Light*, religious ideas and imagery gradually assume increasing prominence in Huston's work, chiefly as a source of irony or as part of the characterization of unsympathetic figures. Conventional Christianity has an equivocal role in *Moby Dick* and is often repulsive in such films as *The Unforgiven, A Walk with Love and Death*, and *Wise Blood*. In the last, the distortion of human impulses toward love and friendship by fundamentalist Christianity constitutes a central theme. At the end of his career, with *Under the Volcano* and *The Dead*, Huston turned toward a less judgmental, more problematic view of Christianity; but in neither of those films, despite the abundance of religious imagery, is the issue of Christianity of central importance. Huston's most sympathetic portrayal of Christianity may be found in *Heaven Knows, Mr. Allison*, made six years after *The African Queen*. His most sustained thinking about religion in general appears in his most overtly mythopoeic films, *The Bible, The Life and Times of Judge Roy Bean*, and *The Man Who Would Be King*. At the time in his career that he made *The African Queen*, his ninth feature film, Huston began to approach issues of religion and to use the ideas and images of Christianity in what would be his most characteristic fashion, as foils for opposing ideas and human tendencies that his films portray more sympathetically.

A relatively minor motif in *The African Queen*, the use of foreign languages in the dialogue, is equally characteristic of Huston's movies almost from the beginning of his career. Though it is central in none of his films, untranslated foreign-language dialogue reappears in the majority of them after Huston first used the technique in *Across the Pacific*. In *The Kremlin Letter* and *The Man Who Would Be King*, it plays a considerable role in emphasizing cultural conflict and intrusion. In those and other films it reinforces the opposing assumptions on which people of different cultures base their lives.

Among the generation of Hollywood directors who rose to sustained prominence after World War II, Huston is perhaps most conscious of, and self-conscious about, the degree to which the identities of his protagonists result from cultural construction. He consistently puts those socially constructed identities under a pressure that brings their fundamental assumptions into question. Whether they include foreign dialogue or not, virtually all of Huston's films subject to intense scrutiny the propositions on which his characters conceive their identities. We have already seen that many of his films introduce foreign cultures, especially primitive ones, as contrasts or alternatives to problematized civilizations represented by the central figures. This tendency appears in the first film he directed, *The Maltese Falcon*, in the sexual and cultural otherness of the antagonists and in their physical strangeness: Sidney Greenstreet's monstrous corpulence, Peter Lorre's effeminacy, Elisha Cook, Jr.'s jejune fragility as the gunsel. Looking at the next four Huston films, the African-American characters of *In This Our Life*, the Japanese in *Across the Pacific*, the Indians and Spanish-speaking natives in *The Treasure of the Sierra Madre*, and the Indians in *Key Largo* all give emphasis to contrasting cultural groups. In the two that followed, *We Were Strangers* and *The Asphalt Jungle*, a subculture occupies center stage, with the dominant culture at the edges. Huston's fascination with the issues raised when cultures meet persisted; *The Barbarian and the Geisha*, *The Unforgiven*, and *Victory* are among the movies in which cultures and/or subcultures clash.

The African Queen keeps such issues largely in the background, but the Babel of hymn singing that opens the film and the heavy dose of German speech near its end bracket the story in cultural contrasts. At the center, when Charlie and Rose come under fire as they pass Shona, the officers in the fortress above the river speak German and, we presume, the language of the African recruits. The latter, with lighthearted ineffectual enthusiasm, do most of the shooting. The Germans contrast

sharply in their dress and demeanor. Yet the behavior of the African soldiers is as ruthless in its cheerful way as that of the Europeans. Neither
group shows significant feeling about their mission; neither acts as if they
have any personal stake in, or regret about, the homicide they attempt.
Only Rose at first and then Charlie take the war personally. In effect, the
Germans and the native soldiers are dehumanized in much the same way.
They seem empty of personal conviction and largely devoid of sympathetic human qualities; and they act without apparent curiosity about
why they are shooting or whom they are shooting at. The episode at
Shona echoes the early action in which a force of black soldiers led by
two German officers burns Kung Du and takes prisoner its inhabitants.
In that sequence, the Germans and the Africans are equally alien and
show equally little empathy with their victims.

In contrast to the separation of the Germans from the English and the
Africans from the Europeans, Rose and Charlie, for all their superficial
differences, share a culture within which emotional connection is possible. If the joy of unexpected survival and the bonds created by overcoming danger together are the immediate stimuli to their falling in love, their
common language and shared culture play a role as well.

The protagonists occupy a similar position with regard to nature.
Among the affinities and contrasts that structure the film, the opposition
of Charlie and Rose to human antagonists and the nonhuman world is
practically equivalent. They are the single locus of human affection and
sympathy in an otherwise indifferent environment of political alliances
and natural forces. They come together in part because only they can.

Through them, moreover, Huston invokes an Edenic solitude of two,
an Adam and an Eve uniquely mated in an aboriginal garden. The first
morning of their life as lovers, they notice flowers that they have never
seen, flowers that they feel "perhaps no one has" ever seen. Like Adam
and Eve, they are the original witnesses of the world around them, with
which – for a little while, at least – they are in perfect harmony.

Without any capacity for sympathy, both nature and humans other
than the hero and heroine in *The African Queen* have a rather rudimentary moral status. Both tend to function as instrumentalities, good or evil
according to whether they are threatening ruin or promising relief for the
protagonists. As a consequence, the more common use of nature and/or
natives in Huston films to criticize the corruption of intruders is almost
absent. The conflicts are not so much between Euro-American and other cultures as between Rose and Charlie on the one hand and everyone
and everything else on the other. As in romantic comedy in general, the

lines of character division are between those who love and those who do not.

Nature and human others have a shifting emotional charge for the audience according to whether at any moment they are obstructing or enabling the journey of Charlie and Rose. Natives appear both innocent and vicious, sometimes simultaneously. Flowers are beautiful, and emblematic of the heroine and the courtship between her and Charlie; but when the river stinks, it reminds Rose of "stale marigolds." Nature is what humans are put on earth "to rise above," lectures Rose at her most priggish. In reaction, the audience may be inclined sympathetically toward carnal manifestations that disrupt such spinsterish propriety: Charlie's rumbling stomach at tea, his frankness about the need in a hot climate to bury Samuel promptly, his adolescent mimicry of hippos and monkeys after he and Rose have become lovers. His imitations of the animals suggest something like a unity with nature while maintaining a human identity – an apparently ideal solution to the natural–human dichotomy in the film. But the mosquitoes and the leeches, the crocodiles, and the storm that sinks the *African Queen* before she can torpedo the *Louisa* represent a nature less in harmony with human aspirations. Even the pervasive imagery of water, regenerative as it mostly is, creates tremendous threats in rapids and the labyrinthine delta.

The poise of *The African Queen* and the ultimate resolution of most of its ambiguities in unequivocal romantic cadences may be symbolized by the symbolic unification of the imagery of fire and water. The combination of those apparently opposed elements leads directly to the marriage of the protagonists – an unlikely and extreme unification, itself – and to their triumph over the Germans. From the beginning of the film, the mixture of water and fire is associated with overcoming obstacles. Separately, they tend to be destructive or dangerous, as in the burning of the village and the violence of the rapids. Together, they lead to triumphant consummations.

When the *African Queen* steams into the picture in the second sequence, the efficacious conjunction of fire and water is established. The boat's whistle announces an arrival that shortens the comic ordeal of the hymn singing and brings to an end the sweaty church service. The whistle and the engine derive their power from steam – that is, heated water – and the boat ingests river and forest and turns them to motion in its mechanical digestion.

Impasses are overcome by the proficient conjunction of fire and water. Her drive shaft twisted and a propeller blade broken after the tremendous rapids, the *African Queen* seems to have reached the end of her inanimate life. But Rose and Charlie descend into the river to work the damaged parts free, then take them onto the bank where they forge the shaft straight and weld a new blade into place. In the same sequence, we witness the increasingly intimate partnership of the lovers, the distant, constrained woman and the rude mechanic. It is Rose who has the idea to repair the damaged parts with charcoal and a stone forge, but when she offers to help Charlie free the drive shaft, he dismisses her irritably. A few moments later, she nonetheless joins him beneath the boat.[19] The repairs are accomplished by the two together. The imagery of fire and water so important in this episode will be repeated when Charlie constructs the torpedoes and when the *Louisa* runs into them, explodes, and sinks into the lake in a tumult of smoke and flame.

The deluge that frees the stymied boat combines water and fire fundamentally in images of rain and sun. The storm begins with crackling thunder from a sky that mixes bright blue and gathering clouds. During the lyrical succession of images that follows, the rain falls paradoxically through conspicuous sunshine. The poetic interlude of sixteen shots and one pan ends when a ray of light streams through a crack in the dark clouds.

The imagery here anticipates that of the Noah episode in *The Bible* and anticipates the extended images of water and heat/light that initiate the creation sequence of the same film. Similar lyrical interludes are inserted into a number of other Huston films: the shots of the forest fires of *In This Our Life*, the subjective camera that walks us through the farmhouse in *Wise Blood*, images of sea and sky at the end of *A Walk with Love and Death*, and the gray Irish countryside that concludes *The Dead*. Such poetic visuals typically mark or prepare for epiphanies, moments in which characters understand their connections to the world and other people with a comprehensive, often grieving, acceptance. In the comic romance of *The African Queen*, the grief is absent but the lyric impulse remains.

As Charlie and Rose paddle out of the frame in the last shot, they end the movie on a note that has been the dominant tone in its imagistic scale. The uniting of man and woman, of working-class mechanic and middle-class lady, and the visual marriage of fire and water are intimately connected. In the romantic world of *The African Queen*, the pathetic fallacy is as natural a law as gravity. Natural and human obstacles to both the marital and the military destiny of Rose and Charlie finally capitulate, even cooperate. The German captain marries his two captives and inadvertently dooms his ship. In a reassuringly absurd moment, a German officer bobbing amidst the wreckage of the *Louisa* salutes his spluttering commander. His preposterous gesture reasserts the comic mode of the film and assures viewers that they need not be distracted from the happy ending by anxiety for the losers. The wish fulfillment and reassertion of a benignant universe that conclude *The African Queen* are unusual for a Huston film, but only in their unequivocal realization. The hopes and desires themselves and the images, rhythms, and characters through which they are expressed remain perfectly typical.

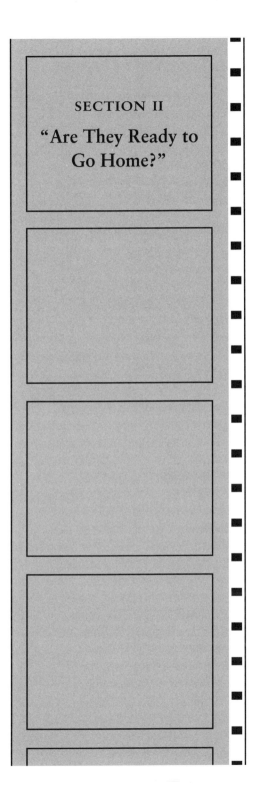

SECTION II

"Are They Ready to Go Home?"

The Misfits
The Night of the Iguana
Let There Be Light

CHAPTER IV

The Misfits (1961) and the Idea of John Huston's Films

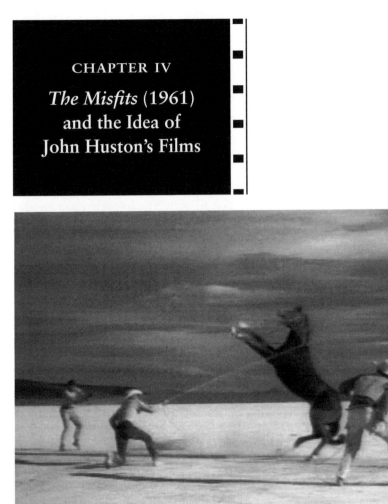

To be alive in any authentic way, the characters of The Misfits *(including jackrabbits and mustangs) must be free.*

The Misfits was released in 1961, twenty years after Huston's first film and twenty-six before his last; it is number seventeen of the thirty-seven feature-length movies he directed. Enormous anticipation attached to its famous director and brilliant cast: Clark Gable, Marilyn Monroe, Eli Wallach, Montgomery Clift, and Thelma Ritter. Its screenwriter was the much-honored Arthur Miller, whose improbable marriage to the voluptuous Monroe was disintegrating, as was Monroe herself, in the glare of publicity and the relentless Nevada sun. (Much of the screenplay in general and Monroe's lines in particular can be read as a melancholy medi-

75

tation on the failing union of the playwright and the star and, perhaps, as a last plea to save it.)[1]

The personal histories of the makers of *The Misfits* were as spectacular as their struggles during its filming, and sadder. Gable died of heart disease before the film opened and, more poignantly, shortly before the birth of his only child. Monroe had to struggle desperately to complete her performance and died of an overdose of sleeping pills before she could finish another film. Though Clift made several more films, he was in serious personal decline after *The Misfits*. His hypothyroidism and other medical problems intensified, as did his alcoholism. When he arrived in Ireland to make *Freud* with Huston the next year, he had so deteriorated that he could not memorize his lines and needed the aid of prompt cards on the set – then an uncommon practice. In 1966 Clift also died.[2] When Thelma Ritter died in early 1969, four of the five stars were gone within about seven years of the release of the film. Only Eli Wallach was (and is) still alive.

Made in the midst of "real life dramas," *The Misfits* undertakes an imaginative exploration of pain and change and death. If the circumstances surrounding its production do not finally affect the images and words of the movie itself, they nonetheless attach to it an aura of tragic richness as an avatar of its ill-fated cast. The biographies of its makers resonate forlornly with the sadness of much of its story. But they also resonate with the courage of its gritty characters, written and played by damaged human beings who were as brave in their professionalism as they were afflicted in their destinies.

Not that the movie needs a biographical setting to intensify its portrayal of desperation, endurance, and hope. Dejected and diminished, its central figures seek a way to come to terms with change and to repair their battered lives. Their quest, as in *The Treasure of the Sierra Madre* and many of Huston's other films, turns toward a home that has been lost or never found. Freedom and trust in self and the world are the medicines that make possible discovering or re-creating a sense of personal fitness, of knowing a home. The characters of *The Misfits* need a place on earth, among other people, and in themselves where, as Gay (Clark Gable) says, they can "just live."

From opening credits on puzzle pieces that do not fit together, *The Misfits* portrays people who are disconnected, out of place, lost. Shortly after he meets Roslyn (Marilyn Monroe), Gay tells her a joke that begins with a "city man out in the country" asking a roadside bumpkin to tell him "how [to] get back to town." The bumpkin can't do it, nor can he tell the wanderer anything else. "You don't know much, do you?" the city dweller finally exclaims in exasperation. "No, but I ain't lost," comes the punch line. Knowing things, as Guido (Eli Wallach) does most conspicuously, will not keep one from being lost; and being able to find one's way obviates the need for other knowledge or, perhaps more accurately, gives meaning to what one knows.

Across the desert highlands of Nevada – a vastness emphasized by heavy doses of panoramic long shots – the universe looms trackless. Although most of the movie takes place in interiors or among crowds of other people, the background of uninhabited mountains and high plateau is of constant importance. As in a number of Huston's films, the most intense crisis of *The Misfits* takes place when its characters go into the wilds. Huston was conscious of the city–country aspect of the movie. "The essence of *The Misfits*," he told Gerald Pratley, "really concerns the environment, what civilization does in the way of tarnishing the life around us and our souls."[3]

The departure from city, court, or farm into a wilderness on a quest for treasure, military glory, or sanctuary is a popular plot structure in narratives of all kinds – from folk tales, through Greek and Roman literature, medieval romances, Renaissance epics, and the Romantics, and on to the novels and movies of the twentieth century. Shakespeare used it again and again. No film director loved it better than John Huston. In *The Misfits* the central characters go "mustanging," in *The Treasure of the Sierra Madre* they go into unexplored mountains seeking gold, in *Across the Pacific* the characters take a ship to Panama to thwart Japanese spies, another boat in *The African Queen* carries the heroine and hero through a trackless jungle to attack a German warship, and in *Moby Dick* still another ship removes the plot to the remote seas of all the world in quest of whales and The Whale. And so on, for most of Huston's career. Even modern California, in Huston's next-to-last movie, *Prizzi's Honor*, functions structurally in much the same way as the wilds of earlier films. In a parody of the more ordinary removal to pastoral self-discovery, the East Coast protagonist goes west as to a wasteland and returns to accept his place in the crime family that he has learned he can live neither without nor outside of.

Unless one has a home in the land or a place to return to among other people, the emptiness of wild nature obliterates human identity. One will be lost. In *The Misfits*, social disconnection and geographical disorientation coincide. "Do you belong to Gay?" Perce (Montgomery Clift) asks Roslyn. "I don't know where I belong," she replies sadly. Later that evening, a drunken Gay confronts her, "Where you at? I don't know where you're at." "Gay, I'm with you," says Roslyn, making again the instinctive equation between connections with other people, orientation in space, and identity.

As *The Misfits* begins, none of its central characters know quite where they're at. The most alienated of the central characters, Guido, at the same time feels most painfully his disconnection from the physical world. He visualizes himself stuck in an airplane that is literally going nowhere: "I can't make a landing and I can't get up to God, either." With the death of his wife he lost his home, an uncompleted house that he can neither inhabit nor relinquish. In comparison, the cheerfully single professional witness for divorce proceedings, Isabel (Thelma Ritter), is better connected to life. She, at least, understands her unsuitability for marriage, understands that one has to have a place and a degree of self-possession before one can find a shared identity with another person: "Charlie never would have stayed married to me. I even lost the vacuum cleaner once . . . they still haven't found it." To Roslyn she gaily confesses that she lost her wedding ring on her honeymoon. Less cheerful, but equally aware of his personal weightlessness and his loss of physical and social place, Perce has been pushed out of his family and off the ranch he expected to inherit. His isolation and uprooting is reflected in the rodeo announcer's confusion about his hometown. For the bucking-horse event he is introduced as "a cowboy out of White River, Wyoming"; on the Brahma bull he is sent into the arena as hailing from "Black Hills, Colorado." According to him, he comes from California. It does not matter which nonexistent nonhome he is assigned, however; both animals unseat him, just as he was thrown from the place in which he had expected to spend his life.

The remaining main characters have connections with the world and with other people that are at best equivocal. Gay claims the open country as home, but his marriage broke up because of his wife's infidelity with his cousin and his family life consists of seeing his children once or twice a year at rodeos. Like Gay, Isabel has adjusted with courage and good humor to being single, but her most enduring romantic connection is the potted rose her former husband sends her every year on the anniversary of their divorce. The place that she calls home she also calls "the leave-it state." It is a state where she has been left at least twice, by her former husband and by the cowboy who "just didn't come back." Roslyn keeps returning to where she began but nobody is at home: "I always end up back where I started. Never had anybody, much . . . Here I am . . . They [her parents] both weren't there."

Loss of home and of bonds to the land frequently represent in Huston's films the loss of an innocence that his characters struggle to recover. The opening sequences of *Wise Blood* express that loss as eloquently as anything in Huston's work. Natives in films like *The Treasure of the Sierra Madre*, *Key Largo*, and *The Man Who Would Be King* have connections with their earth that anglophone intruders lack and threaten to corrupt. In *The Misfits*, the native mustangs are hunted for pet food or simply shot and left to rot because they compete with cattle for forage. Desert jackrabbits get into gardens and then into the sights of proprietary shotguns, and resident eagles are exterminated by ranchers who pay Guido to kill them from his airplane. Human intruders, mostly wanderers, cluster around Reno in the leave-it state, where they lose their money and dissolve their marriages.

Everyone in *The Misfits* needs a home, or hope of a home, or maybe just a plausible conception of one. What might a home be? Love, attention, and – the geographic in this film is always joined to the social – well-understood directions. It is where people worry about you, as Isabel and Gay do about Roslyn and as Roslyn does about Gay and Perce. As in *The Night of the Iguana*, home is something that two people make for each other; in *The Misfits*, people find their way to a life together and to a place where they can just live. Over the first breakfast he has ever prepared for a woman (a comically austere single pancake each), Gay remarks, "I wouldn't know how to say good-bye to you, Roslyn. Surprises me." His sense of personal connection creates a sense of connection to the house: he follows this confession by observing, "There's a lot to be done around this place." After the epiphanies of the mustang roundup, as the movie ends, Roslyn and Gay achieve the mutual trust and commitment they began to work toward when they started living together. They give each other a place and at the same time locate themselves in the universe. "How do you find your way home in the dark?" asks Roslyn, no longer afraid of winding up where she started. "Just head for that big star straight on," answers Gay. "The highway's under it. It'll take us right home."

Two together, fitted to a place they can leave and come back to, make possible a family, make possible human life itself. Going home at the end of the movie, Roslyn and Gay talk about having a baby, "one person in the world, a child who could be brave from the beginning." To the stallion that Perce releases, Roslyn says simply, "Go home." It does indeed go home, but not to the mountains. Rather it returns to the creatures who give it a place in the world, the colt and the mare.

During much of *The Misfits*, however, its characters dwell not among beloved places and persons but among absences, ghosts, nobodies, and nowheres. To Kevin McCarthy, playing the husband Roslyn divorces at the beginning of the movie, Marilyn Monroe declares, "You're not there, Raymond. If I'm gonna be alone, I want to be by myself." (Casting McCarthy to receive those lines may be an insider's allusion to Don Siegel's *Invasion of the Body Snatchers* ['56], in which McCarthy stars as a man resisting aliens who strip people of their capacity for emotion and turn them into automatons who "aren't there" as human beings. Siegel, coincidentally, worked with Huston on *Across the Pacific*.) Guido's wife is dead. Gay's wife is gone and his children are rarely seen; after the rodeo in the bar, they drift away like smoke. Isabel's former lover and ex-husband are mostly absent and Perce is abandoned by his girlfriend and his buddies while he lies in a coma.

Even Roslyn, despite her potential for connection to persons and places, appears diminished and disconnected. Like her husband, her parents were never there. She enters *The Misfits* as an intimation, a ghostly image half-visible through the reflections of a second floor window. A mirror shot gives us our initial view of her face and, when her divorce is final, she appears in Harrah's as another reflection, this one sharply slanted in a mirror hanging above the bar. In *The Misfits*, mirror shots tend to remove some of Monroe's substance and to suggest displacement, as if divorce threatens to propel her through a looking-glass into a haunted world of bars and slot machines. Between the court and Harrah's, Roslyn and Isabel cross a river into which the newly single customarily throw their wedding rings in hopes of preventing another divorce – a prophylactic that could equally signify no future broken marriages or no future marriages at all. Roslyn does not cast away her ring, but she nonetheless appears to pass some kind of a boundary, one that is perhaps distantly related to the mythological Styx, across which wait the unquiet dead. However that may be, the river in Reno is doubtlessly related to those that other characters in other Huston films cross en route to adventure and self-discovery or self-loss, the rivers that the heroes encounter in the opening minutes of *Sinful Davey*, *A Walk with Love and Death*, and *The Life and Times of Judge Roy Bean*, for example.

Loss, injury, and evocations of death suffuse *The Misfits*. Yet in no way does the movie suggest that these maladies are wholly the fault of the characters who suffer them. Guido, though he eventually becomes an unattractive and untrustworthy figure, speaks with an understanding that the film partly authorizes when he says, "Everything just happened wrong. It'll do that sometimes." Misfortune, as in most of Huston's movies, occurs as an ordinary part of ordinary life. The grace and humor with which characters acknowledge their injuries, on the other hand, and the courage with which they persevere, are matters they can control. The responses of Huston's characters to their catastrophes, not their good luck in avoiding them, determine their success or failure.

Roslyn's dented Cadillac and Isabel's broken arm and house full of stalled clocks initiate a motif of damage and injury. To Guido, Isabel explains that she hurt her arm when she "misbehaved"; she goes on to exclaim, "I'm so sick and tired of myself!" Guido, more desperately sick and tired than Isabel, also exists amidst dilapidation: an unfinished house, an overgrown lawn and garden, an old plane that needs its engine replaced. Perce has been in and out of hospitals since he left the ranch and will be injured twice more during his next rodeo.

Roslyn and Gay appear less battered. Although Roslyn's car is immobile and a drunken Gay tumbles to the pavement after the rodeo, neither seems dominated by misfortune. Both appear capable of finding better places, better connections. When Gay first tries to kiss Roslyn, she tells him, "I don't feel that way about you." Neither defensive nor demanding, he affably replies, "Well, don't get discouraged, girl, you might." (Very soon, she does.) Gay, like Roslyn, has the resiliency to look hopefully ahead, to trust that things can get better. Such resiliency characterizes Huston's most sympathetic – though not always triumphant – characters from Miss Roy (Olivia de Havilland) of *In This Our Life* through Rosie (Katharine Hepburn) in *The African Queen*, Billy Tully (Stacy Keach) in *Fat City*, and the title character (Aileen Quinn) of *Annie*.

By contrast, Guido appears hopelessly stuck. He wallows in his misfortunes, his errors, his anger. Querulous, demanding, and narcissistic, he makes no trusting connections with other people. He exhibits but does not reveal himself to them and parasitizes them in relationships to which he finally brings only his own needs.

Roslyn responds to Guido's anguish, which is real enough, with both sympathy and a shrewd understanding that he bears considerable responsibility for having chosen the path of isolation and death. He could not dance with his late wife, Guido tells Roslyn, as he can with her. Roslyn replies that he could have taught her to dance if he had loved her and continues, "We're all dying, aren't we? All the husbands and all the wives. And we're not teaching each other what we really know." As she comes to realize that all three of the men have to some extent embraced their injuries, her accusations become more outspoken. At the rodeo:

"People dying and people just standing around – don't you [Gay] care?" During the capture of the mustangs: "Murderers! Liars! Why don't you kill yourselves and be happy? You're three dead men! . . . You're three dear, sweet, dead men." And finally, to Guido: "You never felt anything for anyone in your life."

Earlier, looking straightforwardly at life and death, Gay declares, "dying's as natural as living . . . a man that's too afraid to die's too afraid to live." But this stoic, perhaps undeniable view falls short of comprehending the twists and involutions of life's mutability. During the confrontations of the mustang hunt, Gay's amiable confidence turns defensive and baffled. "They changed it around. . . . nothing can live unless something else dies. . . . everything else is wages." But he will soon come to realize that his resentful arguments are self-serving. In his capacity to confront his own weakness and uncertainty, he discovers his real courage. His temporary bewilderment is finally stronger than his self-assurance, for life does not stand still and the ability to change distinguishes the living from the living dead.

The alternative is self-absorbed stasis. Renouncing his impulse (compromised as it is) toward Roslyn and life, Guido reverts to bitter certainty: "They're [women] all nuts." Like Shannon in *The Night of the Iguana*, Guido directs his baffled rage against women. Having been unable to draw Roslyn into his isolated, motionless existence, he attempts to do the same with Gay, assuring him that "we don't need anybody in the world." The aggressive mendicant of the "Church Ladies Auxiliary" resembles Guido in her preying on the living to support the rigid dead: "We're going to buy a fence around the graveyard, keep these cowboys from pasturing their horses on the graves." In contrast one remembers William Blake, always the advocate of life and energy, urging, "drive your cart and your plow over the bones of the dead."

The deepest lesson *The Misfits* teaches has two linked parts. Gay articulates the first: "Nothing's it, not forever." The second is that one must make commitments anyway; one need not take the inevitability of death as a reason to stop living. If no thing is forever, then the thing we call nothing is also not forever. For nothing to persist, life must cease. So long as change continues, life continues; and nothing dies so long as nothing is forever. Not even death can be forever.

Life, then, is change – a doctrine as old as recorded Western culture – and living means accepting, even embracing, impermanence. Across Huston's career, most of his protagonists struggle to learn that fundamental truth and to understand its implications. "What do you do out in the country?" Roslyn asks Gay. "Just live." "How," she continues, "do you 'just live'?" "You start by going to sleep. You get up when you feel like it. You scratch yourself. You fry yourself some eggs. You see what kind of a day it is. You throw stones at a tin can, whistle." You live by doing things without the promise or expectation of anything beyond the living itself and the certainty of change. Here, as elsewhere in *The Misfits*, aftershocks of existentialism rumble beneath the surface of the text. Indeed, ideas central to existentialism pervade much of Huston's filmmaking.

Roslyn has, as Guido says, "the gift of life." But she must learn to accept her gift, and to develop it. Early in the film she laments, "That's what I can't get used to, everything changing." Both her perception of change and her inability to get used to it are part of her gift; when she embraces change – which is very different from getting used to it – she will realize fully her ability to engage life. "I don't know what to do," she says early in the film, "but if I knew, I'd do it." Then she dances, first with her new friends and later by herself. In her dancing, she is just living; she is enacting her equivalent of Gay's getting up, looking around, and whistling.

Dancing is another Hustonian motif that recurs throughout his career as a director. Its symbolic valences, as in *The Misfits*, usually encompass engagement with life, art as self-discovery and self-expression, vitality, and connection with other people. Howard's exuberant jig when he finds signs of gold in *The Treasure of the Sierra Madre* exemplifies much of what is characteristic in Huston's use of dance in his films, as does the equally impromptu, joyous dance that Rose and Charlie leap into after they safely pass the German fort and the appalling rapids in *The African Queen*. Dancing is a central image in *Moulin Rouge* and in *The Barbarian and the Geisha*, and it is of considerable importance in *The Dead*. In *The Night of the Iguana*, as Maurice Yacowar notes, Maxine's (Ava Gardner) constantly dancing beach boys "frolic through the film as restless energies."[4]

Though he suggests that the beach boys "personify innocent pleasure," Yacowar also suggests that there is "something ominous" in the persistence of their "constant music." In Huston's most ironic films, the energies of dancing are equivocal. Bette Davis dances by herself, in *In This Our Life*, to a Victrola that she and her husband cannot afford but that she nevertheless insists on buying. Elsewhere, her dancing is also associated with her selfishness and indifference to other people. A jitterbugging teenager so distracts the cleverest of the criminals in *The Asphalt Jungle* that he is caught by the police and the whole scheme unravels. The underground Moscow disco in *The Kremlin Letter* is a resort for despair, drug addiction, and licentiousness.

The sequence in *The Misfits* in which Gay and Guido dance with Roslyn typifies both the innocent, connective symbolism that is usual in Huston's films and its dark inverse. Gay's dancing is simple, slightly awkward, affectionate. Guido shows off. He aggressively controls Roslyn and takes the occasion to complain that his late wife had "no grace." At the end of the sequence, Roslyn asks Guido to smile, joy or even pleasure beyond that of exhibiting his skill having been absent from his performance. This sequence also introduces the sharp contrast between Gay and Guido that will eventually bear much of the symbolic argument of the movie.

The harpy for the Church Ladies Auxiliary, after relieving Roslyn of some money, croaks a benediction at her, "Go reborn." However hypocritical the source, the blessing is sound. To be alive is to be reborn continuously and to be dead is to keep coming back to the same emptiness. Perce asks Roslyn, "How come you got such trust in your eyes? . . . Like you was just born." Later he asks her, "Who do you depend on? Who?" "I don't know," murmurs Roslyn, "maybe the only thing is the next thing that happens. Maybe you're not supposed to remember anybody's promises." *The Misfits* in its totality suggests that you're not, that promises impose the past on the future, stifle life and change. In accepting the possibility that life is only "the next thing that happens," Roslyn confirms her gift. More slowly than Roslyn but with as much puzzlement and courage, Gay also comes to acknowledge the necessity of change and uncertainty. After a tremendous struggle with the stallion – a sequence that reads metaphorically like his wrestling with Roslyn and himself and all the issues of their life – Gay recaptures the animal only to cut it loose again. "I just don't want anybody making my mind up for me," he declares to Guido. Then, mostly to himself, "Just got to find another way to be alive, that's all."

To be alive in any authentic way, the characters of *The Misfits* (including jackrabbits and mustangs) must be free. Achieving freedom is a necessary condition of continuing to live. For Gay, Guido, and Perce, loss of freedom is comprehended in the idea of wages: "Anything's better than wages." There may be a biblical overtone in this terror of wages, but whether biblical or existential, the wages of sin are captivity and the choking of freedom is death.

Roslyn's attempt to buy the horses, a gesture that Gay responds to as if he were being threatened with a salary, strikes at his very identity: "I was just wondering who you think you been talkin' to since we met."

Whatever way Gay finds to live, he must be free to make up his own mind. It may be partly for that reason that Susan, who offers him a place in "the second largest laundry in St. Louis," is bundled back to the Midwest by Gay, who later says that cowboys secretly laugh at such women.

But becoming free, like breaking up even an empty marriage, cannot be done without pain. "Well, you're free," says Isabel to her sorrowful friend. "Maybe the trouble is, you're not used to it yet." A critical moment in Roslyn's progress toward life and freedom comes when she and Gay make a simple concrete-block step for Guido's front door. Delighted, Roslyn swirls back and forth, chanting "I can go in . . . and I can come out." As much as anything else, this freedom to come and go transforms Guido's house into Roslyn's and Gay's home. There Roslyn finds a place and a relationship very different from her childhood and her lonely, entrapping marriage. A home and a family, in *The Misfits*, can be left and returned to freely.

As freedom makes possible love and a place where one fits, so truth – something like existentialist "good faith" – empowers freedom. Roslyn cannot learn the irrelevant speech that her lawyer has given her to recite for the divorce court: "I can't memorize this; it's not the way it was." She cannot begin her journey to self-liberation with an expedient lie. Appealing to both freedom and truth during the critical test of their relationship, Gay says, "Roslyn, we've never kidded, you and I. . . . I hunt horses to keep myself free, so I'm a free man."

Lying smothers reality in a plastic bag of egotism and self-interest. It cuts one off from other humans and embraces death. "Dropping a bomb," says Guido with an anguish only partly affected, "is like tellin' a lie." During the crisis of the story, when the cowboys bind the stallion and begin to think about how much money they will get from the dealer, Roslyn denounces them as "liars" and "dead men." She understands that the reverse of Guido's simile also applies: lying is like dropping a bomb. It destroys, along with truth, everything else Roslyn is seeking – connection, place, a way to live, love.

For Huston too, across his half-century career as a writer and director of films, confronting and remaining faithful to truth is at the center of heroism. Both *The Maltese Falcon* and *The Dead* end with protagonists struggling to articulate and come to terms with agonizing understandings of the world and themselves. Sam Spade (Humphrey Bogart) must "send over" a woman he loves and who may love him. As *The Dead* concludes, Gabriel Conroy (Donal McCann) faces excruciating insights about the "poor part" he has played in his spouse's life, about human isolation and decay, and about his own emotional poverty. Like Roslyn's perception that "we're all dying, all the husbands and all the wives," Gabriel's understanding that "one by one, we're all becoming shades" has a force at once terrible and liberating. If reality is never admitted, it can never be faced, and its power to constrain remains infinite. To acknowledge the worst is to regain one's dignity and integrity, one's freedom. Roslyn accepts that "maybe you're not supposed to believe what people say" and in doing so becomes free and brave enough to find her own place. Only after he realizes that his cowboy life has become "like roping a dream" can Gay begin to seek "some other way to be alive."

The choice between facing the truth of one's existence or fleeing it and dwelling on the threshold of death is also at the center of the unjustly neglected *In This Our Life*. As elsewhere in Huston's work, confronting truth in that film is painful, but evading it fatal. Similar perceptions lie at the center of movies as diverse as *The Red Badge of Courage*, *The Unforgiven*, *A Walk with Love and Death*, and *Under the Volcano*. Truth at once terrifying and liberating occupies the thematic center of *Freud*, Huston's next film after *The Misfits* and one that was of particular personal significance to its director. The restorative power of the truth also constitutes one of the essential points of the documentary that Huston did about an army psychiatric hospital, *Let There Be Light*, another film of great importance for understanding his career.

Giving utterance to the truth is always difficult in Huston's films and his characters often border on the inarticulate when they attempt it. Their speech becomes formal, blunt, hesitant. At the end of *The Maltese Falcon*, Sam Spade, slick and glib elsewhere in the movie, stammers diffident, uncertain monosyllables. Facing death during *The Man Who Would Be King*, Peachy (Michael Caine) and Dravot (Sean Connery) address each other with eloquent plainness. In the last moments of *Fat City*, words entirely disappear in favor of the minimal but encompassing gesture of sitting together over coffee. The plain adieu and spiritual plighting of troth near the end of *Heaven Knows, Mr. Allison* is a splendid example of Huston's ability to render the most affecting moments of his films in his simplest, most direct writing.

When Perce takes leave of Roslyn, his life profoundly changed by the two days he has spent in her company, he gives his feelings formal, intense expression: "I'm pleased to have met you, Roslyn." Gay speaks most plainly and resonantly to Roslyn when the two of them, not yet sure that they will stay together, are driving back in Gay's truck: "God bless you, girl." That simple benediction conveys his love, admiration, and gratitude toward Roslyn. It conveys as well his acceptance of the new life he is about to undertake because she helped him to face the personal and social anachronism of the one he had been living.

The Misfits concludes with Gay going to a new life and Guido returning to his old plane, an ending that emphasizes the pervasive, systematic comparison of Gay and Guido that has been a central structural principle of the film.[5] In their friendship, their places in society, world views, and disconnection from family and other close personal ties, the two men begin at much the same point. Beneath those similarities, however, are differences of character that account for their eventual divergence and summarize most of the central dichotomies of the movie.

Both Guido and Gay have lost wives, Guido when his pregnant wife became ill and died and Gay more ordinarily when he found his mate "all wrapped up in a car with a fella." Guido idealizes his marriage and refuses to accept any responsibility for his spouse's death or for strains in their union that may have contributed to it. Unpersuaded, Roslyn sees through Guido's not having a spare tire to get his wife to the hospital and his claim that "she didn't seem that sick." To Guido's insistence that his wife stood by him "uncomplaining as a tree," Roslyn hesitantly returns, "Maybe that's what killed her. I mean a little complaining helps sometimes, maybe." When he tells her that his wife lacked grace, Roslyn comes right to the painful point: "If you loved her, you could have taught her anything." Later, Guido will confirm Roslyn's intuitions during the mustang hunt: "They're [women are] all crazy. You try not to believe it because you need them. . . . I know this racket, I just forgot what I knew for a while." If Guido has been unable to resolve his feelings about his wife's death, the reason is not the intensity of his suffering but a bitterness for which his lost marriage is more an excuse than a cause.

Although Gay has not entirely come to terms with the loss of his family, neither has he invested himself in lies and evasions. Without rage or shame, he tells Roslyn of his wife's infidelity. He speaks openly of loneliness and regrets: "If I had a new kid, I'd know just how to be with him." Once burned twice shy, he admits that he has thought about getting married again, "but never in daylight." Unlike Guido he has grieved for his losses and, as a result, he has attained the hopefulness that accompanies healing. When Guido says, "everything just happened wrong," Gay later adds what Guido never would, "remember, it goes the other way sometimes too." His optimism and self-irony, in contrast to Guido's posturings as a tormented soul, signal his balance in much the way that Isabel's sense of humor signals hers.

The ability to find a way through the wreckage of one's life to a place of shelter and love defines, in most of Huston's films, both heroism and salvation. Guido owns a house but has no home. Gay, relatively at ease with himself, finds something like a home wherever he happens to be. He and Roslyn improvise a step, cultivate a vegetable garden, plant flowers, build a relationship. Guido, drunk and desperate, tries to hammer up boards in the night and succeeds only in crushing Gay's and Roslyn's heliotropes. In order to "say hello" to Roslyn, he turns to threats and bribes. Guido supposes home to be something someone does for him, not, as Deborah Kerr says in *The Night of the Iguana*, "something two people have between them."

In Roslyn's presence, Guido and Gay discover themselves. For Guido, Roslyn becomes an occasion for reflection on his own injuries; Gay's admiration is unmixed with self-pity. Where Guido begs Roslyn to "help me," Gay offers her sympathy: "I think you're the saddest girl I ever met." Gay accepts Roslyn's rejection of his first advances by offering himself again, without demands, "I may not amount to much in some ways, but I am a good friend." Guido reacts to Roslyn's evasion of his attempted kiss with rage. Gay desires to befriend Roslyn and Guido attempts to seize her; Gay approaches her with amiable generosity and Guido with amorous egotism. Such contrasts embody fundamental dialectics in *The Misfits* between love and selfishness and between the energy of life and the entropy of self-pitying isolation.

At the end of her first evening with Gay and Guido, Roslyn does a primitive, moonlit dance – for her a characteristic engaging of the world. Gay respects Roslyn's dancing and understands its innocence. If her nightclub audience corrupts her art into pornography, she bears no responsibility for that: "You started out just wantin' to dance, didn't you? But little by little it turns out that people ain't interested in how good you dance; they're gawkin' at you with somethin' entirely different in their minds." Guido joins the corrupters. Inside the closet door of Gay's and Roslyn's bedroom are a cluster of publicity stills of Roslyn. Gay had asked her to pin them up, but shows no inordinate interest in them. Guido, however, keeps staring at them, despite Roslyn's attempts to close the door. He prefers the frozen, posed image of a woman to the living, spontaneous one who is present with him, the prurient representation to the person.

Discussing character and thought in *The Poetics*, Aristotle identifies the former chiefly with what characters do and the latter with what they say.[6] There are, of course, hidden complexities in this formulation: in some contexts speech functions to indicate choice (Aristotle's primary category for determining character), and in others actions may communicate concepts rather than achieve consequences. Whatever its complications, Aristotle's distinction often applies to Huston's movies; in *The Misfits* it brings into sharp definition one of the central differences between Guido and Gay. Both speak with wisdom and insight, but the actions of Guido are consistently aggressive and devious, whereas Gay encounters the world with friendly interest. Roslyn articulates the difference between Guido's words and his real character when she declares, "All you know is the sad words; you could blow up the world, and all you would feel is sorry for yourself." Her response to Gay is the reverse: "You were worried about me. How sweet!" Guido wants help and approval from Roslyn but he returns little more than resentment and the lachrymose poetry of his "sad words." Gay offers Roslyn sympathy, affection, and freedom.

Yet there remains, especially during the opening sequences of *The Misfits*, something equivocal in Gay's relations with women in general and with Roslyn specifically. His evasive dismissing of the woman from St. Louis has its unattractive, exploitative side. More alarming perhaps are the mildly incestuous overtones in his relation to Roslyn. Besides the obvious difference in their ages, we may notice Gay's habit of calling Roslyn "girl." We may notice also that the dress size of Gay's daughter Rosemary is the same as Roslyn's and that their names are pointedly similar. Gay sometimes reacts to Roslyn with a distinctly parental combination of doting and distance. The brief sequences of their horseback riding and their outing to the beach both show Gay responding rather paternally to his companion.

When Perce enters the action, it appears that he may win Roslyn from her fatherly lover. A cowboy like Gay, he is both younger and equally unencumbered by a home or mate. If Perce were to replace Gay at Roslyn's side, the shadow of incest would be lifted. The ascendency of the younger man, moreover, would be a thoroughly conventional development.

But Perce has not grown quite that strong yet, nor has Gay grown that old. *The Misfits* raises and squelches the threat of incest at almost the same time. If Roslyn's name parallels Rosemary's, so does Gay's parallel that of his son Gaylord. When Perce proposes to toast "old, elderly Gay," Roslyn quickly contradicts him: "Gay's not old." A few minutes later, Guido notices Roslyn and Perce dancing together with a sour "Nothing like being young, is there, Gay?" Drunk but undaunted by this second allusion to his age, Gay responds, "You know what they say, some keeps gettin' younger all the time."

Miller and Huston ring surprising changes on the standard narrative bells of young woman/old man/young man. Middle-aged but youthfully open to change, Gay preserves Roslyn from the unfitting embrace of a static, embittered Guido. Indeed, Guido first meets Roslyn and invites her to his country house, so Gay has already taken Guido's place quite early in the film. When Perce redirects his toast to "old, elderly Pilot [Guido] and his five-dollar elderly airplane," Roslyn smiles tranquilly, offering no correction. Clark Gable's Gay looks older than Eli Wallach's Guido, but Gay's hopeful flexibility allies him more closely with Roslyn. As for Perce, he's too young. He needs to replace a mother, not a mate. His proper relation to Roslyn is figured when he relates his sorrows with his head in her lap while she strokes his bandages and salves his emotional wounds.

Four years after finishing *The Misfits*, Huston spoke with Gideon Bachmann on the set of *The Bible*. Thinking aloud about "how I make films," he remarked,

The most important element to me is always the idea that I'm trying to express, and everything technical is only a method to make the idea into clear form. I'm always working on the idea: whether I am writing, directing, choosing music or cutting. Everything must revert back to the idea; when it gets away from the idea it becomes a labyrinth of rococo.[7]

Huston's remarks on this occasion go to the center of his art. They also go a good way toward explaining some of the formal qualities that characterize *The Misfits* and most of his other movies: the unobtrusiveness of Huston's camera style, his tendency to encourage broad audience identification with most of the important characters in his films, the precisely modulated, consistent performances he elicits from actors, the emphasis – universally noted by commentators – on telling a story. In general, Huston achieves the subordination of all formal elements of a film to a unifying effect, to what he calls "the idea."

Huston's "idea" is something larger, more abstract, and more perfusive than words, images, plot, or music – either individually or as a simple sum. For *The Misfits*, the central components of "the idea" have to do with the emotional and physical clutter of the human landscape and the sublime desolation of the natural one, the connections between home and identity and healing, the necessity of facing and coming to terms with inevitable change and failure and death, the need to find some sustaining understanding of life, and the centrality of truth and freedom to all human aspirations.

Huston's subordination of all elements to a central idea also partly accounts for some of his filmmaking practices: his eagerness to collaborate with art directors, writers, cinematographers, and others under his direction; his alertness to the fortuitous opportunities of location shooting; his reluctance to intrude into the performances of actors. Once Huston understood his "idea" – which is neither to say that he would have been able to articulate it precisely nor to assume that it didn't undergo modification as he worked on his movies – he had created an opportunity for landscapes, animals, and human collaborators to add their harmonizing richness. Only a filmmaker who is very confidently in control of his creation can say, as Huston did, "I court accident."[8]

The controlling idea at the center of *The Misfits* has a complexity that more than supports the explication of it offered here. It is typical of John Huston's work in its ramification, human sympathy, and depth. The easy characterization of Huston's films as consisting typically of a story about a group of men who either fail to achieve a quixotic goal or succeed in doing so only to find the fruit of their achievement turning to ashes has some obvious truth and a less obvious but equal inadequacy. It goes about as far with Huston as calling Hitchcock the "master of suspense" goes with him. Of more use in thinking about John Huston is the recognition that such stories (and others like those of *The Misfits* or *The Night of the Iguana* which do not answer to such a description) allowed him to think cinematically about ideas that he brooded throughout his career. What it means to be human, the points at which love and courage confront the abyss of sorrow and meaninglessness, the human community of failure and doubt, the fragile abundance of nature, the choice between facing the truth or evading it – these and related preoccupations interweave in *The Misfits* and recur in most of Huston's work. In his mid-career collaboration with Arthur Miller, the collocation of these themes is particularly resonant and delicately balanced. Life and death, earth and the heavens, man and woman orbit each other with stellar attraction and independence.

CHAPTER V

"No Betrayal of Despair": *The Night of the Iguana* (1964)

Directed by
JOHN HUSTON

The Night of the Iguana begins with a cluster of sequences reminiscent of other Huston films. They suggest both the extent to which *Iguana* recapitulates Hustonian themes and the degree of Huston's stylistic transformation of his original. The opening shot repeats Huston's favorite pan down from the sky. The pre-credit flashback of the Reverend T. Lawrence Shannon (Richard Burton) railing at his congregation recalls the sermon early in *Moby Dick*. The imagery of the credit sequence itself – moon, clouds, and a gigantic close-up of an iguana – resembles the simple, vivid images in the credit sequences of a number of Huston's other movies, especially *Under the Volcano*. After the credits, the narrative present begins with another downward pan. Again, a church steeple and facade fill the screen near the end of the shot. The penultimate crisis of *Iguana* is introduced by the camera's descent from a sky full of lightning and thunder to the earth, where human distress echoes meteorological tumult.

Other shots and sequences in *Iguana* recall other Huston works. The waves that abet Charlotte Goodall (Sue Lyon) in defying Miss Fellowes (Grayson Hall) resemble the turbulent sea foam in *Heaven Knows, Mr. Allison*. In *Heaven Knows*, the indecipherable patterns of waves and foam suggest forces beyond the characters' power to affect or fully understand. In keeping with a well-traveled (and often parodied) Hollywood convention, the sea also suggests the depth of feeling that Mr. Allison and Sister Angela have for each other. The unruly breakers that soak Miss Fellowes's skirt are a comic variant of that convention. They underscore her powerlessness before the increasingly open passion of Charlotte for Shannon.

When Hannah Jelkes (Deborah Kerr) removes broken glass from Shannon's feet, we may remember Rose pulling a thorn from Charlie's foot in *The African Queen*. The adolescent sensuality of Charlotte's dancing on the beach modernizes the teenager's jitterbugging that undoes Doc Riedenschneider (Sam Jaffe) in *The Asphalt Jungle*. A slanted reflection of Hank in the rear-view mirror of the bus recalls other Huston mirror shots, most of which – as I argued in Section I – are associated with deceitful characters or equivocal actions.

Few of these moments exist in the Tennessee Williams play that premiered in New York on December 28, 1961. In making the film, Huston and Anthony Veiller heavily rewrote the script on which it is based. All the sequences before the arrival at Costa Verde, the first third of the movie, are additions; Williams's lines are frequently revised or reassigned; and Williams's main subplot, which involves a vacationing family of German Nazis, disappears. The importance of Charlotte and Miss Fellowes is increased.

Most significantly, Huston fundamentally changed the ending. The hopeful commitment of Shannon and Maxine (Ava Gardner) brightens Williams's more grudging version of a half-hearted promise from Shannon for a one-night stand. At the end of the film, Hannah is ready to continue her journey, whereas Williams leaves her on stage alone with the body of her Grandfather at the end of the play: "*In a panicky moment, she looks right and left for someone to call to. There's no one. Then she bends to press her head to the crown of Nonno's and the curtain starts to descend.*"[1] Maurice Yacowar summarizes the changes in terms of the broad contrast between Williams's artistic temperament and Huston's:

"John Huston has always expressed a more robust spirit than Williams has, a vision less bleakly lined with defeat and destruction and one where the joys of life and the quest make up for loss and defeat."[2] John Mc-Carty generalizes the point: "*The Night of the Iguana* is yet another John Huston film whose upbeat reworking of the source material it's based on contradicts all those critics who still see Huston as a pessimist ruled by a philosophy of failure."[3]

For all of the changes that Veiller and he made, Huston also adopted a great deal directly from Williams's play. Its main themes are among Huston's own lifelong preoccupations: people who have reached the end of their emotional endurance, the necessity to confront one's own weakness, the equivocal connections between love and sex, people's desperate need to make a place for themselves in the world and among other people. Huston found these concerns waiting for him in Williams's play.[4] His additions and alterations do not so much transform the original as intensify aspects of it that were already congenial to him.

The film also demonstrates Huston's aptitude for matching actors and characters – his talent for what Andrew Sarris labeled, disparagingly, "casting coups" and Naremore called, admiringly, "assembling such presences."[5] Yacowar notes of Huston's casting that "much of the film's power derives from the personae of its cast. . . . Richard Burton was a resonant Shannon because he was considered a huge, wasted talent. . . . Burton's persona already expressed a fleshly weakness of heroic dimensions." Sue Lyon was recapitulating her Lolita of Stanley Kubrick's 1962 film. Consequently, as Yacowar notes, "there was something of a mythic confrontation in Charlotte's siege of Shannon." Yacowar also argues that Ava Gardner was important to "Huston's optimistic shift of the play." The more dangerous, unsympathetic Bette Davis (whom Huston had directed as one of the leads of *In This Our Life*) had done Maxine in the Broadway production. Gardner's Maxine "vitalizes the role, cheers the play, and embodies the virtues of the hearty life."[6] As for *The Misfits*, the professional and personal reputations that its cast brought to *Iguana* created a resonant aura around the film. Grayson Hall's casting as the pinched, angular Judith Fellowes also seems especially apt. The judges of the American Academy of Motion Picture Arts and Sciences nominated her, alone among the famous cast, for an Oscar.

Like *The Misfits* in another respect, *Iguana* is peopled by alienated, displaced characters desperately in need of homes. Huston said, "The theme of *The Night of the Iguana* is of loose, random souls trying to account for themselves and finally being able to do so through love."[7] As in most of Huston's other movies, making a home has a great deal to do with giving and accepting love. Home is the end of a journey toward coming to terms with the natural world, with society, with other people individually, and with one's self. Making a home requires discovering and accepting the truth about who one is and what one wants, needs, and – on what Shannon calls the realistic level – can have.

At the beginning, Shannon has managed to accommodate neither the world nor other people nor himself. Nature for him is chiefly a body of evidence convicting humankind of dirtying and devastating its surroundings. In the pre-credit flashback, he rages in the pulpit, drives his frightened parishioners into the rain, and delivers what is virtually a declaration of his resignation from the church. The fictional present begins with his half-recumbent figure, a newspaper over his head, a quantity of alcohol in his bloodstream, and his back against a wall – metaphorically as well as literally. The world he is attempting to escape soon comes to pursue him, first in the dangerously attractive Charlotte, then in the less alluring persons of his clients on Blake's Tours of Mexico, the women faculty of Baptist Female College. Shannon at the beginning of his story is in full retreat from everything and everyone, including himself. He looks like a derelict, what we now call a homeless person.

He observes life from the point of view of an alienated modern for whom the world and other people have assumed an overlay of the demonic. While leading his bottom-of-the-line tours, "On the side, Shannon has been collecting evidence . . . of man's inhumanity to God . . . the pain we cause him: we've poisoned his atmosphere, we've slaughtered his creatures of the wild, we've polluted his rivers." As in most of Huston's work, nature and nature's god are equivalent. In a Hustonian moment, Shannon stops the tour bus to look at native women and children washing clothes, bathing, and playing in a river, a sequence that repeats a similar moment in *The Treasure of the Sierra Madre* and anticipates one in *The Man Who Would Be King*. For Shannon the scene allows "a fleeting glimpse into the lost world of innocence." This line better describes the speaker's nostalgia for his own hopeful youth, however, than it does Mexican peasant society.

Shannon is as alienated from himself as he is from the country in which, ironically, he serves as guide. Spiritually homeless, he can find no more shelter in his own soul than in the world among his fellows and Fellowes. He exemplifies the text of his aborted sermon (Proverbs 25:28):

"He that hath no rule over his own spirit is like a city that is broken down and without walls." When Charlotte nearly seduces him in his bedroom, he prays, "Lead me not into temptation." Then, with equal futility, he murmurs to his temptress, "Go on home. I'll find my way all by myself."

He will find his way, but not by himself. *Iguana* insists that one cannot make such a journey without other people. Again, Shannon's sermon is germane. "We cannot," he haltingly tells his congregation, "rule ourselves alone." To find a home in the world and in his own spirit, he must also find a place among other human beings. The most authoritative voice in the film is that of Hannah Jelkes. Speaking of the homes that people make for each other, she says, "What is important is that one is never alone."

Always among other people, Shannon is nonetheless painfully alone until the closing movement of the film. *Iguana* often looks like an amplification of the Sartrean idea of hell as other people whom one can neither escape nor make authentic contact with. Indeed, most of Huston's films echo the existentialism of such writers as Sartre, Camus, and Simone de Beauvoir. In 1946, Huston directed the U.S. premiere of *No Exit*, and he worked for several years on and off with Sartre on a screenplay for *Freud*. To an interviewer in 1958, Huston observed that his French viewers regard him as "an existentialist who preaches a philosophy of failure," and he went on to "admit there's a lot of that in my films."[8] Stuart Kaminsky relates that "Huston describes himself as a 'philosophical atheist' with existential ideas" and Martin Rubin argues that Huston's conception of heroism is deeply implicated with "existential notions of perseverance in the absence of expectations."[9] For Naremore, "many of [Huston's] pictures, despite their superficial realism, are like existentialist morality plays."[10] Arthur Miller, with whom Huston made *The Misfits* three years before *The Night of the Iguana*, was another of Jean-Paul Sartre's collaborators, Sartre having scripted a film version of Miller's *The Crucible*.[11] In *The Misfits*, as we have seen, existential formulations are often especially clear; but its universe is more or less the rule for Huston's films. Within it, his characters attempt to create places of shelter and trust; they must find the courage to offer and accept love without promises.

The church, the place of shelter and faith in which Shannon should be both a member and a leader, appears to him as a parochial parody. He berates his congregation for reverting to isolation and self-serving hostility. "You've turned your backs on the God of love and compassion and invented for yourselves this cruel, senile delinquent who blames the world and all that he created for his own faults. Close your windows, close your doors, close your hearts against the truth of our God."

Associated with this exclusionary institutional deity is a visual geometry that stands in sharp contrast to the amorphousness of the natural landscape. It appears in the hexagon above Shannon's pulpit and the arches surrounding it, in the lines of the pulpit itself, and in the orderly curves of the black umbrellas that his fleeing congregation open as they leave the church and its stricken minister. (The white umbrella under which Hannah shelters her grandfather contrasts with the ominous black ones of the churchgoers.) The contexts of these neat lines consistently suggest that attempts to tidy life and give it a simple structure are part of the pattern of cruelty and denial that turns away from the "God of love and compassion."

Later, this motif will be associated with Miss Fellowes, an adversary even more scandalized by Shannon and less responsive to his ministry than his congregation. When she goes to send a telegram requesting her brother to check her tour guide's background, she is photographed through a leaded glass window with symmetrical lines that echo those of the church. Her inquiries, as ruinous to Shannon as his lapses with his congregation, result in his dismissal from Blake's Tours and drive him deeper into emotional collapse. When Miss Fellowes returns and pointedly ignores Shannon's pathetic greeting, the geometries of the previous shot are repeated.

Like the tidy lines of pulpit and leaded glass, those inscribed by stairs and railings look down on Shannon as he writes "a letter of complete capitulation" to his bishop. Charlotte will take over that point of view when she begins her penultimate assault on the remaining fragments of Shannon's chastity. Sharply downward-angled shots and downward camera movements, like the pans from sky to church, suggest both an imperfect world below the heavens, or Heaven, and an infernal world still lower. The demonic overtones of downward-looking camera positions appear early in *Iguana* when Shannon flees his crippled bus and its passengers for the relief of a solitary swim in the ocean. As he strokes through the clear water, an overhead shot delivers a startling image of Charlotte swimming up from the depths to continue her assault on his broken-down, unwalled person. She pops to the surface like a mermaid from hell – a sharp reversal of the more usual reviving promise of water in this and other Huston films.

Demonic associations attach to Charlotte throughout the film. After the minister wrestles her from his cabin at the Costa Verde, Hannah

Jelkes enters to ask him, "What is it, Mr. Shannon?" He replies, "Hell
and damnation." Earlier, the shadowy bedroom of Charlotte and Miss
Fellowes is vaguely reminiscent of a vampire film.[12] Charlotte rises like
a specter from misty mosquito netting and sets off to stalk Shannon in a
diaphanous nightie and robe. Her weapons are not the hypodermic ca-
nines of the usual cinema bloodsucker, but a voluptuous body and skin
so soft "she should be licensed." When she corners her prey, she assures
him, "I'll rule your spirit. I'll hold you."

When she shifts her attentions to Hank, Charlotte remains a seductive
parasite. She attracts the bus driver to the beach and urges him on as he
is beaten up and made a comic spectacle by Maxine's hired boys. A little
later, while Hank pinions Shannon's arms, she extracts the distributor
head of the bus from the minister's pocket. Since that bit of hardware
represents Shannon's last source of control over his tour group and, apparently, his life, Charlotte accomplishes by force and stealth what she
didn't quite achieve through enticement. She dances around him, chirp-
ing "I got it! I got it! I got it! That's to show I hate you! I hate you!" Charlotte's love and her hate, as the audience and Shannon are likely to feel
at this moment, have little to distinguish them.

The other vengeful spirit on Shannon's trail is Charlotte's desperately
possessive chaperone. For Miss Fellowes, sex is an abomination. Her vi-
tuperative passion arises both from her prudish horror at the attraction
between Shannon and her precocious charge and from her unconscious
rivalry with the minister. When Shannon emerges from the ocean in his
briefs with the scarcely more clothed Charlotte, the older woman slaps
the girl as if Charlotte were her faithless lover.

That evening, after Charlotte has slipped away, Miss Fellowes is
roused by the sound of dogs. Unaware of her companion's absence, she
begins a languorous apology – very much in the mode of a bedroom reconciliation after a lovers' quarrel. The dogs may remind us again of a typical motif of the vampire movie; more generally, they tend in narrative
film to be associated with menace and, harkening back to classical precedent, with the underworld. After Miss Fellowes's humiliating discovery
that she has been asking forgiveness of an empty bed – empty for reasons
all too easily deduced – the barking returns. Later, when Charlotte steps
on a dog while dancing with Maxine's beach boys, it howls and scurries
away, its noise once more associated with sexual desire as threat. Huston's addition of the dogs as emblems of anger coupled with lust adapts
from Williams's play an incident in which Shannon, acting the dog directly, "cocks his leg." In the original, he urinates on the luggage of all

the ladies on the tour; in the film, he sprays only the baggage of Miss Fellowes. (Huston repeats this action in *The Life and Times of Judge Roy Bean* when Paul Newman raises one leg as he walks away from a confrontation with the whores-turned-ladies-turned-prudes, the wives of his deputies.)

Asexual as Miss Fellowes appears, her capacity for harm nonetheless takes its energy, like Charlotte's, from a combination of desire and self-absorption. Miss Fellowes is intensely concerned with her comfort, for the sake of which she turns an unpitying eye on Shannon's crack-up. The deeper source of her hostility, as Maxine perceives, is rooted in the attraction that Miss Fellowes feels toward Charlotte but that she cannot acknowledge, even to herself. She spurns the toy birds that Shannon holds out as a peace offering and that suggest both his spirit and his masculinity. The birds end in the gutter, a destination that seems to prefigure the minister's own. When Miss Fellowes brushes aside Shannon's confession that his life is on the rocks with a frigid "How does that compensate us?" she establishes one of the low points of the film. Her dismissal of Shannon's appeal is accompanied in the background by the relentless, mechanically sexual maracas of Maxine's gigolos. At that moment, humanity in *Iguana* seems to be made up of desperate weakness, snarling self-interest, and mindless appetite. The world appears to be without peace or help for pain, and Shannon to be hopelessly alone in it.

He is as alone, as tied up and desolate, as the tethered iguana. When he attempts his "long swim to China," Maxine's beach boys pursue him through the jungle underbrush just as they earlier pursued the iguana. After they catch him, Huston intercuts a brief shot of the captive lizard, then returns to Shannon, now bound and struggling. He appears to have suffered the fate that, from the opening credits, the film has had in store for him. We may at this moment also recall native boys holding up captured iguanas for sale or Charlotte scampering past the tethered reptile on her way to Shannon's cabin.

Shannon's interpretation of what has happened to him is misogynist. Sounding like Guido in *The Misfits*, he declares that "All women want to see a man in a tied-up situation." His unhappy progress to a hammock straitjacket seems indeed to have been propelled by women: the smitten Sunday school teacher in his past, Charlotte's temptations and subsequent betrayal, Miss Fellowes's hostility, even Hannah's and Maxine's collaboration in tying him down. But his own contributions to his plight more than match those of his female tormentors, and the last two are not tormentors at all.

Shannon's self-indulgence, though its expression is different from Charlotte's or Miss Fellowes's, is nearly as extreme. His eviction of the elders (and everyone else) from the temple and his contriving to get himself lashed into the hammock are, as Hannah perceives, gestures in imitation of Christ. His is a luxuriant, sensual version. As Hannah insists, "Who wouldn't like to atone for the sins of themselves and the world if it could be done in a hammock with ropes instead of on a cross with nails? On a green hilltop instead of on Golgotha, the place of the skulls?" Like Miss Fellowes's solicitude to Charlotte, this motive of Shannon's masochism is probably unconscious, but Hannah's assessment is consistent with everything he does and says. Her understanding of his character goes a long way toward explaining Shannon's most vicious, self-destructive action, his urging of Maxine back into the uncomforting arms of her beach boys. Maxine, as the conclusion of the film will confirm, represents his best realistic possibility for a loving relationship. But precisely for that reason she threatens the perverse satisfactions that he finds in declaring the civilized world a place of infinite depravity and in his personal imitation of the martyrdom of Christ. Shannon cannot easily relinquish the miserable security of his grievances and posturings for the hopeful risks of an honest human connection.

His imitation of Christ is limited to crucifixion and a harrowing of hell; thus he recapitulates Christ's anguish but omits His strength and joy. The pre-credit sequence has overtones of a sacrificial death when Shannon invites his congregation to "get out your tomahawks, sharpen your scalping knives . . . scalp me." The crucifixion he invokes introduces action after the credits that spans the three days more or less requisite for a harrowing of hell and that concludes with the promise of Shannon's resurrection as a human being.

Until Nonno's death after he finishes his poem, "the God of love and compassion" seems to be dead or distracted, to have forsaken the world. The response that Huston gave to interviewers who asked about his religious beliefs during his work on his next film, *The Bible . . . In the Beginning*, can be applied to the crisis of faith that Shannon and Hannah suffer. "In the beginning," Huston would reply, "the lord God was in love with mankind and accordingly jealous." Later he starts to lose interest. Finally he forgets about humans entirely: "He's taken up, maybe, with life elsewhere in the universe. It's as though we ceased to exist as far as He's concerned. Maybe we have."[13] In Huston's personal mythology, one can trace outlines of intersections between theology and existentialism that were very much in the air in the 1950s and 1960s. When Shannon agrees to free the captive iguana, he conceives himself as doing what God should do, "We'll play God tonight. We'll cut the damn lizard loose so he can go back to his bushes because God won't do it and we are playing God here tonight."

Insofar as God exists in *The Night of the Iguana*, he seems to be the judgmental, threatening spirit that Shannon accuses his congregation of inventing – the divine version of a series of shadowy, dangerous, off-screen figures of masculine power hovering in the background. Miss Fellowes's brother is the most important. Like a vengeful god, he knows all of Shannon's sins and has the power and inclination to punish them. When Miss Fellowes confronts Shannon with his past and announces that she is going to have him fired, the beleaguered minister protests that he has a contract with Blake's Tours. "Your contract is worthless," Miss Fellowes announces scornfully, "My brother is a judge." Two other unseen masculine presences, Mr. Blake and the authority figure that Shannon calls "my old Bishop," are also immanent at crucial moments. Shannon himself, at his worst, invokes a similar spirit of judgment when he taunts Maxine about consorting with her beach boys while her late husband Fred was still alive. "Old Fred," like "my old Bishop," both carries the hope of succor and serves as a God of righteousness to be called upon for Shannon's own – sometimes least admirable – purposes.

The emptiness underlying Shannon's miseries, according to Hannah, comes from his "need to believe in someone or something, almost anything." Like the minister, Hannah sustains deep uncertainties about the existence of God, but she has nonetheless found "something to believe in, . . . broken barriers between people, wanting to help each other." For Shannon, believing in other human beings is tantamount to conceiving a plausible God of love and compassion. It is also tantamount to belief in himself. His anguish results from his loss of faith in humanity, his own and that of other people. He projects his fears, as he accuses his congregation of doing, onto the specter of a vengeful deity, an "angry, petulant old man."

Shannon's first steps out of the pit into which he has cast himself begin with the advice implicit in the title of his sermon: "The Spirit of Truth." When Hannah tells the minister that "acceptance of life is surely the first requisite for living it," she articulates a conviction that occupies the center of much of Huston's strongest, most humane work: before weakness and fear can be overcome, they must be accepted. Shannon proclaims that Hannah is "a lady, a real one and a great one." Her greatness originates in her firm connection to reality, her acknowledgment

without shame of life's vagaries, and her undaunted confronting of its necessities. Like the more tentative Roslyn in *The Misfits*, she understands
that chances and mischances simply arise. With neither shame nor pride,
Hannah tells Maxine that she and Nonno are broke and that being broke
"happens to be what's happened to us."

"I had a spook like yours once," Hannah admits to Shannon during
their long night together. She goes on to relate her victory ("I couldn't afford to lose") over her "Blue Devil" after "subterranean travels that the
spooked and bedeviled take through the unlighted sides of their own natures. . . . " For her disillusioned companion, her terse narrative of
doubt, sorrow, and despair offers profound inspiration. In Hannah,
Shannon can rediscover what is best about himself, shorn of the self-pity
that has grown up to obscure his own courage and integrity. He has a
spirit that she recognizes as the mate of her own, albeit that theirs will
be a companionship of only one crucial night. She tells Shannon – at his
most unsympathetic, just after he has dismissed Maxine to her beach
boys and called Hannah "Miss Thin, Standing Up, Female Buddha" –
that he is "a person I respect." She thus expresses her respect for Shannon's goodness and decency when he seems to have least of both. Human beings must be cherished for the virtues that they manage despite
their blemishes, not because they have no flaws. Without weakness there
can be no strength, without temptation no goodness. In this respect – in
however few others – Huston is very much in accord with traditional
Christian thinking.

Shannon devalues Maxine's humanity when he declares her to be "in-
destructible." On the contrary, Maxine's strength, like Hannah's, derives
from her intimate knowledge of weakness. Shannon seems not to penetrate her facade of tough self-sufficiency, but that has more to do with his
absorption in his own anxieties than with her concealment of hers. One
of her lines begins, "people with troubles, and that's everybody. . . ." On
the life buoy that decorates the front of the resort's drink trolley is written "HELP!," an advertisement that we may take as both an offer and a
plea.

When Maxine implicitly admits her need for someone to live with
and love, she also demonstrates her strength. As thunder and lightning
crackle overhead, she tears herself from her beach boys and runs back toward Shannon and Hannah. Earlier, she had angrily told Hannah that
"even I know the difference between lovin' somebody and just goin' to
bed with 'em. Even I know that." But she seems disinclined to stop sleeping with boys she doesn't love or to act on her desire for the man she

does. When Shannon offers to stay, her tears express present joy and past desolation. In strength that accepts its weakness, Maxine regains her innocence. To underline that point, the music track returns at the end of the movie to a theme first associated with the peasants washing and playing in the river and then with Hannah and Nonno.

Maxine's strength will suffice for both herself and Shannon, who has also learned something of the power that comes from self-acceptance. After Shannon reverses their usual roles by offering Maxine a rum-coca, "speciality of the Costa Verde," she asks him to go with her to the beach – where we last saw her in dark embraces with her boys. "I can get down the hill, Maxine, but I'm not sure about getting, uh, back up." His doubt increases her certainty: "I'll get you back up, baby, I'll always get you back up." Maxine's amiably indecent pun prevents the sentimentality of the moment from being overwhelming. If Shannon can be strong enough to acknowledge his need for her, she can be strong enough to do the same for him, and to raise him in return – in most senses of that verb.

The completion of Nonno's poem moves Maxine to face her deepest needs. It is again typical of Huston's films that the power to accept daunting truths and to confront loss should be associated with the creation of art. "Love's an old remembered song / A drunken fiddler plays," Nonno declaims, summing up much of the action of *Iguana*. Fragments of the old man's last work sound through the final third of the movie like a chorus. His poem at once pays tribute to courage in the face of inevitable decline and, when Nonno completes it just before he dies, stands as an example of what it expresses. Hannah, too, confronts despair when she sketches Shannon. "Are my eyes as wild as this?" he asks her. "Yes they are, Mr. Shannon." Shannon denies the insight in her drawing: "I have fever," he explains. (It appears that the director himself did the sketch of Burton that Kerr is represented as drawing, for it exists, signed by Huston, in a file of Huston sketches in the Huston Collection of the Margaret Herrick Library.)

Judith Fellowes teaches voice at Baptist Women's College, but her art – to call it that – is trivial and evasive. Unwilling to acknowledge her motives or her situation, she leads her colleagues in "Down by the River in an Itty, Bitty Poo" and "Happy Days Are Here Again." The first is a debased musical parody of the river scene that Shannon calls a glimpse of lost innocence; the second epitomizes Miss Fellowes's ugly determination to evade truths about herself and the chaos into which the tour has fallen.

The deepest betrayal of art and of life consists in denying reality, in refusing to confront self-doubt and loss. The heroic characters of the film

– Hannah and Nonno first and then Maxine and Shannon – muster the courage to face their weakness and to do what must be done. That is the integrity and strength of the art both in and of *The Night of the Iguana*.

Shelter from storms of despair generally arises as a product of what *Iguana* calls "decency." By that word, we are led to understand something like Hannah's response to Shannon's denunciation of her second "love experience" as a dirty little episode. "You weren't disgusted by it?" he asks incredulously. "Nothing human disgusts me, Mr. Shannon, unless it's unkind or violent." Decency consists of gentleness, acceptance of human weakness, and kindness toward other people. Like the word "kind," the idea of decency is rooted in fellow-feeling, in sympathy toward humankind. As regards decency, Miss Fellowes again reverses a central value of the film, embodied ironically in her name – which also invokes her latent lesbianism. She is neither jolly, nor good, nor, precisely, a fellow.

Decency begins with an understanding like Maxine's that everyone has troubles. It leads to treating other people as reflections of one's self. In Maxine's case, decency shows in such actions as opening the Costa Verde to Shannon and his flock of tormentors and to the penniless Hannah and Nonno. Decency is part of her sympathy for Shannon's regular breakdowns and even her attraction to him. It is manifest in her explanation to Hannah of why she suppressed that attraction rather than tell Shannon the reason her impotent husband wouldn't mind: "It didn't seem fair to Fred."

Hannah's decency is obvious in her dedication to her failing grandfather and her sympathy for Maxine, Shannon, and even Miss Fellowes. She describes how, as a lonely, recently orphaned sixteen-year-old, she refused to press charges against a young man who pestered her in a movie house. When she sees that Shannon's feet are bleeding, she immediately bandages his wounds. This incident was added to the film by Huston and Tennessee Williams during location shooting; as already noted, it recalls a similar moment between Rose and Charlie in *The African Queen*. In *The Night of the Iguana*, however, Hannah's gesture signals not a growing intimacy that will lead to love, but her capacity for mitigating the anguish of other people. It also anticipates her later understanding that Shannon is engaged in an imitation of Christ. Tending the minister, Hannah recalls the woman (Mary, sister of Lazarus) who washed Christ's feet, dried them with her hair, and anointed them.

If Shannon does not strike us as especially Christlike, he nonetheless retains what Hannah calls "his bit of decency and goodness." He inter-

cedes with Maxine on behalf of Hannah and her grandfather and he refuses to take advantage of the delectable Charlotte's adolescent infatua-
tion. (A less sympathetic figure in Williams's stage play, Shannon there
has a history of sexual predation upon his female clients, especially young
ones.) His most charitable act, ironically, benefits his chief tormentor, Judith Fellowes. He refuses to allow Maxine to confront the music teacher
with her lesbianism. "Miss Fellowes is a highly moral person," he explains. "If she ever recognized the truth about herself, it would destroy
her."

Within the larger ethical context of the film, however, Shannon's char-
ity toward his enemy could be construed as discounting the possibility of
her redemption. As we have seen, acknowledging one's weaknesses must
be the first step to overcoming them. When Shannon protects Miss Fellowes he effectively blocks her chance to confront her self-delusions. The
injury from which he shields her would be pointless and cruel precisely
because he judges her incapable of the self-knowledge requisite for real
humanity.

Achieving one's humanity, faith in the humanity of other people, and
faith in God as well, are intimately linked to what Hannah calls "broken
barriers between people, a wanting to help each other." Consistent with
his direction of other films, Huston in *Iguana* signals movements toward
human connections among his characters – and the failure or impossibility of such connections – through the placement and choreography of
figures within the photographic frame. Separating or bringing characters
together with respect to distance from the camera (depth) is especially revealing. Horizontal proximity also emphasizes psychological intimacy or
alienation, especially when those qualities are already evoked by the
closeness or separation of characters along the optical axis of depth.

Characters who escape the confines of ego come together in typical
framings. Those who cannot overcome psychological distances, or who
are temporarily antagonistic, tend to be placed both at different depths
in the frame and on opposite sides. The morning after Miss Fellowes discovers Charlotte in Shannon's hotel room, Huston sets the minister front
right in the frame and Charlotte, in sharp contrast to her proximity to
Shannon the previous night, back left. A triangular variant of this composition, with obvious symbolic functions, signals conflict as well as distance among three figures. At the Costa Verde, Charlotte truculently announces, "I want a room of my own!" She is in the right foreground;
Miss Fellowes stands left rear; and Shannon occupies the middle, between the two angry women.

This sort of choreography might remind us that *Iguana* began as a work for theater. The neat, compact timing of entrances and exits also recalls the theatrical origins of the screenplay. At the same time, we should remember that much of Huston's early experience as an artist was in the theater, with his father Walter serving as mentor. One of Huston's first works as a writer was a play for marionettes, *Frankie and Johnny*; and he had a brief career in his early twenties as a stage actor. Huston also relates that he spent weeks watching Eugene O'Neill and director Robert Edmond Jones rehearse the cast for the premiere of *Desire Under the Elms*. "What I learned there during those weeks of rehearsal," he wrote, "would serve me the rest of my life."[14] We ought not to be surprised that this early training and experience left lasting traces on his direction of movies – just as it is visible in the work of other directors, like George Cukor, with strong connections to theater. Huston's controlled, frequently schematic handling of visual relationships among figures is characteristic of his other films as well, works that have no previous history on stage.

As characters become more intimate their relationship within the frame signals their progress. While she tells Shannon of her own "spook," Hannah is placed in the front left of the frame with Shannon in the middle right, listening and responding. Similarly, as Shannon and Hannah listen to Maxine's "proposition" near the end of the movie, the minister is shot in medium close-up screen right; Hannah is slightly farther from the camera on the left. A few minutes later, when Shannon gives Hannah his cross to pawn for her trip home, they are reversed horizontally, but Shannon is still slightly closer to the camera. These framings express both the increase and the limits of their intimacy. It is not with Hannah that Shannon will achieve full trust and commitment, and he will never be stationed precisely next to her in the same photographic plane. The closest approximations of that placement come on two occasions: when Shannon agrees to set free the tethered iguana, and just after Nonno dies.

Only with Maxine does Shannon approach full commitment and connection. And only with her does he occupy the same photographic plane in the film. They do so briefly just after Shannon frees the iguana and at length as they listen to Nonno dictate his finished poem to Hannah. Jameson comments upon a similar use of photographic space in *The African Queen*. In that film, he remarks, Huston "develops complex planar separations for the two protagonists, but only so that [he] can describe their movement toward consolidation as one flesh."[15] Huston's similar compositional practice is also striking in *The Man Who Would Be King*. There it traces and underlines the vicissitudes of friendship between the two protagonists.

Nonno's completion of his poem marks one of the climactic incidents of *Iguana*, and the clustering of characters at that moment prefigures the final outcome of the action. Shannon and Maxine listen together in one framing, Maxine's head intermittently on Shannon's shoulder; in the framing that alternates with that one, Hannah takes the poet's dictation, then comes forward to embrace her grandfather and tell him that he has written a "lovely poem." With a gesture similar to Maxine's, she too puts her head on his shoulder briefly. Another climactic moment is the final sequence of the film, in which Maxine and Shannon establish their partnership. As the image fades out over the last scene, Maxine moves from behind him into Shannon's photographic plane and starts to help him remove his tie. The compositional motif is consummated, as it were, at the same moment as the oblique, unconventional love story.

Institutionalized religion in *Iguana*, as in most of Huston's movies, tends to be portrayed as sanctimoniously destructive, ethically self-contradictory, and associated with alienation from nature and from other people, people outside the sect.[16] At the same time, deep sympathies among human beings in this film are closely related to the possibility of faith in an attentive, benign deity. Even religion has its reverse, its honest, sustaining side. Set against its hypocrisies and vengeful patriarchs is a personal reverence in which people express their individuality rather than lose it and in which they experience an embracing fellowship rather than the exclusivity of pious crowds. The emotional rebirth promised by Shannon's discovery that unknowingly he has been making a nest with Maxine also promises a spiritual rebirth. The cross that he lends to Hannah will be redeemed; when we saw it previously, its chain was serving as an improvised hacksaw with which its owner appeared determined to behead himself. Shannon can be "a man of God" – with the emphasis of the phrase equally on both nouns – when he rediscovers himself and a world in which innocence exists, and in which God plays God and humans can be themselves.

After Nonno finishes his poem, he murmurs, "I'd like to pray now." A shot of the moon and clouds then repeats part of the credit sequence. Huston cuts back to Nonno's face, then to Hannah's, as she prays in turn: "O God, can't we stop now?" As with the saving flood near the end of *The African Queen*, a benignant nature or fate or god takes control of this moment also. Grandfather's cane clatters to the flagstones. He nods for the last time. Shannon puts his hand over the old man's heart to search for a pulse, then announces, "God has played God and set him free." He has also set Hannah free and evoked from Shannon his clearest expression of faith, whatever the irony of the ambivalent verb "played."

However provisional the deity may be for him, Shannon descends from a line of clergymen as well as from a "collateral branch" of frontiersmen "with men's hearts, the wild and free hearts of men. They knew hunger and they fed their appetites." What this conflicted offspring of bishops and adventurers needs to find, as Hannah asserts, is "something or someone to believe in." For Shannon that something must include God and the natural world along with men and, especially, women. Across the breadth of Huston's work, from screenplays like *Jezebel* (Wyler, 1938) through mid-career films like *A Walk with Love and Death* to the final frames of *The Dead*, the divine, the natural, and the human are inextricable. To be in harmony with one is to be in harmony with the other two. A vote of no confidence is equally inclusive.

Trust in self and confidence in other people and the world, as we have seen, is intimately associated with finding or making a home. The early shots of the tour bus recall the opening shots of *Key Largo*, another Huston film in which an uprooted protagonist eventually rediscovers his faith in himself, other people, and the world. In the process, he too finds a home. The urgency of Shannon's quest is reflected by the spinning wheels and careening of the bus as he guns it past the scheduled stop and on to the Costa Verde. Shannon's erratic progress toward the recovery of himself and his god is also a journey toward a home, something that he and Maxine may eventually create for each other but that is not a part of this movie to show.

Hannah observes, "I think of a home as something that two people have between them, in which each can nest, rest, live in, emotionally speaking." Most of the central figures of *Iguana*, indeed, are engaged in some form of a search for home. After her husband's death, the Costa Verde no longer offers shelter and companionship to Maxine; she will consequently offer to turn over its operation to Hannah and Shannon while she goes to El Paso to seek human warmth in the relative civilization of its bars and beauty shops. As broke financially as Shannon is broken emotionally, Hannah and her grandfather have no place to stay; when they arrive at the Costa Verde, it is their last chance for refuge. Even the callow Charlotte, after Shannon expels her from his cabin, melodramatically tells the concessionaire on the beach, "I have no home."

Recall again how the camera pans from sky to earth. Between the heavens and the world below there is no boundary but a continuity. Thunder and lightning accompany Maxine's furious descent to the beach with her young stallions, and the camera pans down from the same storm to where Hannah and the trussed Shannon are talking of panic and blue devils. But they are also talking about how to prevail. Maxine jerks away from her beach boys and reascends to the patio, where she finds Shannon unbound and the tethered iguana cut free. The sky mimics human emotions, rage as necessary and fertile as rain. The storm accompanies, off screen, the completion of Nonno's last poem. Clouds clear and the moon emerges. The characters can indeed "stop now." People have broken the barriers between them and become human together. God has played God, all in good time.

What remains takes place in the light of day. Neither Huston's nor Tennessee Williams's artistic worlds in general nor that of *The Night of the Iguana* can assure us of anything as unequivocal as a "happily ever after," but the end of this film does at least promise an "after" with hope of happiness.

Earlier it appeared that an idealized nature and a primitive peasantry were the only alternatives to the anxious, lonely world of the Americans. The bus stops on the bridge to witness the river and the natives, "the lost world of innocence." But Huston was not wont to romanticize either natives or nature. Down the road from the bridge native boys hold aloft captured iguanas that they offer to passing vehicles. The remedy for human misery cannot be found in escape to a simpler human world or a nonhuman one; it comes from persevering together in the time, place, and humanity that people share.

For *Iguana*, the world is surrounded and revived continuously by the sea – perhaps the most persistent, all-purpose, inclusive symbol across Huston's career. As death approaches, Nonno returns to "his beloved sea"; Shannon, at the end of his rope, comes to the same place. Maxine's late husband spent the end of his life fishing on it. Hannah is an islander, "Nantucket born and bred." Huston himself, imitating his art at the end of his life, would return to the seaside setting of Puerto Vallarta, where *Iguana* was made, and then build his house in the more remote hamlet of Las Caletas, a half-hour boat ride up the coast. Like the fictional artist, the real one would return "to his cradle of life."

But the world and its people must outlast their devils and spooks on land. The central characters of *Iguana* come together on a green hill, the very greenness of which presages its eventual dissolution. Nonno's poem acknowledges and mourns that inevitable defeat. Equally, it celebrates the courage of knowing the fatality of life while at the same time refusing to betray despair either by succumbing to it or by denying it. In those simultaneous refusals, Nonno acts out the conclusion to which the narrative of *Iguana* has been leading its characters and its audience: the ideal and the real can be reconciled. The task equally of art and of living is to discover how to thrive within the dream of innocence while accepting and accommodating the waking reality of life and death, of love and sex and loss. Before he reaches that point, a forlorn Shannon has all but given up: "When you live on the fantastic level, as I have more and more lately, but have to operate on the realistic level, that's when you get spooked." But the "New England spinster" to whom he is speaking is less pessimistic; for her, the real and the fantastic are as contiguous as heaven and earth. If we judge by the films of his lifetime, Huston took the real and the fantastic to be equally actual, and closely connected. It is when one dominates or suppresses the other that Huston's characters and their worlds become unbalanced. After he loses the distributor head, his tour party, and his livelihood, Shannon believes himself to have exhausted all hope: "There's nothing lower than Blake's Tours." As far as the minister is concerned, "He's [God has] proved there's no place for Shannon on the realistic level." He then embraces a theatrical – and real – despair and dives into the bay for his suicidal swim to China.

In human affairs as well as in the natural world, day follows the longest, stormiest nights. By the end of the film, Shannon will have proved Hannah's declaration that "we are operating on the realistic level when we are doing the things that have to be done." As Gay maintains in *The Misfits*, death must be faced, and life too. Remarkably, the minister will discover that the things that he has to do can be perfectly fantastic as well as realistic. "Yes, Mr. Shannon," says Hannah, for once confirming his understanding rather than anticipating it, "fantastic is what it is."

In a universe the possibilities of which are at once infinitely fecund and crushingly barren, the artist and his audience can do nothing braver or more hopeful than to affirm the things that happen during the creation of love, trust, and a home, the redeeming moments of contact between human beings. *The Night of the Iguana* faces the grief that Huston faced in all his art, the knowledge that death finally cancels all actions and affections. But it confronts that apprehension, as does "The World's Oldest Living and Practicing Poet," with no betrayal of despair.

CHAPTER VI

Let There Be Light
(1946, released 1980)

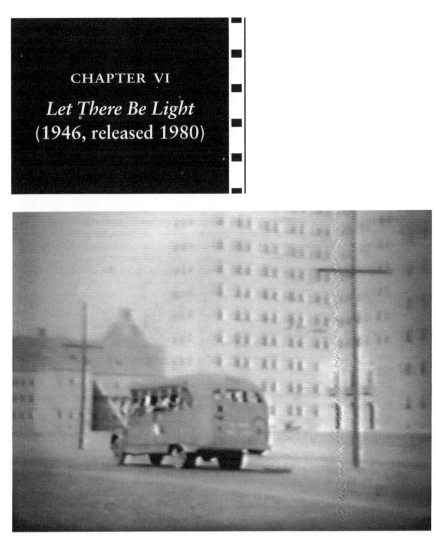

As the bus carries the discharged men from the hospital, it passes utility-pole crosses that mark their psychic resurrection.

At the end of World War II, Huston made *Let There Be Light*, his third and last documentary for the Army. Set in Mason General Hospital, Long Island, it dealt with the rehabilitation of "the psychoneurotic soldier." The Army wished to reassure anxious civilians, especially potential employers, that soldiers who received treatment for acute, battle-induced "nervousness" were not dangerous lunatics or permanently damaged personalities. *Let There Be Light* accomplishes that job very well indeed. The Army's dogged suppression of the film, which it refused to release for thirty-four years, is hard to understand. Huston and others felt that

111

it had to do with a sort of corporate denial: "They wanted to maintain the 'warrior' myth, which said that our American soldiers went to war and came back all the stronger for the experience, standing tall and proud for having served their country well."[1] Only in December of 1980, on the orders of Vice-President Walter Mondale, was Huston's long-proscribed film released for general distribution.[2]

For Huston, the making of *Let There Be Light* became more than an exercise in informational propaganda. It became a meditation on human existence, an essay responding to a question asked in its voice-over narration: "What is the mysterious ingredient that gives joy and meaning to life?" Huston wrote that the time he spent in Mason General, about three months, affected him "almost like a religious experience."[3] He called making the film there "the most hopeful and optimistic and even joyous thing I ever had a hand in" and described the work that resulted as being "wonderfully hopeful and even inspiring."[4]

Jameson calls *Let There Be Light* a "cardinal film in the Huston canon. . . . nothing less than the discovery of the sources of neurotic complication in Huston's world-view, and . . . the compositional style that will dominate his work for the next decade."[5] David Desser asserts that the effect on Huston of his Army movies, "thematically and technically, cannot be overestimated."[6] For Gary Edgerton, "John Huston's three wartime documentaries . . . are pivotal works in the evolution of Huston as a movie maker."[7] "Every man has his breaking point. And these, in the fulfillment of their duties as soldiers, were forced beyond the limits of human endurance." Quoting these sentences from Huston's voiceover, Scott Hammen comments, "It is a theme central to almost all of John Huston's work, but he never found so apt a medium for its expression as in his final war documentary."[8]

With these assessments I am in agreement, but I wish to add a cautionary note and some further observations. First, for all of its importance to Huston personally and its power to illuminate his career, *Let There Be Light* does not represent an epiphany that left its director changed utterly from the boy that he was before – as one of the psychiatrists says to a soldier. While it profoundly influences the films that follow, it also reflects what Huston had already learned in his life and career before he enlisted in the Army. His wide reading and his socializing with an extremely diverse group of intellectuals, artists, friends, and lovers all leave traces on his last documentary just as on the films that follow it. Existentialism and psychoanalytic theory, two strands of obvious importance in *Let There Be Light*, can be seen in the pictures that he directed before the war and also in those on which he worked as screenwriter in the 1930s and 1940s. *Let There Be Light* displays certain Hustonian thematic and stylistic preoccupations with particular clarity, but we overstate the case, I believe, if we think of it as the efficient cause of career-long tendencies. It is of a piece, finally, with the rest of his films.

On the other hand, considering the assertions that critics have made about the importance of *Let There Be Light* in Huston's oeuvre, they remain vague as to specifics. It is unclear, indeed, whether *Let There Be Light* has had much effect on characterizations of Huston's career. Desser's remarks are the most precise. He sees paired thematic concerns arising out of the documentaries and other films that Huston directed during the 1940s, "a binary opposition" between what he calls "the *noir* vision and the *therapeutic* vision."[9] The *noir* vision dominates in Desser's understanding of Huston. Desser only briefly considers the therapeutic side of the binary, nor does he argue for extending his pair of categories beyond Huston's "wartime films and their extensions throughout Huston's career."[10] It seems to me, however, that Desser's insight applies to all of the director's films and that the therapeutic is as powerful and central as the *noir*.

The lack of influence of *Let There Be Light* on popular or scholarly conceptions of Huston has to do with its long unavailability and with the generality of existing descriptions and analyses. In any case, the movie that Huston shot in Mason General Hospital does not fit the standard account of Huston's work as portraying the adventures of a small group of men (usually) failing (usually) at some quixotic enterprise. On the contrary, it portrays a rather large group of men making a surprisingly successful effort to understand and heal themselves, accompanied by doctors, nurses, and orderlies. As Jameson puts it, "We are witnessing the first movement of the 1962 *Freud*'s 'descent into a region blacker than Hell itself,' the unconscious, and an earnest attempt to provide, if only temporarily, that a man need not walk there alone."[11] Its director's understanding of his film as "joyous," "optimistic," and "inspiring" accords well with Jameson's description but poorly with the generally circulating notion of a movie by John Huston. Hammen and Edgerton express what I suspect to be a widespread view of *Let There Be Light*, one heavily influenced by the standard conception of a Huston film. Hammen writes, "The one false note in the work is its implausibly optimistic ending. . . . Yet the sense of all that Huston has captured earlier leads the viewer to just the opposite impression."[12] Edgerton responds similarly: "The major flaw in the film certainly is [the] strong disposition to believe in the unfailing powers of the various military psychiatrists at Mason General."[13]

The perky, vapid music track that accompanies the obvious tendentiousness at the end of the film may have something to do with the rejection of its optimism. Yet the score probably sounded less idiotic – and certainly less dated – in the 1940s than it does now; and the propagandistic purposes of the movie fell so far short of the Army's desire that it was suppressed for a generation. The widely accepted view that psychotherapy must be a protracted, uncertain process may also contribute to the tendency of critics to dismiss the final movement of *Let There Be Light*. Huston himself notes in *An Open Book* that "there was no pretense at effecting complete or lasting cures, which can only be achieved by deep analysis, for the underlying cause of a neurosis usually dates back to childhood."[14] But *Let There Be Light* is about an eight-week immersion course of treatment for combat-induced symptoms. Recently, moreover, there have been studies suggesting that relatively brief, intense therapy may be as effective as protracted analysis, even when applied to peacetime, nonmilitary emotional disturbances. The end of *Let There Be Light* openly concentrates on men whose experience has been successful and who can be released following a relatively brief course of treatment; it never asserts that everyone achieves this happy success. Indeed, by implication it suggests the opposite: "Are they ready to go home? That will be for the doctors to decide."

I see no reason to regard *Let There Be Light* as unrepresentative of Huston's work or as rendered unconvincing by its institutional occasion and rhetorical purposes. The claims made for its influence on Huston's later films and for its importance in understanding the tendencies of his art are just. Its formal and thematic balance, richness of ideas, compassion and empathy of tone, rhythmic deftness, striking composition and cinematography, and precise structure sum up many of Huston's qualities as a filmmaker.

The clarity with which *Let There Be Light* can be seen as a paradigm for Huston's other work results from its concentration. Although it has a rudimentary narrative in the admission, treatment, and discharge of a particular group of patients, the proportion of ideas to story is higher than usual in a fiction film. To adopt a term commonly used in talking about Hitchcock, *Let There Be Light* largely dispenses with the McGuffin, the sought-after external object that provides occasion or motive for a story whose principal concern is finally the internal life of the protagonists. The spiritual and emotional life of the patients is presented with unwavering directness.

The film begins with men coming home and ends with them going home. "The guns are quiet now; the papers of peace have been signed. The oceans of the earth are filled with ships, coming home. In far away places, men dreamed of this moment. But for some men, the moment is very different from the dream." We have already seen the importance of the idea of home in Huston's fiction films; it is of equal importance in *Let There Be Light*. The ironic sorrow of the initial homecoming for the physically and emotionally wounded is intense, because their return does not signal an end to war but marks its continuing effect. *Wise Blood* will reverse the beginning and end of *Let There Be Light*; the recently discharged Hazel Motes revisits his childhood home at the beginning and suffers a terrible return to the boarding house at the conclusion. *In This Our Life*, *Moulin Rouge*, and *The Unforgiven* work variations on similar openings and conclusions. *Key Largo*, a movie Huston made within two years of *Let There Be Light*, begins and ends very much as the documentary does. It opens with a discharged soldier (Humphrey Bogart) on a bus traveling to visit the family of his dead Army buddy and it closes when he comes to terms with himself, reaffirms his deepest beliefs, and discovers a home for himself.

Ideas and images of home are also important, though less emphasized, in Huston's other wartime documentaries. *Report from the Aleutians* ends with the twin triumphs of damage to enemy hangars and the safe return to base of all nine bombers involved in the raid. The last words on the sound track are of men singing "as we go rolling, rolling home." *San Pietro* concludes with the emergence of townspeople from their caves and cellars to plant their fields and reconstruct their homes, and with the faces of children, who represent both the future of the devastated village and testimony to the survival of its families.

(The end of *San Pietro*, however, like the rest of the film, is complicated by its irony, in particular the counterpoint between the cheerfully overstated clichés of the voice-over and the disturbing images of orphaned and semi-orphaned children, heaps of rubble where dwellings used to be, coffins, and bodies being pulled from destroyed houses. The children and their mothers – very few fathers are in evidence – do represent the future of San Pietro; but we can hardly believe that the past will simply disappear, that "tomorrow it will be as if the bad things never existed.")

Why is the idea of home so important for *Let There Be Light*? The most direct answer comes from one of the psychiatrists, addressing a group therapy session: "Not all the learning in all of the books is half as valuable in getting over nervousness as to find someone that you esteem, that you can learn to feel safe with, where you can get a feeling of being accepted, of cherished [sic], where you get a feeling that you're worthwhile and that you're important to someone." His statement answers the question of the voice-over about what gives joy and meaning to life. Huston will implicitly reiterate these ideas in his films of the next four decades: home is something people create together in which they can feel valued and secure. Some of Huston's movies will detail the successful struggle to achieve such a home, others the failure; in all, however, the general idea of a home will remain, with modest variations, constant.

The patients confirm the centrality of family and home to psychic health. The melancholic private sobs as he speaks of his sweetheart, "the one person that gave me a sense of importance." The soldier whose brother died at Guadalcanal recounts a dream of familial harmony: "sittin' around the table we were laughin', talkin', just admirin' each other, and then it ended." The soldier with a severe stutter has partly lost the support of his military buddies, and with it his ability to communicate with other people. He became isolated and his condition acute when "the fellas laughed at me." The paralyzed soldier tells of a disappointing reunion with an ailing, abrasive mother and a hot-tempered father. His is an ironic return to a home that provides little love or security. These interviews demonstrate what the voice-over makes explicit: to become whole again, the men must be reconnected to the homes and families that the war, in various ways, has deprived them of. "These are the people they are coming back to, whose lives are bound up with theirs. Without their understanding, all that has been accomplished in the last few weeks can be torn down; with it, their return to life can be doubly swift and sure."

The alternative is fear, loneliness, gradual psychological and physical dying. "However different the symptoms, these things they have in common: unceasing apprehension, a sense of impending disaster, a feeling of hopelessness and utter isolation. . . . through all the stories run one thread: death and the fear of death." The imagery of the first shots of *Let There Be Light* reflects these themes: a single pair of nurses, diminutive in long shot, enter the mysterious, slightly forbidding portals of an unidentified institution; a solitary sentry paces in shadows and mist; a ship drifts silently into harbor. The *noir* vision will continue to be associated with the sorrows and fears of war. "In the darkness of the ward emerge the shapes born of darkness: the terror of things half-remembered, dreams of battle, the torments of uncertainty and fear and loneliness." The heavily shadowed compositions that express this anguish look back to *The Maltese Falcon* and ahead to films like *We Were Strangers*, *The Asphalt Jungle*, and *Freud*. One of the soldiers anticipates Dobbs in *The Treasure of the Sierra Madre*. Asked where he was during an especially terrifying attack, he simply replies, "I was in a hole." The first shot of a returning injured soldier is of his shadow preceding him down the gangplank. Huston himself was not immune to the dark horror of war: "I remember saying to myself one day in Italy that I was really seasoned at last, a proper soldier. That same night I woke up calling out to my mother."[15]

At the end of the film, fog and darkness give way to brilliant sunlight; the nurses are a waving, smiling crowd; and the men depart together after a joyful valedictory ceremony. Community replaces isolation. Light, health, and happiness replace dark sorrow and illness.

The road home leads through the foundations of the self. "It's almost the core of all our treatment methods," says a psychiatrist, "development of knowledge of one's self, with the accompanying safety that brings." In Huston's relatively optimistic films, self-knowledge is usually key to the prospect of future happiness. The protagonists of more ironic or tragic movies typically fail to connect with their communities or to achieve self-knowledge. The longest sequence in *Let There Be Light* is devoted to the soldier who has forgotten his name and identity; the second longest to the one whose buddies laughed at him and who can no longer get his words out. The constructive communal activities of art, crafts, and sports ease the men back into themselves and the world of other human beings. As for Gay in *The Misfits*, "a new way of living begins." Woodworking, sports, and guitar playing are devoted to "building rather than destroying." The making of *Let There Be Light* itself contributed to this building. "The presence of these cameras" was pointed out and explained to the men when they arrived at Mason General; the psychiatrists later reported that "the cameras seemed to have a stimulating effect, and that the patients being filmed showed greater progress than those in the other groups."[16] Internal representations of art in Huston's fiction films – *Moulin Rouge* is the preeminent instance – strongly invoke his therapeutic vision and often contrast pointedly with *noir* aspects.

Self-knowledge leads disturbed soldiers both to an understanding of their fundamental sanity and to reconnection with other people, from whom they learn that they are no different. The frights and sorrows of the patient are not seen to be exclusively those of traumatized soldiers, but rather reflect "troubles [that] have always gone on, in all time, through all the centuries . . . conflicts, with variations, common to all men." The condition of the patients, far from reflecting disgrace, is doubly honorable. It results not only from the "fulfillment of their duties as soldiers" but also from their gentleness and decency before they "were overnight plunged into sudden and terrible situations." We come to see them – and they perhaps come to see themselves – as normal and sane. Their symptoms are evidence of their kindness, their horror of killing and destruction. Most civilians would respond similarly, the patients are assured; and the civilians for whom the film is primarily intended, after listening to their stories, are likely to agree.

Like Huston's next film, *The Treasure of the Sierra Madre*, his third Army documentary has an unemphasized but important religious imagery. A close-up of a cross on the side of a vessel – the designator of a hospital ship – accompanies the opening words of the voice-over narrative. The imagery of the end of *Let There Be Light* recalls that of its beginning. As the bus carries the discharged men from the hospital, it passes three utility-pole crosses that mark their psychic resurrection, a celebratory leaving behind of their Calvary. As one of my students put it, the doctors and nurses "replace God." They accomplish the miracles of making the halt walk, the dumb speak, the broken in body and mind mend. The title of the film, taken from the opening of Genesis, emphasizes the underlying Christian mythology at the same time that it declares its purpose of revealing truths that were previously concealed as too frightening or shameful for acknowledgment. Among the first fluent words of the stuttering soldier are "Oh, God, listen! I can talk!" When he made *The Red Badge of Courage*, Huston reintroduced this religious motif: the Happy Soldier (Andy Devine) and the General (Tim Durant) both find peace by putting themselves in God's hands. (Another echo that Huston's cinematic adaptation of Crane's novel brings from *Let There Be Light* can be heard in the tribute both works pay to "the natural regenerative powers of youth.")

The technique of *Let There Be Light* will be repeated, explored, varied, and elaborated for the forty years that follow it in Huston's career. Huston brought to it a stylistic conviction that he had already developed and to which he would remain faithful: images and compositions are best that tell the story best, and technical flash-and-dazzle can distract from the actions and ideas that give narrative film coherence and its profoundest expressive powers. Huston's sense of visual and narrative rhythm – among his greatest strengths – is also evident in *Let There Be Light*. One example may suffice. The early interviews between soldiers and psychiatrists establish two of the central tenets of the documentary: the simultaneous uniqueness of each man and the universality that underlies their individual identities. We hear and see in considerable detail their stories and the symptoms of their nervous afflictions. The first five interviews have screen times of a minute and a half to two minutes each. Then, in rapid succession, we witness revealing fragments, often no more than a sentence or two, of seven more interviews. Every man is himself; every man has his anguish in common with others.

Let There Be Light represents one of Huston's most intense meditations on human life. Its understanding of health and happiness, as in the fiction films, is sympathetic, balanced, and humane. "He is breaking out of his prison into life, the life that lies ahead, offering infinite possibilities for happiness and sorrow. How does a man find happiness? Is there a secret to discover?" In most of Huston's films there is. It has to do with honest connections with other people, with self-knowledge and fidelity to one's deepest beliefs, with understanding that one has control over one's self if not over the world. "Underneath 'I can't,'" says one of the psychiatrists, "you usually find 'I won't.'" Most important is love. "The time at Mason General . . . made me begin to realize that the primary ingredient in psychological health is love, the ability to give love and to receive it."[17] The view of Huston as a macho manufacturer of cynical, gynophobic adventures and tall tales, of the *mythe de l'échec* (failure), is wholly inadequate to the emphasis on love, self-knowledge, and community that underlies *Let There Be Light* – and that also underlies virtually all the thirty-seven feature films that Huston directed. These themes, explicit in *Let There Be Light*, make sense of the famous quests in the fiction films and give them meaning. They also make sense of the films – from *In This Our Life* and *Moulin Rouge* to *Under the Volcano* and *The Dead* – that have nothing to do with masculine adventure but everything to do with love, integrity, and self-understanding.

SECTION III

"Trying to Account
for Themselves"

Heaven Knows,
Mr. Allison

The Maltese Falcon

Reflections in a
Golden Eye

*T*HE *Treasure of the Sierra Madre, The Man Who Would Be King, The African Queen, The Misfits, The Night of the Iguana,* and *Let There Be Light* all develop thematic centers in the discovery, creation, or recovery of self by figures who need to achieve a sense of personal coherence and the regard of others. Indeed, these themes are central, one way or another, to most of the films Huston directed. The five fiction films detail quests for external goals as well: gold, a kingdom, an improbable naval coup, a way to live without collecting wages or preying on other free beings, a desperately needed place among other people. By metaphor and association, these external quests become identified with internal pressures for self-knowledge and a realistic coming to terms with the world. The latter, in turn, is frequently summarized in the idea of home as a place, an attitude, and a relationship with one or more beloved people. In *Let There Be Light*, the external desideratum – the return of fighting men to resume their identities as sound, functioning participants in their homes, families, and jobs – is only alluded to; the film documents their direct attempts at self-discovery or recovery. Among the five fiction films, *The Misfits* most nearly approaches the explicitness of these psychological and spiritual preoccupations.

The three films discussed in this section – *Heaven Knows, Mr. Allison, The Maltese Falcon,* and *Reflections in a Golden Eye* – all explore the quest for self-realization through a sharpened focus on the conflict between an individual's autonomy and desires on one side, and the opposing weight of social institutions, both as outside forces and as internalized aspects of a character's fundamental identity, on the other. Social institutions – whether religious, political, military, national, ethnic, or class-based – do have importance in the films analyzed thus far, but they mostly receive secondary or tertiary emphasis. In *The Night of the Iguana*, however, the personal values of Shannon are deeply involved with conventional religious issues, which have a central position in the matrix of conflicts that motivate the film. Among the leading figures of *Iguana*, reverence for and misgivings about God, nature, and humanity are crucial to conceptions of self and home. Similar fusions and conflicts involving institutional and personal agendas are of great importance to the films analyzed in this section.

Like all of Huston's movies, those discussed in this section include both external and internal quests, here strongly conditioned by severe contradictions between the social placements and commitments of the protagonists and their more private needs for love, a coherent sense of self, and a secure place in the world. From the discussion of *Heaven Knows, Mr. Allison* through that of *The Maltese Falcon* to *Reflections in a Golden Eye*, we shall see that the conflicts become more acute, more desperate, less resolvable. In none are private and institutional goals and roles fully reconcilable, but in *Heaven Knows, Mr. Allison* partial accommodation proves possible and satisfying. Such partial resolution also occurs in *The Maltese Falcon*, but the satisfactions it offers are equivocal, both to the protagonists and to the audience. *Reflections in a Golden Eye* can posit no durable reconciliation between the needs of personal love and self-expression and the demands of society on a military base. The murder at the end of the film solves nothing, resolves nothing. On the contrary, it expresses the impossibility of relieving pressures that result from the inability of central characters to understand or acknowledge their own desires and identities in a rigid social setting in which "a square peg in a round hole" can only be conceived as a "mess."

CHAPTER VII

Heaven Knows, Mr. Allison (1957)

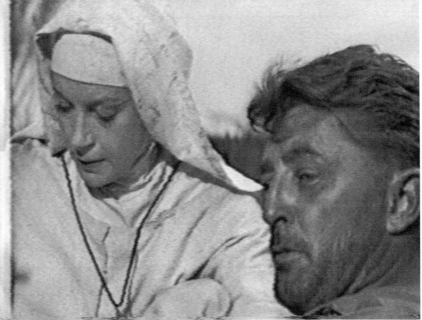

The knowledge of each other that Sister Angela and Mr. Allison possess is deeper and more transforming than sexual experience or even marriage.

Of *Heaven Knows, Mr. Allison* Huston remarked, "*Allison* is seldom referred to, but I think it was one of the best things I ever made. It was unostentatious, had very simple, clear dialogue and was built on a first-rate foundation."[1] This assessment seems just. *Allison* is also emphatically characteristic of John Huston in stylistic tendencies and themes: its imagistic oppositions and blending of fire and water, of nature and civilization; its thematics of home, self-creation and self-discovery, love and integrity; its characteristic choreography of actors and camera, the lively rhetoric of its editing and pacing; its sense of humor and sense of play;

its precise, expressive writing; and the collaboration of director and actors that develops its strong sense of character in central figures and links personality firmly to fate.

Allison is perhaps most illuminatingly Hustonian in its explicit, complex relationship to *The African Queen*, which its director made six years earlier. Although the likeness of the two films is obvious enough to have been generally noticed, the implications of their similarities have not been seriously pursued; neither have commentators thought about the contrasts between them that become important issues precisely because of their pointed similarities. The pervasive resemblance between *Allison* and *The African Queen* suggests a relationship that exceeds the sharing of a creator; it implies that the later film comes into being, in part at least, as a commentary on the earlier one, a set of variations upon its themes.

Allison brings to the dramatic situation of two people isolated in a world at war slightly less fantastic assumptions and more realism than Huston applied to the same *donné* in *The African Queen*. Generically, *Allison* has less of romance and more of irony than *The African Queen*. Mythologically, the consequences of the Fall are more present in *Allison* than they are in the earlier film. The civilizations that exist elsewhere and that periodically impinge upon the protagonists' solitude in both films have more power to affect the lives of the central figures in the later one. Sister Angela and Mr. Allison are less able than Rose and Charlie to recreate themselves in a latter-day Garden of Eden, to escape the effects of history and of the world beyond the jungle, or to achieve a personal, private salvation.

The first sequence after the credits of *Allison* both recalls and condenses the images of the opening of *The African Queen*. Mr. Allison's life raft brings him, as the *African Queen* brought Charlie, to a village of huts. In *Allison* they have been deserted, evidently recently and suddenly. We soon learn that the Japanese have abducted their inhabitants, as we saw the Germans do in the earlier film. Everywhere, as in *The African Queen*, the jungle is emphatically present. Mr. Allison investigates a deserted cottage, very much like that of Rose and her brother and complete to such details as a broad porch with a chair and railing. A church with steeple and surmounted cross recalls the "1st Methodist Church / Kung Du." The dialogue of *Allison* also occasionally echoes that of *The African Queen*. When Mr. Allison asks, "You're alone here?" Sister Angela's reply is quick and emphatic: "God has been with me." We may remember Rose's pointed correction of Charlie: "God has not forsaken this place, Mr. Allnutt, as my Brother's presence here bears witness." Most obviously, *The African Queen* and *Heaven Knows, Mr. Allison* share status as virtuoso exercises in the dramatic possibilities of an essentially two-person cast; in *Allison*, supporting figures are almost entirely absent.

Strikingly parallel actions, revealing of both affinities between the two works and persistent tendencies in Huston's art and thinking, occur during similar moments of apparently imminent catastrophe, the grounding of the *African Queen* among the reeds and the discovery by the Japanese of the cave in which Mr. Allison and Sister Angela have taken refuge. At both moments, the heroines pray. Sister Angela recapitulates the fundamental plea of Rose's prayer, which is not for rescue but for divine acceptance and admission into heaven. The simplicity and generosity of Sister Angela's utterance is characteristic of Huston's most powerful writing: "Dear God, Mr. Allison here is not of the Church. He's only a marine, but he is a good man, brave and very, very honest. I humbly implore thee when his time comes to be merciful and receive him into Thy [inaudible word] presence." Unlike Rose, Sister Angela does not include herself in her prayer; her vocation and the chastity of her relationship with Mr. Allison make self-advocacy unnecessary. We might notice even at this dire moment a bit of characteristic Hustonian wit, amused and resonant: "He's only a marine. . . . " In retrospect, such a touch – like the spluttering German's aqueous salute after the sinking of the *Louisa* – signals the relaxed, confident hand of the writer-director who exercises his benignant control over the fate of his creations.

The heavenly response to both prayers is unexpected, improbable, and wonderfully easy for an audience to accept. As we have seen, a vast rainstorm frees the *African Queen*. In *Allison*, the bombs of American airplanes prevent a threatened Japanese grenade. The *machinae* of both films descend carrying a godlike filmmaker ready to work miracles for characters who love, are brave, and ask for nothing beyond divine recognition of their innocence and devotion. (A similar idea, similarly executed, reappears at the conclusion of Albert Brooks's 1991 *Defending Your Life*.)

The water and fire that served as dominant and tonic tones on the imagistic scale of *The African Queen* reappear in *Allison*, but without the tendency to synergy that we saw in the earlier film and with a stronger emphasis upon their opposition. As is usual in all but Huston's most ironic films, water in *Allison* is mostly associated with life, fertility, rescue, and revival. And, in storms, with truth. Fire is generally connected to warfare, violent destruction, and the dangers of the civilized world beyond the island.

Mr. Allison's first act upon reaching land is to drink fresh water from the lagoon. Later he will immerse himself in the sea to catch a turtle, spear fish, hide beneath the waves from a Japanese patrol boat. In the first and third actions the camera submerges itself with him, as it did beneath the hull of the *African Queen*. The sea conceals the breech blocks that Mr. Allison removes from the Japanese 105-millimeter cannons, thereby allowing the U.S. forces to land without significant casualties. In a small, related detail, an aging Japanese officer takes off his glasses while showering and thus allows Mr. Allison to reach the enemy storeroom unseen. When the Japanese temporarily leave the island and Sister Angela and her companion can emerge from their cave, the first use they find for their freedom is to bathe in the sea, a sequence that Huston treats like a rebirth and a baptism. As Robert Mitchum floats in the water, we see him clean-shaven and youthfully handsome for the first time; off camera, we hear Sister Angela singing – the only occasion on which she expresses such secular high spirits.

Set against the reviving water, the fire of bombs and of "battle wagons sluggin' it out" beyond the horizon embodies the violence and danger of the outside world and its war. The Japanese burn the foliage of the island in order to discover the hiding place of the nun and the marine. Both the Japanese and the American forces prepare the way for landings by setting the island aflame with their bombardments. "Thank God there was no one out there to be killed," Sister Angela murmurs gratefully after the first bombing of the island by the Japanese. In the next shot, however, she and Mr. Allison emerge just in time to watch the burning steeple collapse into the ruins of the church. A slower-working irony is created by the American bombs that save the lives of the protagonists, for we realize later that the arrival of the U.S. troops means that the time together of Sister Angela and Mr. Allison must soon end.

In this complex movie, the imagery of water does not entirely escape the irony that attaches to fire. The symbolic associations of the sea move in at least two directions at once when it serves as a watery grave for the enemy soldier whom Mr. Allison kills – a grave that gives up its secret all too quickly. The violence of the rainstorm into which Sister Angela flees and from which she takes fever has the positive values associated with the strength and truth of her feelings and the negative ones associated with her attempt to evade them and with Mr. Allison's drunkenness. Of the sake that helps to precipitate the whole episode we may remain in doubt. Is it water or fire?

Most complicating in Huston's treatment of water in *Allison* is the systematic distinction that the film makes between the water of the ocean and that of the lagoon. The credit sequence shows an unknown soldier adrift in an unprovisioned life raft. (It shows an unknown star, as well; we do not see Robert Mitchum's face until nearly the end of the credits, when he rolls over to face the camera.) The credits are followed by a title, "1944 SOMEWHERE IN THE SOUTH PACIFIC," that announces the beginning of the story. The first sequence emphasizes the life-saving fresh water that the marine drinks and then swims through to discover Sister Angela and, ultimately, something like the meaning of his life. Overtones of birth or rebirth are strong in this sequence. The ocean waves bring representatives of the world of wars and social complexities to the island, a commodious green land to which the word "pacific" applies far better than to the salt water that surrounds it. The lagoon separates the island from the ocean; and across the lagoon – insistently shown during turning points of the film – a rickety bridge connects the island and the sea beach. Mr. Allison, who comes peacefully, significantly avoids the bridge in favor of immersion in the fresh water. When the Japanese or the Americans prepare to land, we see a long shot of the lagoon, with the bridge and behind it the sea, carrying its burden of violent death. Near the end of the movie, we will see the American marines bathing in the lagoon, unaware that many of them owe their lives to the disabling of the big Japanese guns in the foreground.

(We might be puzzled by the fact that Mr. Allison and Sister Angela run across the bridge to pursue and catch the turtle that they share for their first meal. With a single idyllic exception of gathering coconuts, the food that Mr. Allison acquires comes from the sea or the civilization associated with it. He spears fish at risk of discovery by the Japanese, and, when Sister Angela proves to be a queasy snapper of raw mackerel, he goes into the enemy camp for more palatable provisions.)

The principal theme of *Heaven Knows, Mr. Allison* may be seen as the conflict between the idea of persons as autonomous and innocent (the protagonists approach that condition when they are alone on the island) and persons fully implicated in defining social settings. Like the lagoon and the sea, such contrasting psychologies are connected by bridges as fragile-looking but durable as the foot bridge between the island and the ocean beach.

After the most telling moment of conflict between innocent and socialized perspectives, the episode in which Mr. Allison proposes marriage to Sister Angela, the imagery of sea and lagoon resonates with the action just passed. When Mr. Allison responds to the nun's explanation about her engagement to Christ by concluding that he had "no right to speak,"

Huston cuts to a shot of the bridge across the lagoon with the beach and ocean in the background. The next morning, when Sister Angela comes to the lagoon for a bucket of water, she sees the marine walking pensively along the verge of the Pacific and crosses the bridge to join him. Shots of waves and sea foam bracket the conversation that follows, in which Mr. Allison recants his proposal and we are left wondering if Sister Angela was about to recant her refusal. As they talk, between them across the lagoon in the background we see the cottage, a slightly out-of-focus image of domesticity forgone or unattainable. The sequence ends with a dissolve from Mr. Allison's face to another shot of waves and foam – inscrutable and expressive abstractions. Each framed, ambiguous pattern is abruptly erased by a wave creating the next. As Raymond Chandler wrote in a novel that Huston would almost surely have read, "the surf curled and creamed, almost without sound, like a thought trying to form itself on the edge of consciousness."[2] A little later we will see Mr. Allison looking through a Japanese book, its characters as significant and mysterious as the patterns of spindrift foam. The film ends as it began, with a title and a crossing of the lagoon. The conclusion reverses the opening: Mr. Allison and Sister Angela cross from the island over the bridge toward the sea and the closing title follows, dropping a curtain on the action that the opening title announced before Mr. Allison plunged beneath the surface of the lagoon to swim to the demi-paradise of the island.

Between those two titles, the dominant metaphor in *Allison* is the myth of the paradisiacal garden. As in *The African Queen*, the religious affiliation of the heroine evokes the specifics of Christian myth, an evocation that is made explicit in the dialogue. Like Rose and Charlie, Sister Angela and Mr. Allison approach the status of Eve and Adam in a tropical Eden, an uncultivated garden whose abundance is insisted upon graphically and verbally. From the opening sequence, the fecundity of the jungle is visually pervasive. As the protagonists eat their first meal together, Mr. Allison remarks, "There's no question about us surviving. We could go on here for years – and I mean years." Though the marine wants to try to sail to Fiji to rejoin the fighting, the dialogue enforces our sense of a paradise that exists in contrast with an infernal world elsewhere. Mr. Allison himself notes the apparent folly of leaving "this place where there's plenty to eat, good water, and go sailin' off to hell an' gone – beggin' your pardon, M'am." He and Sister Angela are hardly acquainted at this moment; after they know each other better the idea of leaving the island "for hell an' gone" will produce more ambivalence. But at this early stage of the story the inferno of the world has greater attraction than the placid abundance of the island. "What if I myself would like to try, Mr. Allison?" "Then I'd say you was crazy too, M'am."

We may recall here Northrop Frye's description of what he calls the second phase of romantic myth,

> a phase most familiar to us from the story of Adam and Eve in Eden before the Fall. In literature this phase presents a pastoral and Arcadian world. . . . The archetype of erotic innocence is less commonly marriage than the kind of "chaste" love that precedes marriage [and] the sense of being close to a moral taboo is very frequent, as it is of course in the Eden story itself.[3]

His sketch of the setting of such romantic narratives as "a kind of prison-Paradise or unborn world from which the central characters long to escape to a lower world, . . . a world of action" describes quite precisely the situation of Sister Angela and Mr. Allison at this early point in the film and in their relationship.[4] After they come to know each other and after the Japanese bring the "lower world" onto their island, both will take more seriously the idea that leaving their paradise may be "crazy." Neither, however, will finally repudiate that idea, for reasons that this discussion will explore later.

To continue for the moment with Frye as guide, what he called "displaced mythology" appears in *Heaven Knows, Mr. Allison* in the fact that the marine is of unknown birth and origin, having been left as an infant "at the Allison Street entrance one morning in an empty egg crate." (An evocation of Moses may be reflected, as well, in Mr. Allison's floating to the island on a raft and in his later receiving a command from God.) Sister Angela's origins are at least as mysterious; we know nothing of her before her novitiate. She appears to Mr. Allison as Eve appeared to an awakening Adam, a gift from heaven to care for and cherish as a helpmate. Both aspects of her role are evident early in the film. Before Mr. Allison allows himself to rest after his arrival, he asks Sister Angela if she is okay. When he sets off in pursuit of the turtle a little later, he tells her, "I'm gonna need your help."

Further displacements of Christian myth (and more generally of the myths of heroes that Joseph Campbell and folklorists have detailed) are discernible in *Mr. Allison*. Not only is the marine of mysterious birth, but he also disappears and returns three times for Sister Angela: first, when he goes to the Japanese camp for food and she thinks that he has been killed; second, when she is delirious and he returns there for blankets (his disappearance in this case occurs during her loss of consciousness); and third, when he leaves to disarm the cannons and reappears to her like a ghost in the smoke and haze of early dawn. In each case, Mr. Allison descends into the lower world of the enemy and returns to a higher place after his mission is completed. But the fact that he is not Christ – albeit he may in some details suggest Him – is crucial. Unlike Charlie's replacing of Rose's brother in her life, Mr. Allison's attempts to substitute himself for Christ as Sister Angela's spouse are bound to fail.

The African Queen, as we saw, took the form of an unusually (for Huston) straightforward romantic comedy. Though the comic elements are diminished and complicated in *Allison*, they remain worth noting. The central narrative of Christianity is structurally comic and its evocation in the title and characterizations of *Heaven Knows, Mr. Allison* partly signals the genre of the film. We may further note that *Allison* repeats one of the commonest plot structures of romantic comedy, what Frye calls "the rhythmic movement from normal world to green world and back again."[5] The action of the film takes place almost entirely in the middle section of that rhythmic movement, but we have seen that the opening and closing strongly allude to the "normal world" from which Mr. Allison and Sister Angela come and to which they return. Frye's discussion of green world comedy illuminates another of the details of the film: "as the forest in Shakespeare [the jungle in *Allison*] is the usual symbol for the dream world in conflict with and imposing its form on experience, so the usual symbol for the lower or chaotic world is the sea, from which the cast, or an important part of it, is saved."[6]

The marine and the nun explicitly confront the implications of their enforced absence from the world of experience after the possibility of sailing to Fiji has been exploded by Japanese bombs, the enemy soldiers have left the island, and the American forces have apparently decided to ignore it on their way east. Energized by having consumed most of a large bottle of sake and frustrated by the unavailability or irrelevance of the nun's "big blue eyes and a beautiful smile, (pause) freckles," Mr. Allison smashes the late Father Ryan's pipe against the cottage wall. "What good is it without tobacco!" He unhappily goes on:

We're gonna be on this island for years and years, till the war's over, anyway. . . . We've been bypassed. . . . Just you and me, see. Now what's the point of your bein' a nun if we're all alone? Answer me that. Can't, can ya, 'cause there ain't no point. No more than my bein' a marine. What would ya do all day? Pray? And I, uh, I drill, I guess, huh? . . . All we got is it and each other. Like Adam and Eve, like we was the first two people on earth and this was the Garden of Eden.

Sister Angela begins to sob, then runs out of the cottage into the storm when Mr. Allison approaches to comfort her. Later she will tell him that she was running not from the threat of his sexual advances but from "the truth."

The truth is that nuns and marines are irrelevant in Eden. The point of both exists only in a postlapsarian world in which sin and violence are present and must be constantly ameliorated or fought. In a latter-day Garden, praying and drilling have no use, no logical place. Uncorrupted nature requires no more than harvesting; and uncorrupted humanity there can only be plausibly imagined as participating in the fecundity of nature.

But Huston knew, and Sister Angela and Mr. Allison swiftly learn when the Japanese return, that the modern world (after the Fall) is nowhere uncontaminated. To exaggerate Donne's formulation, no island is an island. When Corporal Allison assures the nun that "anybody with any sense believes in God," Huston cuts ironically to bombing and strafing by the Japanese. The editing urges that anybody with any sense also believes, as the Kirk Douglas character says in *The List of Adrian Messenger*, that "Evil does exist. Evil is." The bombing destroys the island's buildings, the raft that its inhabitants were fitting for their voyage to Fiji, and the garden-jungle itself: "This island is sure beat-up. Fruit's all blasted; there isn't a whole coconut left." At the moment that Eden is shattered, it becomes inescapable. Much of the rest of the action will take place under the threatening surveillance of the Japanese reconnaissance tower, a panopticon that the marine and the nun – and the camera – only look up at, never down from.

Even without the Japanese, the island cannot be Eden to its inhabitants, because they bring to it the knowledge of good and evil that began human history. Moving warily through the deserted village at the beginning of the film, Mr. Allison is startled by the rustling of a large, ratlike creature. Later, in the Japanese supply building, he must lie motionless while a similar rodent crawls frighteningly over his body. It is finally evident that neither creature is dangerous, but the fear with which Allison responds to them underlines the fact that he comes onto the island with a preexisting conviction in the danger of the world. If the island fully re-created Eden – and we have seen that it cannot – the marine and the nun still could not live on it with the innocence of Adam and Eve. The impossibility of the perfect innocence of the protagonists is a theme relatively common in what we may call "desert island fictions," a kind of narrative that stretches back through *Robinson Crusoe* and *The Tempest* to the *Odyssey*. In film, it is an idea that *Allison* shares with Lena Wert-muller's 1975 *Swept Away*, though Wertmuller's film gives the point most emphasis after the two central figures have been rescued and returned to their original situations.

In Huston's reworking of the themes of Genesis, evil brings God and religion – and marines – into existence. Other people and their civiliza-tions are the vectors of that evil. Without it, there would be no need for gods, religions, nuns, soldiers, discipline, or identities outside of one's self. Huston's is an existential, Sartrean version of Christian mythology: *"L'enfer, c'est les Autres"* (Hell is other people). The director adds what Sartre's formulation logically implies: *L'enfer, c'est nous-même* (Hell is ourselves).

Because civilization and its ambivalences are taken seriously in *Alli-son* in a way that they are not in *The African Queen*, the later film is a more complicated work thematically. Despite being even more austere in casting and plot, it generates a denser dialectic. Although they are like Rose and Charlie in finding themselves temporarily isolated in an Edenic jungle, Sister Angela and Mr. Allison are shaped by societal identities stronger and more fully internalized than the affiliations of nation and class of their earlier prototypes. The power of their institutional identi-ties is signaled by the fact that neither has two names, the place of a sur-name being taken by "Sister" for Angela and that of a given name by "Mr." or occasionally "Corporal" for Allison. The conflict of institu-tional identities with both basic human nature and the individualities of the protagonists shapes the film's themes and the significance of its rather scant action.

From his first appearance, Mr. Allison does everything very much ac-cording to regulation: the elaborate, slightly comic maneuvers of his first landing, his declaration of a blackout in the church, the raw-fish-eating lesson he gives to Sister Angela. He finds his identity, as he tells the nun, in being a marine. His language – sometimes incomprehensible to his companion – is the jargon of the Corps. Going into the shade is "trans-fer[ring] out of the sun"; rumor is "scuttlebutt, you know, the poop, . . . like guys beatin' their gums"; and his most earnest exhortation is "hub-ba hubba." Without resentment, Mr. Allison describes the submarine captain submerging and abandoning him under fire, "which is according to his book, but a little tough on us gyrines."

In his adherence to his own military book, Mr. Allison resembles the Japanese, in whom the weakness of such subordination of personal au-tonomy is evident. While the Japanese are absorbed in an assembly for a formal flag-raising (a scene that will be duplicated by the Americans later), the marine takes advantage of their distraction to slip back to the cave. With an irony more evident to the audience than the speaker, Mr. Allison explains to Sister Angela why the Japanese come ashore firing rifles and machine guns onto an island they suppose deserted: "It wouldn't be a proper landin' without shootin'." When Allison is discovered stealing blankets by an enemy soldier who is in the midst of traditional fencing exercises, the enemy's rigid continuation of his samurai identity allows the free-lancing American to quietly kill his discoverer. The dissonant comic overtones of this moment recall Bergson's assertion that we laugh at characters when they show the inflexibility of machines, in this case fighting machines. Similar overtones attach to Allison's dismissal of Sister Angela's dismay when she learns what happened: "It's my duty to destroy the enemy. I been neglectin' it, you might say, 'count a you."

Like Mr. Allison, Sister Angela follows her book and her procedures; and like the marine, she is part of a "tough outfit" into which she was initiated by a formidable "D.I." (Drill Instructor). The emblems of her vocation are prominent throughout: the white habit in which she is always dressed (with two brief exceptions); the ring that signifies her engagement to Christ; and, most insistently, various crosses, including the one suspended on a chain from her neck – as important a stage property as Shannon's crucifix in *The Night of the Iguana*. We see her lighting tapers and worshiping before the altar and its elevated cross in the church. She is also associated with crosses by subtler images, those that she weaves in her thatching of a sail, for example.

When Mr. Allison snuffs the votive candles and when he pushes Sister Angela down and conceals her with palm fronds from a Japanese reconnaissance plane, we are forcefully reminded of the differences in their professions, the opposing axioms of their books. A marine, he is trained to suspect and fight evil; a nun, she is trained to seek out and support good. Their conflicting vocational dispositions are evident when Sister Angela proposes to surrender herself to the Japanese. She assumes that the enemy will respect her vocation and her person; Mr. Allison seems to make the contrary assumption. Just before that dispute, as the nun and the marine hide motionless in the cave, they make a *tableau vivant* symbolic of their opposing stations. Mr. Allison stands with drawn knife and "USMC" (United States Marine Corps) stenciled prominently on his shirt pocket; Huston then cuts to Sister Angela in her habit, her cross suspended on her breast.

Balancing the institutional oppositions of the protagonists are less predictable consonances: shared values, habits, circumstances, and assumptions to which Huston gives frequent emphasis. "Now you look at me, M'am," says Mr. Allison near the beginning of the movie, "What do you see besides a big dumb guy? I'll tell ya, a marine! That's what I am. All through me. A marine. Like you're a nun. You got your cross, I got my globe an' anchor." He describes becoming a marine as if it were a religious conversion: "then I seen the light, and I started bein' a marine." It becomes evident as the movie progresses that both Sister Angela's and Corporal Allison's careers require a withdrawal from the ordinary business of daily life and a simultaneous engagement with the world's deepest needs and dangers.

When Mr. Allison uses his knife to lift the altar cross from the smoldering ruins of the church and carry it to Sister Allison, the camera moves in for a close-up of the two objects. They emblematize the central themes of *Allison* very much as the close-ups of the Gila monster on the sack of gold or the empty bag on the small branched cactus did for *The Treasure of the Sierra Madre*. The juxtaposition of knife and cross figures forth the differences and similarities of the objects and the ways of life that they symbolize. The closing shot of Sister Angela carrying the cross and walking next to the stretcher on which Mr. Allison is at last smoking the cigarette that he asked for in the opening sequence has a similar emblematic quality.

Mr. Allison's social, institutional role as a marine has been more than internalized; it gives him an identity that he did not have before and that provides him with personal coherence. Sister Angela is a nun in the same way. When Mr. Allison receives word from God as to how he can assist the American landing, both the internalization and the affinity of his vocational identity with Sister Angela's are vividly dramatized. The sequence begins with Mr. Allison directing a startled look in the general direction of the camera (a look that replicates those that accompanied his learning that Sister Angela's vows were not yet final and his sniffing the bottle of sake). In response to the nun's assurance that God need not speak in thunder, that His voice "usually comes from within," Mr. Allison announces, "He just told me the way [to put the Japanese artillery out of commission] – so simple I should have thought of it myself." We may smile at the innocence of Mr. Allison's understanding of what has happened to him; but if we do, we are more naive than the marine. The identities of the soldier and the nun are so thoroughly defined by their vocations that voices "from within" are truly both the directives of the causes they serve and their own, simultaneous and indistinguishable. As

André Bazin once remarked, "the individual transcends society, but society is also and above all within him."[7] This fusion of social identity and personal integrity is recurrent in Huston's movies. We encounter it in his first film when Sam Spade explains to Brigid O'Shaughnessy the obligations of being a detective.

When the protagonists prepare to separate at the end of the film, their action expresses and preserves their identities. However much their return to the world and its divergent paths pains them, the alternative is worse. To marry would be personal annihilation. By the end of the film, we can add what Mr. Allison leaves unsaid at the beginning: the soldier and the nun have equal claim to the famous motto of the U. S. Marine Corps, "*semper fideles.*" It is also clear that their faith addresses their own needs as much as it does the demands of their institutions.

"Goodbye, Mr. Allison. No matter how many miles apart we are, or whether I ever get to see your face again, you will be my dear companion always, always," vows Sister Angela. Despite their parting, the nun and the marine achieve a real coming together, one that the movie does not belittle as a consolation but represents as a fulfillment, a marriage of true minds in which each remains faithful both to self and to the other. *Allison* is finally a love story with a happy ending.

Broadly conventional in its plot sequence of meeting, courtship, and commitment, the romantic narrative of *Heaven Knows, Mr. Allison* derives most of its interest and resonance from the obstructions to love thrown up by the institutional identities of the protagonists, especially the nun's. The novel of Charles Shaw on which the screenplay was based dwells on the sexual temptations of its situation more insistently than the film, though it does not verge on the pornographic. But the erotic energies of the film are quite thoroughly sublimated. Early in the movie, a couple of hints threaten – or promise – sexual love. When Sister Angela goes into the church to rest, Mr. Allison's shadow darkens the door as she closes it behind her. That shot dissolves into an action familiar from certain risqué folk tales in which Sister Angela holds up the skirt of her habit to catch coconuts thrown down by Mr. Allison. Such mild erotic gestures are not amplified, however, and the film proceeds with a discretion that the most punctilious censor would find exemplary.[8]

The getting-to-know-you phase of the story occurs with a swiftness in establishing and developing character that is among Huston's greatest strengths. Sister Angela learns the marine's argot rapidly: "They don't seem to beat their gums on very hopeful poop." Huston's camera underscores the growing intimacy of the protagonists. As Sister Angela questions Mr. Allison about a near–faux pas, "mackerel sna—," the camera shoots her through the palm frond sail she is weaving. After she makes him admit what he was going to say and he recovers his social balance by telling her that Catholics "are good marines, M'am," the camera moves around the sail to shoot her without visual obstruction. In doing so it quietly expresses what was called in *The Night of the Iguana* "broken barriers between people." Other movements toward intimacy have the economy of familiar movie conventions: Mr. Allison calms and reassures Sister Angela during the first Japanese bombing; he nurses her through her fever and she doctors him after his excursion against the Japanese; he instructs her in the lore of the marines and she enlarges his religious education beyond orphanage lectures about the evils of cigarettes and – Mr. Allison can't say it – masturbation.

But the conventions of courtship are recurrently deflected by the situation and professions of the protagonists. When Mr. Allison gives the sister a comb that he carves and wraps in palm-leaf paper with an hibiscus bow, he learns that the short hair required by her order makes his offering useless. It is a gift for an uncommitted woman, not a nun. Yet if Angela, as a nun, cannot use it, she does not, as a woman, reject it. She will "cherish it always," as a "keepsake" – her "always" anticipating the doubling of that word at the end of the movie in her farewell to Mr. Allison. Significantly, however, after Sister Angela finds her companion's gift but before she allows herself to open it, she completes her morning prayers. By including this detail, Huston keeps her priorities evident to the audience if not to the sleeping marine. We witness a similar suggestion of Mr. Allison's deepest allegiances when he learns that the nun "could still pull out" before taking her final vows. At that moment, he is distracted by the sound of distant guns, and leaves Sister Angela's side to investigate. His action anticipates his later recanting of his proposal: "I must've been off my rocker last night. A marine oughtn't to get married. . . . You do me a favor, huh M'am, just forget I opened my big mouth?"

After the Japanese leave the island, the marine sings, "Don't sit under the apple tree with anybody else but me," and swings the smiling nun into a rough dance. That evening, the courtship intensifies. "Some moon, isn't it, M'am. . . . Funny, it seems bigger than the stateside moon, huh?" "It's a lovely moon," answers Sister Angela in her lilting Irish accent; then, after a short pause, "to sew by." Huston shows us the moon, pans characteristically down the palms, and returns to the nun, who asks the marine whether a sweetheart awaits a "big, handsome fellow like you." He has no one, and the next move is conventionally his. Mr. Allison has learned earlier (along with the audience) that his companion has not yet taken her final vows, and since we now know that both are free of romantic entanglements, his next words are predictable: "I want to ask you to marry me. . . . So tell me if there's a chance. Is there?" But the fact that Sister Angela has not sworn her permanent vows does not make her available; it makes her fidelity to her vocation voluntary rather than a matter of obligation. Her answer to the marine will set the problem for the rest of the film, how to achieve love and marriage without marriage or – corporeal, at least – love. "No, Mr. Allison, you see I've already given my heart, to Christ our Lord."

There will be a second crisis of this sort brought on by Mr. Allison's drinking of the sake – as effective a stimulation to amorousness as the moon – and by Sister Angela's attempt to teach her companion to play draughts (checkers). In perhaps the most nearly explicit sexual line in the movie, Mr. Allison speaks both his desire and his confusion. "You don't want to play?" asks Sister Angela. "No, M'am. I mean yes, M'am. I mean I don't want to play no game of draughts."

The developing closeness of the nun and the marine is supported by a series of images of domesticity. After they capture the turtle, Huston shows his protagonists side by side in the raft, a framing that the director uses rarely and one that usually signifies close companionship or unity of purpose. The cave is the setting for a sort of semi-marital housekeeping. When Mr. Allison and Sister Angela move in they look over their new dwelling like a couple assessing their first apartment. "Well, this isn't too bad, is it?" says Mr. Allison judiciously. "It's a very pleasant cave, indeed," replies his agreeable companion. Continuing this sort of conventional interaction, he fetches water for them and she makes the beds. Inside the cave later, as they listen to the American shelling of the island, the pair will again be framed side by side.

The significance of such scenes approaches the explicit when Mr. Allison first goes to the Japanese camp. There he finds parallel images of domesticity: the enemy soldiers bathing, shining their boots, playing go, even receiving what looks like a parental scolding from an older officer. What is missing, however, is the configuration that Sister Angela and Mr. Allison define in their cave: a man and a woman dwelling together. As they listen to music, the Japanese soldiers must dance the women's parts themselves. The absence of the feminine in the Japanese camp is emphasized through montage that includes a match-dissolve from Mr. Allison prone on his side to Sister Angela sleeping on her side in the cave. A little later Huston will cut from the Japanese camp back to the cave where

Sister Angela awakens, finds herself alone, and calls for her companion. Then back to Mr. Allison, in danger amidst the enemy.

A final image of domestic tranquillity is so conventional that it approaches parody. Mr. Allison sits at table reading while Sister Angela prepares dinner and promises that the rice is almost ready. As we have seen, however, the writing is in Japanese characters incomprehensible to the marine, his food will be replaced by sake, and the emotional limitations beneath the domestic surface will erupt to become explicit and critical.

Despite such moments of frustration, the partnership of the nun and the marine approaches something like marriage or engagement. Indeed, after she runs from "the truth" and later recovers from her fever, Sister Angela seems almost to look forward to some such outcome. "Dear Mr. Allison, they [the Japanese] might not be here tomorrow. Tomorrow might not come. Perhaps God doesn't intend me to take my final vows. Only He knows what'll happen to us." Mr. Allison gloomily adds, "An' He won't tell anyone." To which the nun calmly replies, "He might."

In the next sequence, the Japanese begin their search of the island and Mr. Allison proposes to draw them away by leaving the cave so that they will see and follow him. Sister Angela's response both underlines her commitment to the marine and recalls Mr. Allison's earlier determination that she should not surrender herself. "No, Mr. Allison. We'll remain here, or we'll go out – as you wish – but together." (We may remember here the quarrel between Rose and Charlie about who should pilot the *African Queen* to attack the *Louisa* and its resolution in the decision that both would go.) Sister Angela's insistence that they remain together intensifies her plea to Mr. Allison when he returns from the Japanese camp: "Promise me you'll never go without tellin' me, because I'll never sleep, I'd be afraid to close me eyes. Promise me, now. Promise."

As traditional "husband," Mr. Allison goes out to fish and to raid the enemy camp for food and blankets; in fact, most of his contacts with the enemy until he disables their artillery are on his companion's behalf. As "wife," Sister Angela stays home, makes dinner, does the sewing, offers counsel. Their intimacy becomes physical, though it remains perfectly chaste, when Mr. Allison removes his shirt to cover the delirious nun and later takes off her wet habit.

The parallels with a similar scene between Jimmy Stewart and Kim Novak in Alfred Hitchcock's *Vertigo*, released a year later, are not only striking but include details so specific as to suggest that Hitchcock or one of his collaborators might have taken some cues from Huston. In both sequences, a soaked, unconscious woman is carried like a bride by a man who will undress her and put her to bed. In each sequence, the woman speaks incomprehensibly in her delirium and awakens to ask the man what happened. Both include shots of clothes hanging up to dry, shots suggesting the obvious conclusion (to the woman and the audience, as well) about who has taken them off. The hair of the woman in each is an important point of focus – almost a fetish. Finally, each woman after awakening responds to her rescuer with a simple, significant "Thank you."

But the contrasts between these two sequences are as revealing as their similarities. Kim Novak is almost surely feigning unconsciousness as part of an elaborate scheme to use her attractiveness to entice Jimmy Stewart unknowingly into a murder and cover-up. Hitchcock develops the forbidden erotic energy of the sequence in *Vertigo* from early shots that emphasize Novak's body as she is pulled from the bay until the moment that a mesmerized Stewart covers Novak's hand with his own just before he is interrupted by a telephone call from her "husband." Even though Mr. Allison partly undresses himself as well as the nun in Huston's film, sexual implications remain subdued: there is no husband off camera, no feigning, and only a little erotic energy, forbidden or otherwise. One point of the disrobing, indeed, is Mr. Allison's complete acceptance of Sister Angela's unavailability for love or marriage and the nun's equally complete trust in her companion.

"Very pleased to have met you, M'am. It was a privilege to know you. I wish you ev, every happiness. Goodbye." Mr. Allison speaks just before the Americans arrive to end his time alone with Sister Angela, who responds with her own farewell, already quoted. The union that Huston allows them is the only union they can attain without betraying their integrity. However many miles separate them, they will remain "dear companion[s]." The knowledge of each other that Sister Angela and Mr. Allison possess is deeper and more transforming than sexual experience or even marriage. It is the realization of self through another, a jointly achieved acceptance of fate. It is tragic in its deeply felt understanding of the inevitable connection between what has happened to one and who one is, and comic in its fully accomplished mutuality, the profundity of the sympathy and approval that its protagonists hold for each other.

After the landing, the American flag is raised in the foreground as Mr. Allison, accompanied by the nun, is carried down the hill. When the procession passes American marines bathing in the lagoon, the Hustonian signature shot of innocent bathers observed by more sophisticated characters is varied in an important particular: the witnesses are not within the film but outside it. We who watch the end of the movie are cast as the observers of both the bathers and the nun and marine who pass by them. We are aware of two things that the characters cannot be: how happy they are, and how far from them our regained self-consciousness places us. Huston's use of long shots in the closing sequence reinforces the sense of our sudden distance from a story that we have been intimately involved with, but that we have not, we abruptly understand, been in.

From our new vantage point we are reminded, as Stanley Cavell writes, that "nothing is of greater moment than the knowledge that the choice of one moment excludes another, that no moment makes up for another, that the significance of one moment is the cost of what it forgoes."[9] What Sister Angela and Mr. Allison forgo is the same, in a sense, as what they keep. Like the fusion of their personalities and their callings, what they cannot have is a necessary part of what they can. The multivalent resonance of the closing title bespeaks how much we have learned in two hours. The opening title of *Heaven Knows, Mr. Allison* can be little more than cryptic, a (usually exasperated) colloquial expression the meaning of which we can't even guess. The second time it appears it replaces an absence of meaning with a superflux. There is a heaven to be known by, and to know. Perhaps only heaven *can* know what no one else in the film besides the protagonists could witness. Although we are not within the film, the filmmaker has allowed us into the heaven of his creation, to know what he knows. We may recall from the opening credits the extreme high shot of Mr. Allison, then an unnamed figure bobbing in an unnamed sea – a view, in retrospect, looking down from heaven or from the equivalent divine perspective in the movies, the director's.

But knowledge, as we have seen, has its cost. Daughters and sons of Adam and Eve, we are no more able to abjure the knowledge of good and evil than Mr. Allison ("all sons") or Sister Angela in their brief Eden. And we are less able than they to escape the knowledge of ourselves. The sexual sense of "know" sounds in faint overtones, like the deeply sublimated sexual energies of the film. Along with that meaning, equally faint, the pun on the homonym of know, "no" – what the protagonists must forbid themselves in order to retain the only heaven they can possess, the one they create and preserve within themselves. Our heaven is witnessing theirs, briefly created or re-created in what Sir Philip Sidney called the "erected wit" of art, the prelapsarian remnant that escapes our fallen "infected will."[10] Perhaps, finally, as we leave the theater, we have some inkling that heaven may know the moments that we too have forgone to arrive at the moment in which we exist.

CHAPTER VIII

Theater, Identity, and Reality in *The Maltese Falcon* (1941)

"Wipe the water from your eye, Sheriff. It may hinder ye in your job. We mustn't welch now, we got somepin to do together, – not thinkin' on ourselves, but on what it'll come to. Without it endin' thisaway, they'd be no point to the story."

John Huston, *Frankie and Johnny* [1]

Brigid is a real thing, albeit that that thing is a liar.

Of great importance to *The Maltese Falcon*, but explicit only near the end of the film, is the conflict between people as relatively private, individual selves and as social constructions, players of societally defined roles. (The story of Flitcraft, told by Sam Spade to Brigid O'Shaughnessy in the novel but omitted in the film, develops this theme quite explicitly.) [2] In many of Huston's films, this conflict results in potentially debilitating interference between the identities characters have or desire versus their place in the world and among other people. Sometimes, as in *Heaven Knows, Mr. Allison*, this tension is largely resolved; often, as in *A Walk with Love and Death* and *The Kremlin Letter*, the resolution is equivocal or fails entirely. In *The Maltese Falcon*, which falls into the second category, the conflicts between self and society are expressed as a subset of broader issues of truth and falsehood, and of the consequences of accepting or ignoring the generally agreed upon view of things that people call reality. The dominant metaphor through which these issues are explored, both visually and verbally, is the theater.[3]

At the center of Huston's handling of this metaphor, and therefore at the center of the film as a whole, is a logical dilemma like that known as the Cretan paradox. "All Cretans," declares someone from Crete, "are liars." If he is telling the truth, then he is lying; if he is lying, then he may be telling the truth. His statement cannot finally be judged either true or false. The admission of Brigid (Mary Astor) that she is a liar varies this well-known paradox only by making the self-accusation more direct. In diverse ways, most of the main figures of the film are implicated by similar self-canceling assertions. Such paradoxes finally include one of the paradoxes of art itself, which in announcing its status as imitation – naively, admitting its lies – tells the truth.

Elaboration in *The Maltese Falcon* of themes of truth and falsehood, theater and reality, private and public identities, occurs in three phases that, while overlapping, dominate the story in succession. The first phase occupies most of the film and constructs a world of shifting, unstable appearances, plots, and identities, none of which seem anchored in reality beyond characters' desires to possess the objects (also shifting) of their greed and lust.[4] The second phase, which occurs mainly during the concluding scene in the apartment of Sam Spade (Humphrey Bogart), consists of a sudden validation of a stable world of truth and social cohesion beyond the intersecting circles of plots and counterplots in which the main characters of the film have been absorbed. This world abruptly divides the characters into those who accept the reality of reality and liars whose interested attempts to create a reality of their own collapse into felonies. The third phase recomplicates and makes ambiguous the dichotomies of the second. It might be said to occur largely after the film has ended, either in the audience's later musings or in re-viewings of the movie. It is cued in the film itself by Spade's closing line, "the, uh, stuff that dreams are made of," and earlier by ambiguities that militate against both the clarity of the dichotomies implied by the end and their resolution in favor of reality, social responsibility, and a secure sense of self. At the same time, however, this recomplication does not return to ironic cynicism. Rather, it actively asserts its dilemmas and suspends them unresolved. As we shall see, Spade's last utterance summarizes this ambiguity and invokes a context that confirms its most expansive implications.

From its prefatory historical explanation scrolled in front of a falcon statuette strikingly lit from the side and below, *The Maltese Falcon* is emphatically theatrical in the limited sense of persistently alluding to the theater as well as in the colloquial one of being heavily shaded by the dramatic, the histrionic. Its lighting and its design, often considered one of the first examples of *film noir*, may be characterized with equal accuracy as evocative of the stage. When Spade searches the pockets of Joel Cairo (Peter Lorre), he finds a theater ticket; and when the detective leaves his office in the next sequence we see a theater marquee in the background. A little later he confirms that he is being tailed by looking in the reflective glass of poster cases in the exterior lobby of yet another theater. The language of acting frequently colors the dialogue. Wilmer (Elisha Cook, Jr.) is "made for the part" of the fall guy; Spade tells his secretary to "listen carefully, here's the plot"; and he more or less continuously critiques the acting skills of his client-lover-antagonist Brigid. In a 1981 interview, Huston spoke of his first film as "a dramatization of myself, of how I felt about things."[5] Even without this clue, we might suppose that in emphasizing the theatricality of his film, Huston – offspring of the theater on his father's side, an experienced writer of scripts, and a new director – was thinking partly about himself and his profession when he made *The Maltese Falcon*.[6]

The opening expository sequence with Brigid, "Miss Wonderly" at that point, takes place in front of reversed "Spade and Archer" window signs – behind the scene, as it were. (At the end of her visit, Spade's partner claims her as his sexual prey; like Archer's wife Iva [Gladys George], Brigid will prove to be a woman whom Archer may have claimed first, but Spade will possess.) The camera pans down to the sun's projection of the sign, unreversed, on the floor of the office. The movie has begun in earnest; we are no longer backstage or being fed narrative background.[7] The ending of the film also invokes the theater. Elevator doors draw the curtain on the main action, Spade walks offstage down the stairs, and generic, incongruously perky music plays as the closing credits run. Titles and score proclaim as we leave the movie house that what we've just witnessed was all make-believe.[8]

As theatrical and other fictional motifs develop, they are increasingly associated with lies. Brigid announces herself successively as Wonderly, Leblanc, and O'Shaughnessy; like Brigid, Cairo writes his origins across much of Europe, carrying Greek, French, and British passports along with his theater ticket. As John Anderson notes, "The name 'Cairo' itself hints not only of the origins of the bird, but also of an Eastern otherness."[9] Cairo's inspection of himself in a mirror after Spade punches him may remind us that mirrors in Huston's work are generally associated with the false or askew.

Direct allusions to the theater or other fictions continue mostly to signify falsehood. In the critical minutes after Wilmer has escaped, Gutman (Sidney Greenstreet) and Cairo have left, and Spade has called the police, the detective demands the truth from Brigid: "This isn't the time for that schoolgirl act." A little later, "You haven't played straight with me . . . I won't play the sap for you." Brigid responds in kind: "You've been playing with me, just pretending you cared, to trap me like this." The various performances of Brigid – those that Spade criticizes and those that he lets pass without comment – are associated with more or less obvious fabrications. Lying to him, she consistently moves theatrically about her stage of the moment, "straightening things and poking the fire," as Spade once remarks. Still wearing the fur that she implied she would have to hock, Brigid tells him earnestly that "You know I never would have placed myself in this position if I didn't trust you completely." Spade: "That again?"

Lies in Huston's films are destructive when they are presented – and, equally important, accepted – as the truth. This axiom will be true in various ways during Huston's career as a director. The self-indulgent lies of Stanley (Bette Davis) in *In This Our Life*, the schemes and disguises of George Bruttenholm (Kirk Douglas) in *The List of Adrian Messenger*, the multiple fake identities of the central figures in *The Kremlin Letter*, and the pose of the blind preacher (Harry Dean Stanton) in *Wise Blood* represent only the most obvious examples. Spade never believes much of what Cairo or Gutman assure him, but when Brigid's performance becomes convincing, he declares that "now you *are* dangerous." She is at her most dangerous when she seems to give up on Spade ("I'll have to take my chances") and when she seduces him in order to avoid his questioning. In the first case, he appears to believe her performance (or is unable to resist his attraction to her) and agrees to continue as her protector; in the second, he accepts her performance whether he believes it or not. In both, he puts himself at great risk.

Reality can be dangerous, too, especially in the service of a deception. Perhaps Gutman understands that he will need to give Spade some truth to bait his trap when he tells him the story of the golden falcon. Along with Gutman's "historical facts," Spade swallows enough drugged whiskey to be conveniently out of the Fat Man's way for five or six hours.

The most prominent visual symbol of the theater in *The Maltese Falcon* and the chief vehicle for that metaphor occur in repeated images of curtains and curtain-framed blinds.[10] This imagery becomes conspicuous during most of the turning points of the story. (We know from the testimony of numerous persons involved with the making of *The Maltese Falcon* that Huston sketched virtually every set and camera set-up for the entire film.) Blowing curtains form the central image in the second sequence of the film, when Spade takes the telephone call informing him of the murder of his partner. The mystery of that murder is the motivation for the rest of the story.

Subsequent images of curtains appear increasingly theatrical and are systematically associated with the telling of stories – often, but not always, lies. When Spade returns from the murder scene, the curtains in his quarters are again prominent; but now we can see that they cover windows in a bay at one end of the main room that forms a sort of proscenium arch. Brigid will twice perform her lies and evasions for Spade in front of similarly stagey recessed windows in her apartment. Though the bay there is framed by curtains, the windows are covered by Venetian blinds, an addition that anticipates the closing of the inner bars of the elevator at the end of the film. Back in Spade's room after Cairo and the police leave, Brigid moves to the bay as she starts to answer Sam's repeated questions with a new set of lies. Beneath its arch she admits to being a liar, declares her weariness with "lying and making up lies, not knowing what is a lie and what's the truth." And there she seduces her interrogator, at least in part to evade his questioning. But when the camera pans from Sam leaning down to kiss her to the gunsel waiting across the street in the shadows, it suggests that beyond her private performance reality is biding its time.

The curtains are visible when Cairo is promising money for the falcon during his meeting with Brigid in Spade's office. On that occasion, the detective has to save his two clients (with a particularly ridiculous story) after their fracas has brought in the police. Concluding his implausible skit, Spade stands directly in front of his curtains. Lieutenant Dundy (Barton MacLean), evidently no fan of impromptu theatrics, punches him by way of criticism – a response to Spade's baiting that he might have hoped for, since it brings the scene to an end without anyone going to jail.[11]

In Gutman's hotel room, the Fat Man performs for the detective. The low-angle shots of Sidney Greenstreet are well known for emphasizing his enormous stomach; less obviously but equally importantly, they place him as on a stage in front of a curtained corner window and its projection on the adjacent wall. In that setting, Spade (and the film audience) will twice listen to him "talk about the bird," and Spade himself will reverse the roles of performer and audience with his own acting out for Gutman of a man with "a most violent temper." In front of the curtains and blinds of the windows of the District Attorney's office and with a stenographer writing down his story, Spade will repeat a similar mad scene for different auditors.

While the characters deploy their various stories in the elaborate verbal chess of the last sequence in Spade's room, they take turns in front of the window-stage arch. When Huston directs them into that position, they are generally reciting accounts that may or may not be true but that are unquestionably self-interested. Spade stands before the bay at the beginning of the scene as he establishes that he retains a good deal of bargaining power even in the face of Gutman, Cairo, Wilmer, and their guns. Then Gutman takes his place to tell what happened earlier in the evening, a performance that reiterates his ruthless determination to possess the Maltese Falcon. Spade is again front and center stage as he telephones his secretary Effie (Lee Patrick) to tell her "the plot." Brigid, Cairo, and Gutman are framed by the bay as Gutman discovers that the statuette is a fake. Only once more will Spade occupy that position, when he responds in the film's last line to the query of the policeman about the black bird.

Speeches not delivered in front of the bay windows, visually unframed utterances, occur when characters are speaking the truth, often under duress, or when they have lost control of themselves and have tumbled out of self-scripted roles to display underlying personalities and desires. In the last scene, the bay is absent when Cairo denounces Gutman and deduces how they came to be tricked with a counterfeit statuette. The close-up of Brigid honestly denying having taken the missing thousand-dollar bill does not include the window recess. It is also absent when Spade demands the truth from her after their adversaries leave.

Perhaps most revealing in terms of the theatrical imagery is the *mis en scène* of the sequence in which Spade tries to explain to Brigid why he is sending her over. Elsewhere in the movie he is fluent to the point of implausibility; "You always have a smooth explanation ready, huh," Cairo observes skeptically. At his moment of crucial self-revelation, however, the detective all but stutters. He sits on the left side of the frame, beside rather than in front of the bay window. Through the window streams light, a routine Hollywood convention for the illumination of truth. His speech, taken with moderate editing directly from the novel, is written in the plain style that Huston will characteristically use at moments of intense significance and revelation in other films.

You'll never understand me but I'll try once and then give it up. When a man's partner is killed, he's supposed to do something about it. It doesn't make any difference what you thought of him, he was your partner and you're supposed to do something about it. . . . I've no earthly reason to think I can trust you and if I do this and get away with it you'll have something on me that you can use whenever you want to. Since I've got something on you, I couldn't be sure that you wouldn't put a hole in me some day. . . . And what have we got on the other side? All we've got is that maybe you love me and maybe I love you. . . . If all I've said doesn't mean anything to you then forget it and we'll make it just this: I won't because all of me wants to, regardless of consequences, and because you counted on that with me the same as you counted on that with all the others.

The camera angle and the writing, the light through the curtains, and Bogart's interpretation of the lines all promise that Spade is speaking the truth. Brigid, by contrast, *is* framed in front of the curtained windows; the implication of that framing as well as the manipulative petulance of her words suggest that for her the scene continues as theater, as usual.

Both the use of theatrical imagery and language and its absence at revealing moments in *The Maltese Falcon* support the idea that an objective reality does exist (fictionally speaking) beyond the hermetic lies and self-concealment of the main figures. This reality is intersubjective, something we (the audience as well as the figures within the film) can agree upon. As Spade's explanation to Brigid makes explicit, such a view of things implies group cohesion and social responsibilities. The purveyors of self-interested lies, by their actions as much as their words, ignore or deny such implications.

The exposing of an especially important falsehood leads Spade to suspect that Brigid killed Miles Archer. The moment of truth comes when Gutman recounts a sequence of events that does not allow Thursby's presence near Archer at the time of the detective's murder and that contradicts Brigid's repeated assertions about Thursby's betrayal of her. Shots of Spade looking hard at Brigid during these revelations and a close-up of her anxious countenance alert the audience to the implications of Gutman's narrative.[12] Because Gutman has agreed to "be candid with you" to help Spade deal with the authorities after he hands over Wilmer, the detective can probably believe most of what the Fat Man says. In any event, Spade's dawning comprehension of what really happened to his partner has almost immediate consequences. When the premonitory bars of the elevator replace the images of curtains and windows a few minutes later, those consequences are evident. The film comes to an ending that emphatically favors the truth of reality and affirms the fate of those who fail to realize that truth will out.[13]

Or so it seems. But obvious conclusions do not necessarily count as final in Huston's films. Truth and falsehood, sincerity and feigning, are not always clearly separable. Though Spade behaves as if he were acting after he erupts in Gutman's suite, his hand is nonetheless shaking when he goes to the elevator. There he uncharacteristically fails to observe an important detail, the arrival of Joel Cairo.[14] He has abundant reasons to be truly angry and anxious at this moment, and the role he chooses may be more accurately expressive than we realize or than his demeanor afterward suggests. When Spade gives Tom Polhaus (Ward Bond) "the thousand dollars I was supposed to be bribed with," he again appears to be creating a fiction, since we have just seen him withhold it from the Fat Man "for time and expenses." But after we reflect on Gutman's motives for so easily relinquishing that hefty sum, Spade's representation seems plausible. Brigid's seduction of the detective in front of his windows appears improvised to silence his insistent questions, and her subsequent "*Darling*, someone's been in my apartment" and Spade's broadly exaggerated "precious" and "angel" seem to give the lie of overstatement to their pretense of real affection. But the last scenes show a love that is probably genuine, if compromised. A line of Brigid O'Shaughnessy's that did not get into the movie from the novel sums up much of the ambiguity about play-acting and truth-telling that did: " . . . if it's a pose it's one I've grown into, so you won't expect me to drop it entirely, will you?"[15]

The existence of theater has as much reality in the world as other quotidian facts. So do socially constructed roles. In Huston's films, the separation of a true, private self from an identity compounded of external determinants is either impossible or pathological. All human beings fuse personal and social realities. As was the case for the protagonists of *Heaven Knows, Mr. Allison*, the relation between Spade's love and his identity in society proves complex. Both are part of his integrity. In the metaphorical terms operative in *The Maltese Falcon*, backstage, centerstage, and the street outside the theater adjoin and exist together in a larger world that they partly constitute. The elevator doors closing on Brigid draw the curtain on one role and cast her into another one. Spade has already affirmed that he has a part different from that which he has been playing: "Don't be too sure I'm as crooked as I'm supposed to be." Spade has been crooked about being crooked.

The Cretan paradox returns universalized. We are all liars. But some stories, Huston's films suggest, are truer than others, more comprehensive of human needs and realities in all their complexity. Seeking and accepting such answerable accounts of ourselves, as we have seen in other Huston films, make up an important part of his conception of heroism, integrity, and good faith. Whether as the protagonist's quest, the theme of a particular movie, or a tendency of Huston's career, the discovery and comprehension of one's self, other human beings, and the world is not only represented in Huston's cinematic art but is also associated with art – in particular, as in *The Maltese Falcon*, with theater. In *Moulin Rouge*, by contrast, the artistic metaphor of self-creation is painting. The creation of another self in Toulouse-Lautrec's art, however, like the creations of theater or film, remain tied to the world and to human weakness and need. Toulouse-Lautrec, like Daniel Dravot and Judge Roy Bean, can achieve transcendence or perfection only in death.

A question about art and other fictions remains: how do we know, how does Huston disclose, which are the true, the reviving stories? We might begin to answer that question as it applies to Huston's films by returning to Gideon Bachmann's 1965 interview with the director. "Flamboyance," mused Huston,

is something that people assume when they feel a lack of structure in their own characters. But this, too, is not invariably the case. I've known some flamboyant people who were extraordinary too. Flamboyance is all right when it is a natural expression of something that is really that person. It's like every other characteristic that a person has: it's good only if it's real. I don't like it if people put on false surfaces, and I think by now I can tell when they do. And it always works against my choosing a certain person to play in a film.[16]

There is for Huston real and false acting – whether in professional actors or in people generally – and this distinction applies in his filmmaking. The sympathy we feel for characters in *The Maltese Falcon* roughly correlates with the degree to which their flamboyance appears to be an "expression of something that is really that person." Gutman and Cairo present themselves as performers; their theatrical flamboyance has an unchallenged reality. That of Wilmer does not: "the cheaper the crook, the gaudier the patter." But if his false surface makes Wilmer less sympathetic and less real, it does not make him less dangerous. So we gather from Spade's warning to Polhaus on the telephone.

The Maltese Falcon itself is both false and real. The golden mimicry that the Knights of Rhodes were inspired to send the Emperor Charles V is a more glorious tribute than a real bird. But the leaden imitation Gutman uncovers is nothing but a vulgar fake.

Brigid simultaneously dissembles and appears to be what she claims. She is "bad" and, above all, a liar – presumably about being bad as well as about everything else. Effie's "woman's intuition" that "she's alright" may be accurate at the same time that it is wrong. Like the Cretan, Brigid is unfathomable. The expressive depth of her endlessly refracting stories is evident when we compare her to the widow Iva, also a liar by word and deed, but one whose lies lack the resonance – the reality as it were – of Brigid's. (The difference in screen time matters too, of course.) If Brigid's identity remains protean, Iva's hardly exists.

Spade, professionally and personally flamboyant most of the time, combines much of Brigid's elusiveness with something untheatrical and solid. His involvement with Iva is the most clearly false note in his life. Neither flamboyant nor straightforward, she elicits from him emotions approaching self-hatred. On the other hand, he apparently feels no regrets about his painful, irresolvable love for Brigid, who is falser and far more dangerous to him than Iva. Brigid is a real thing, albeit that that thing is a liar. Iva, like the lead falcon, is an insignificant shape. Spade knows the difference.

As his interrogation of Brigid and his attempt to explain himself to her suggest, Spade's own motives are a disorganized mix of self-protection, respect for truth, feelings of obligation to his profession and to society, love, desire for financial gain, and a wish to be free. Further complicating all this, we know that he does not always tell the truth, either. But the various images of himself that Spade shows to others and the motives that the film lets us infer are, like the theater, part of reality. If the truth emerges upside down or as the product of multiplied errors in Huston's *Freud*, in *The Maltese Falcon* it appears as the paradoxically inclusive sum of performances that are often self-contradictory. It is the measure of Spade's strength and coherence that he can partly control and largely comprehend the babble of competing speeches, postures, and actions. At the same time, it is the measure of Huston's understanding of his film that his protagonist cannot exist above or outside his messy, illusive world.

In his son's movies, Walter Huston's laughter at the end of *The Treasure of the Sierra Madre* is the most famous transcendent gesture in the face of defeat, but the first instance is Gutman's appreciative chuckling after his initial shock at discovering that the falcon in his possession is bogus. It is a response appropriate to him, for he admires the first-rate performances of his adversaries, from his relishing of Spade's volatile persona to his acknowledging that the escape from him of Brigid and Captain Jacoby "was neatly done, Sir, indeed it was." It is also a response appropriate to the film, which has presented its characters and situations from the beginning with a stylish theatricality that asks at least as much for our admiration as for our belief.

The last words – and doubly famous ones they are – are Spade's. His reference to Shakespeare is probably the best known gesture of literary self-consciousness in Huston's work. Holding the spurious statue, Detective Polhaus asks what it is. "The, uh, stuff that dreams are made of," Spade mutters. So far as I know, the allusion has not been remarked by commentators, for whom the debating issue seems to have been whether the last line was suggested by Bogart or Huston.[17] Whoever may have inserted the line (it is not in the novel), a glance at *The Tempest* makes clear that the primary source is Prospero's speech in Act IV:

> Our revels now are ended. These our actors,
> As I foretold you, were all spirits and
> Are melted into air, into thin air;
> And, like the baseless fabric of this vision,
> The cloud-capped towers, the gorgeous palaces,
> The solemn temples, the great globe itself,
> Yea, all which it inherit, shall dissolve,
> And, like this insubstantial pageant faded,
> Leave not a rack behind. We are such stuff
> As dreams are made on, and our little life
> Is rounded with a sleep. Sir, I am vexed.[18]

By referring to these lines Huston emphasizes the artifice of the cinematic performance that the audience has just witnessed and the internal fictions, the lies and acting that its figures have performed for each other. Both are part of "the baseless fabric of this vision" that dissolves at the end of the film, along with the machinations of its characters. The allusion reinforces the deepest meanings of the movie, who Sam Spade is and the laws of the world in which he operates. It also helps to rotate the action from the fantastic realm that it has occupied toward a more realistic, ironic modality.

But the nod toward *The Tempest* does not allow us to choose reality over theatrics, for Prospero asserts that life itself is made up of performances. *The Maltese Falcon* supports such an assertion. If the appearances, the sets, and the characters that constitute a broader reality are more capacious and more durable than the limited dramas of detectives, flamboyant thieves, or movie directors, they are finally no different in kind.

As the last line of the film invites us to remember, the great globe itself (the name, we recall, of Shakespeare's theater) and everyone who appears on it will finally fade away like dreams, plays, and movies. We depart our lives, as Brigid and Spade leave his apartment or as the audience leaves the theater, to go to what another *noir* detective film later in the 1940s called the Big Sleep. Spade, like Prospero, has had a vexing time. He has had to write, perform in, and direct a production whose other actors are determined to take over the stage with their own plots. One supposes that Huston's role as director was not so far different from Spade's. But regardless of whose drama prevails, the final act will be the same, an eternity that makes Spade's promise to wait twenty years for Brigid seem a relatively modest gesture.

CHAPTER IX

Reflections in a Golden Eye (1967)

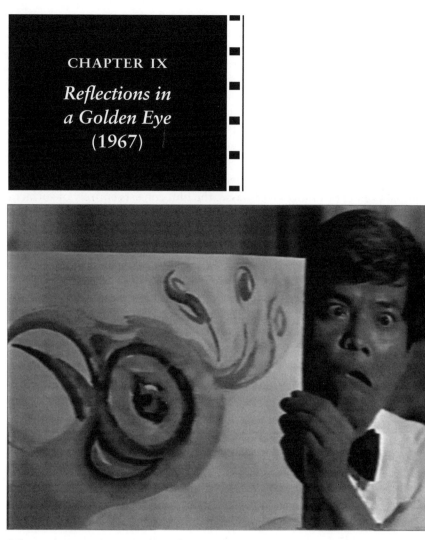

Like eyes, mirrors return images distorted by egotism, desire, and anxiety.

Intense and delicate, Huston's *Reflections in a Golden Eye* has a poise that makes it difficult to analyze without oversimplification. His film reproduces the sympathetic equilibrium of Carson McCullers's precisely balanced novel. Huston's filmmaking is unusual, especially for commercial narrative cinema, in its tendency to distribute sympathy – or to withhold it – equally among central figures. This tendency is especially marked in *Reflections*. At the British Film Institute, Huston spoke of an alternative to creating emotional centers around attractive protagonists:

"I very seldom feel involved with my characters, but rather detached and fasci-

nated. . . . I'd rather have an audience identify with the picture itself than with
a character in the picture, feeling a fascination for the whole material rather than
being emotionally involved with the hero or heroine."[1]

In McCullers's novel, Huston found a similar aesthetic. He was "impressed with how well McCullers understood the people she wrote
about, without hatred or moral evaluation."[2] Jameson notes a similar
quality in the film, its simultaneous "studied dispassionateness" and
compassion.[3] For François Ramasse, the film consists entirely of surfaces
and reflections, impenetrable and without depth; it steadfastly resists all
attempts to break open the characters or motives of its central figures.[4]
Speaking to Rui Nogueira and Bertrand Tavernier about this film, Huston remarked, "Myself, I do the same as all my characters, I watch. I
don't judge."[5] If the director refuses to judge he does not fail to portray
his protagonists with amusement. *Reflections* is often a very funny film
– a quality that finally serves to increase its pathos.

The three movies discussed in this section have an imploded quality,
attributable in part to their isolation from the world outside their settings
and, in *Falcon* and *Reflections*, to the existential loneliness of their characters. The ravine between most of the central figures of *Reflections* stems
principally from the bad fit between fundamental human needs and the
social roles available on the Army base. As in *Heaven Knows*, Huston
found in the institutional saturation of identity by the military a vivid,
extreme exemplification of the double nature of humans as individuals
and as members of groups.

The alienated characters of *Reflections* watch each other with an ob-
sessiveness that is broader than voyeurism. They usually peer across or
through barriers, settings that emphasize their separation. Major Weldon
Penderton (Marlon Brando) stalks Private Williams (Robert Forster),
even stands in the rain staring at his barracks; Williams watches Weldon's
house, fascinated by his wife Leonora (Elizabeth Taylor); Alison Langdon (Julie Harris) sees Williams from her window; at the boxing matches (an episode Huston added to what he found in the novel), Weldon
looks at Williams, Williams and Colonel Morris Langdon (Brian Keith)
look at Leonora, and only Leonora directs much attention to the ring.
"Everybody," as Huston remarked, "watches everybody."[6]

But the characters of *Reflections* virtually never exchange gazes. And
the audience, looking via the camera at figures who do not look back,
watches across its own chasm of unreciprocated staring. The tendency of
such staring to make objects of other people is emphasized by Weldon's

possession, in his little box of treasures, of a photo of a classic male sculpture. A similar photographic fetish appears in *The Misfits*, when Guido becomes fascinated with Roslyn's publicity photos. Again, Huston to Nogueira and Tavernier: "The simple act of looking makes you an accomplice of what is happening in front of you. That's what I wanted people to feel while watching the film."[7]

In Huston's movies, such fetishization is sick. He also generally associates the related imagery of reflections, especially in mirrors, with neurotic distortions or lies. The Filipino servant Anacleto (Zorro David), showing Alison his watercolor of a peacock, tells her that in its eye are "reflections of something tiny and, tiny and . . ." Unable to find the right adjective, he contorts his face. "Grotesque," Alison supplies. On Anacleto's confirmation, Huston cuts from Alison's bedroom to Leonora's. There Williams is scrutinizing Weldon's sleeping wife. The image on the screen alternates between increasingly tight close-ups of the private's eye and the suggestive images it receives: Leonora's thick, curled lashes; her brilliant red lips; the wedding ring on her finger. Fearful of and inexperienced with women, Williams turns Leonora into something tiny and grotesque. What is freakish is not Leonora but Williams's watching, and the distortion and diminishing of her in his eyes.

Like eyes, mirrors return images distorted by egotism, desire, and anxiety. After lifting weights, Weldon stands before a mirror flexing his muscles, drawing up his chest, pulling in his stomach. Later Williams watches unseen as Weldon poses before another mirror, looking intelligent and judicious, smiling, gazing seriously, and talking by turns. Huston remarked,

That was a scene which was written. I wanted to show a man who is trying to protect the image he has of himself. And that image doesn't exist, it's a dream. He goes through a variety of feeling and states of mind: ambition, servility, satisfaction. He sees himself decorated, received by a general, promoted to an important position.[8]

When we see Weldon applying gardenia scented lotion in front of a bathroom mirror, we may remember that the gay Joel Cairo's perfume was gardenia and that he too spends time in front of a mirror. In Leonora's bedroom, Williams sits at her cluttered vanity, smelling and handling her cosmetics, while we watch him and the sleeping woman in reflection.

Pathetic emotional lives in *Reflections* are expressed by habitual watching across walls of half-realized shame and by desires that characters are unable to acknowledge or, often, even to feel. All suffer what McCullers called "the strain of not realizing the truth."[9] Staring and narcissism imply an isolation from other people and an imprisonment within the self that is underlined by images of bars and other barriers. Such imagery is particularly associated with Weldon and Williams. Lonely and constrained, the major repeatedly faces barred windows and closing doors. The first time we see him, he is in front of a window with blinds, a placement that will become familiar. When he watches Williams nursing the horse Firebird, he is photographed through the bars of the stall. Such shots imply that the watcher is himself imprisoned. As in *Freud*, closing doors serve as an extreme image of isolation from other people. The most notable example occurs when Weldon watches Williams enter his wife's bedroom and shut the door behind him.

The parallel alienation of Private Williams is emphasized by the same imagery of constraint and separation. During the first sequence, he looks at Firebird through the bars of his stall; a reverse shot subsequently shows him behind the same bars. Blinds and curtains obstruct his gaze as he stares into the Pendertons' house. When he is in contact with other people, he almost invariably gets into trouble. He brawls pointlessly in the barracks; he once spilled coffee on Weldon, ruining his new uniform; he misunderstands the extent of the pruning to which he is assigned (in part because Weldon's orders are ambiguous); and he is twice found out in the bedroom of Weldon's wife. After he first spends the night in Leonora's room, the private bounds up a rough woodland road in the dawn like an exuberant young lover returning home from his mistress. But the wheel tracks catch the early light and shine like the lines of bars, mirrors, or blinds that elsewhere suggest isolation. Alison's glimpses of Williams near the Penderton house are similarly associated with images of windows, blinds, and shades.

Reflections enacts the psychoanalytic principle that our unlived lives revenge themselves. Such revenge comes through sublimated impulses – oblique, often self-destructive manifestations of feelings that cannot be expressed directly. Alison's abrupt announcement that she is going to divorce her husband appears to result more from acute irritation with Leonora than from outrage about Morris's infidelity. That scene dissolves to another indirect expression of emotion, Weldon's determination to take Firebird out, evidently to assert a control over his wife's horse that he lacks over his wife. The editing links the impotent anger that both Weldon and Alison feel at being pushed around and humiliated by Leonora.

Similar sublimation motivates other actions. Bewildered by sexual feelings he has avoided all his life, Williams picks an unprovoked fight in the barracks. His nude riding before Leonora, Weldon, and Morris may have an element of unconscious purpose designed to reciprocate, as it were, Leonora's unclothed appearance to him the previous night. Anacleto has merged his emotional identity with Alison's, grimacing when she takes bitter medicine and happy, as he says, when she is well. Alison's grief and anxiety leads her to hear an accident that does not occur, while Weldon's tumultuous feelings make him deaf to one that takes place behind him. Even the usually forthright Morris is infelicitously moved to say to his fellow officer and friend, "Weldon, your wife's cheating" – an announcement that speaks to more than her play at blackjack.

The rage that leads Weldon to threaten his wife after she strips in front of him begins with her taunts about Williams and about Firebird's being a stallion. It increases when he overhears her telling her maid Suzie about "these two little queers," a joke that implicates Weldon – albeit probably without his conscious knowledge. But his anger is not a direct response to those utterances; rather, he fastens on noise from the kitchen that disturbs him in his study and on his wife's bare feet. Presented with a panorama of Leonora's womanly rump as she lights the fire, Weldon snarls his disgust, another emotional eruption the sources of which are at least partly disconnected from the immediate provocation.

Weldon's anxieties about his leadership form a further reservoir of unacknowledged feelings. He drives Lieutenant Weincheck out of the Army because he judges that Weincheck (like himself) lacks "certain qualities of leadership." Speaking on "pride and leadership" to a class of junior officers, he is so affected that he fails to complete his lecture. We discover another motive for his ill-judged attempt to ride Firebird when we see him standing by while Morris holds forth about how "the polo grounds have produced more great leaders than the playing fields of Eton."

After he is thrown by his wife's stallion, Weldon implores heaven for succor. Like the consciously devious characters of *The Maltese Falcon*, he occasionally uncovers his truest emotions, usually when he loses control of himself. His most revealing self-encounter arises when he contests Morris's incredulous description of Anacleto.

> Weldon: Any fulfillment obtained at the expense of normality is wrong, and should not be allowed to bring happiness. [inaudible phrase] It's better because it's morally honorable for the square peg to keep scrapin' around in the round hole, rather than to, to discover and use the unorthodox one that would fit it.
> Morris: Well, yeah, that's, that's right, Weldon. Don't you agree with me?
> Weldon: (quietly, after pausing) No. No, I don't.

As usual in Huston's dramatic writing, Weldon's expression of his deepest feelings is delivered in an earnest, somewhat plain prose. Whether he understands himself to be a square peg, however, is not clear.

Weldon's complaint about Williams, "I dislike clumsiness willful or otherwise," seems partly an unconscious expression of self-hatred. Weldon rides badly – falling during a simple jump, failing to control Firebird, presenting a ludicrous posterior view to the men at the stable – and he breaks his wife's ceramic statuette when he bumps it from the mantle, a mishap that he blames on her feminine love of "clutter." His blunder leads to his long speech about the joys of "the life of men among men," with its austerity, chivalry, and "friendships, my lord, . . . stronger than the fear of death." In McCullers's novel Weldon's sentiment is immediately discredited by the narrator's observation that he "was not familiar with enlisted men and his picture of the life inside the barracks was greatly enriched by his imagination" (p. 213). Huston conveys the same message with the subsequent portrayal of Williams's lonely existence in the barracks and his pointless fistfight. The spartan existence of men among men that Weldon romanticizes has to do with his loneliness, his marital misery, and his fierce attraction to Williams.

The stopping up of Weldon's emotions, especially his libidinally charged anger, is suggested by his habit of tugging his hat down when he is enraged. He does so when he notices that Williams has cut away the oak branches the pruning was designed to reveal and he repeats the gesture when he observes Williams riding naked. At the start of the sequence in which Firebird bolts with him – by the end of which he is weeping helplessly – his hat flies off his head.

Within the psychodynamics that Huston establishes, the murder appears less motivated by Weldon's wrath toward the private – though that is part of his feeling – than by self-loathing and rage toward his wife, who thwarts him at every turn, including the amorous one that he passionately desired would lead Williams to his bed. In her mocking of Weldon's displeasure with Williams, her praise of the enlisted man's deftness with horses, and her contempt for Weldon's indignation when they come upon him riding "bareback and bare-assed," Leonora both makes Williams an occasion for belittling her husband and aggravates Weldon's ambivalent feelings toward the private. Williams's death may well be the eventual outcome of Weldon's humiliation when Leonora taunts him: "Have you ever been collared, and dragged out into the street, and thrashed by a naked woman?" The five bullets that Weldon fires into Williams have an intricately sublimated provenance; they explode from Weldon's self-hatred, from its exacerbation by his erotic fixation on the enlisted man, and from his disgust for his wife. In shooting Williams, he also kills himself and his wife by proxy, thus in a sense murdering all three of the figures among whom the camera frantically pans as the film ends.

McCullers's narrator describes Leonora as a little feebleminded, but as someone who "feared neither man, beast, nor the devil" (pp. 153–4). In the movie, she usually expresses feelings, as does her lover Morris, in a manner more straightforward than the labyrinthine emotional twistings of other characters. She has unabashed enthusiasm for going with Morris into the blackberry bushes, and she is friendly and relaxed with people like Williams and Suzie. But like her husband, she too suffers from jealousy that she does not express directly: she envies Alison's share of Morris's affections.

Always eager to assure her lover that his wife is crazy, Leonora practically flaunts her intimacy with him in Alison's presence. Her anxiety about revealing their affair and her expressed affection for her lover's wife are disingenuous. "Does she know about us?" she asks Morris, then continues, "Well, I hope not! I like Alison!" In the novel, Morris pats Leonora's thigh under the card table in front of Weldon and Alison. Huston changed that to having Leonora indiscreetly stroke Morris's leg with her stockinged foot under the table but in Alison's sight. The film thereby adds emphasis to Leonora's rivalry with Morris's wife and her desire to claim all of the Colonel's affection. Even after Alison's death, Leonora's jealousy expresses itself in her suggestion that her lover give away Alison's phonograph records. At one point, she wishes that "Alison would come back," but her longing has to do with the despondency into which Morris has fallen and his guilty preoccupation with his late wife.

Except for the deviousness of her jealousy, however, Leonora is passionately direct. The reds, violets, magentas, and other strong colors in which she dresses stand out among the neutral tans of the uniformed men on the Army base and emphasize her emotional vigor. Although Huston intended a very different look for *Reflections* than that of the conventional Technicolor released in most theaters, much of his systematic use of hue to suggest character or emotion remains perceptible. The process of desaturation that Technicolor developed for *Reflections* did not necessitate a commitment to either normal or desaturated color prior to filming: "the new desaturation process does not require any alteration in normal filming technique. . . . of course, if a particular color were to be accentuated it would be best for the art director to know this early in the design stage so that he could plan his use of that particular color for optimum effect." Technicolor director of research Frank P. Brackett reported that "John Huston chose to work in an overtone of sepia with the pinks and reds accentuated."[10]

Purples are associated with expression of feelings in Anacleto (who dances in a purple shirt) and Alison as well as with Leonora; on one striking occasion red is assigned to Suzie, who flows in a red dress through a sea of khaki during Leonora's party. The brilliant white of the hostess's dress also vividly contrasts with the uniforms and at the same time associates Leonora with her white horse – an effect that Huston went to considerable trouble to achieve. "[Production designer Stephen] Grimes was amused by John's insistence that the stallion, which was called Firebird and was red in the novel, be a white Lippizaner. They got two of them from Austria, along with a groom who was very strict about their workouts."[11] I have viewed a reel of the desaturated version of *Reflections* (at the Film Study Center of the Academy of Motion Picture Arts and Sciences, in Los Angeles), and clear blacks and whites, as well as pinks and reds, contrast strongly in that version with the golden-tan cast of most other hues. This fact may partly explain Huston's insistence on a white stallion for Leonora.[12]

A connection of saturated color to strong feelings that had sharp impact in the desaturated version is the red "Baby Ruth" label on Williams's candy bar. Diminished but still ascertainable in the standard version is the association of a leprous green with its traditional emotional correlate, jealousy. The jealous green of *Reflections* does not occur in the mixed woods and scrub surrounding the base but in the unvarying color of the lawn around the Penderton house and of the field across which Weldon watches Morris and Leonora ride after one of their trysts. (One can infer from the existing desaturated reel of the film that this green would appear relatively unaltered.) Green also conveys predictable suggestions of jealousy when it occurs on a prominent lamp base while Leonora listens to Morris talking about Alison's pending institutionalization and in shots of Williams bathed in green light as he watches his true rival, Morris, play cards with Leonora. These chromatic overtones are keyed to Anacleto's peacock's head of "ghastly green."

Although much of the color symbolism of *Reflections* survives in the standard Technicolor print, the change weakens the general effect that Huston was eager to achieve, an effect that he sought for *The Night of the Iguana* by photographing in black and white. In defense of the desaturated color that he wanted for *Reflections*, Huston wrote, "when we are dealing with material of psychological content it [ordinary color] becomes invariably distracting as it gets between the viewer and the mind he is trying to search into."[13] My own sense of the desaturated version is of a smooth, almost gilded surface from beneath which the reds and pinks flash out occasionally, like flames. The effect suggests emotions running strongly beneath a decorous surface, and it can sometimes be subtle as well as striking. The scattered red berries on the bushes that screen the tryst of Leonora and Morris, for example, would appear more vivid in the desaturated version than in standard Technicolor.

The association of color with emotion occurs systematically in McCullers's novel as well as in Huston's film. At the end of the second of the novel's four sections, Williams leaves Leonora's bedroom and the narrator observes, "Already the sky was a pale blue and Venus was fading" (p. 182). The third section, at which point Weldon is stalking the private, ends similarly: "It was late afternoon and the winter dusk had in it a pale violet tint" (p. 209). Shortly before including that detail, the narrator offers an explicit clue to the significance of the color imagery: "The mind is like a richly woven tapestry in which the colors are distilled from the experiences of the senses and the design drawn from the convolutions of the intellect. The mind of Private Williams was imbued with various colors of strange tones, but it was without delineation, void of form" (p. 209).

Constrained physically and visually by windows, blinds, framed mirrors, and barred stalls, the characters of *Reflections* are more likely to face – if not to acknowledge – their deepest feelings when they are exposed to the openness of the natural world, its unruly landscapes, winds, and weather. In accordance with the color symbolism, Huston sometimes injects a violet overtone into the light of the setting, especially outside. In the opening shot, for example, the dawn sky is colored by purple-pink clouds. At moments of emotional intensity indoors, in Alison's bedroom or just before Williams enters Leonora's room for the last time, purple or red flowers bring inside the emotional energy associated with the outdoors.

Something of a spirit of nature, Leonora makes love in blackberry bushes, swings in a hammock, and wears a purple floral blouse the first time we see her riding. Williams appears most relaxed and tranquil riding or sunning himself alone in the woods, but he does not thrive, as we have seen, indoors or among other people. He is suspended between the indoors and the woods outside when he is spying on the Pendertons; on those occasions, his agitation is suggested by placing him in front of dark branches tossing in the wind, particularly those of a large tree that may be the oak he mistakenly pruned.

Much as the storm in *The Night of the Iguana* echoes the crisis in that movie, night winds in *Reflections* suggest emotional tumult in Williams and other characters. The gusts shake the screen door of the Pendertons' home and the shade on Alison's window. But when Weldon latches the door to stop it from banging, Williams lifts the hook with a dangerous-looking, phallic knife; and on the three occasions when Alison goes to close her window, she first witnesses the disturbing sight of Williams leaving the neighboring house, then thinks that he is a hallucination, and finally mistakes him for her husband.

Like the emotions of the characters, storms and other aspects of the natural world cannot be suppressed or shut out. Weldon dislikes and fears the unruliness that exists beyond study and classroom. His terrifying ride on Firebird suggests that what he dreads is uncontrolled emotion. The passions that Weldon experiences careening through the woods penetrate his home; his final violent outburst is prefigured by the greenish white of repeated lightning flashes in which he sees Williams approach. Besides the storm in *Iguana*, this setting recalls similar symbolic tempests in *The Treasure of the Sierra Madre*, *Key Largo*, and *Heaven Knows, Mr. Allison*; it anticipates the deluge at the end of *Under the Volcano* and the elegiac snowfall that concludes *The Dead*.

Alison is associated with the natural world through representations in her room. She happily watches a paper flower open in a bowl of water, but other images underline her illness and emotional anguish. Huston's editing is suggestive. From Williams lurking in front of the familiar tree outside the Penderton house, he cuts to Alison and Anacleto in her bedroom; behind them on the wall is a framed print of a tree that rhymes with the previous image. On another wall hangs a reproduction of Andrew Wyeth's *Christina's World*, its wind-tossed field and the semi-prostrate woman emblems of Alison herself. Later, in the dining room of the sanitarium, a large potted plant behind Alison casts its shadow on the wall much as the tree shadows the Pendertons' house. The brief shots that allude to her funeral show a church steeple with foliage stirring in the breeze, an image that suggests Alison's release from the confinement of her room and her life.

As usual in Huston's films (and in narrative films generally), themes and actions in *Reflections* are largely organized by antagonisms and affinities among characters. The parody of marriage enacted by Weldon and Leonora includes polar contrasts, overt antagonism, and Leonora's unrelenting exertions to break her husband as one might break a fractious horse. (Ironically, she cherishes Firebird's spirit as much as she dislikes any sign of self-assertion in Weldon.) The struggle between this ill-mated pair, for all of Weldon's superior intellect, almost wholly favors

Leonora. The first time we see her husband, he is lifting weights; his wife calls from off camera; after he answers her, he is unable to do the press that he was attempting. An inconspicuous detail, his small failure can be seen retrospectively as initiating a motif in which Leonora obstructs or disables her spouse. A little later Weldon falls silent in the midst of a lecture when he sees his wife through the classroom window. Her scornful question about thrashing him turns into prophesy when, as punishment for beating Firebird, she whips him with a riding crop in front of his guests and fellow officers. During her next visit to the blackberry bushes with Morris, she chortles that her husband's chastisement has left him "a changed boy. He's even polite to me when we're alone!"

Although Leonora and Williams share an expert's love of horses and a sort of animal absence of intellection, the strongest parallels in *Reflections* are between the downtrodden major and the nearly mute private whom he at once hates and passionately seeks. Underlying their kinship are their repression, their distance from other people, and their inability to understand their own desires. Weldon's suppressed homosexuality is clear enough to most viewers, and it finds an echo in Williams's horror of women and their "terrible disease," a fear that has kept him a virgin. Both are isolated among their peers. Williams's only friends seem to be horses, and Weldon has no close friends at all, with the possible exception of his wife's lover. Both appear abstemious, even miserly; Williams never drinks, Weldon drinks only a little, and each has a personal hoard of a few treasures. Both, as we have seen, are associated with clumsiness, and both like to ride (so far as Weldon likes to ride at all) the black mare. Most obviously and importantly, both are voyeurs obsessed by the objects of their gazes.

Despite physical separation and the cross-purposes of their passions, there is an intimacy-at-a-distance between Williams and Weldon. Because of his constant surveillance of the Penderton house, Williams has a familiar knowledge of Weldon – his relationship with his wife, his habits of work, his posturings in front of mirrors, the objects that he takes out when he is alone. Weldon strives for a similar knowledge of Williams in his tenacious shadowing of him and his inspection of his personnel file. Between the two men Huston also suggests an ironic tactical affinity; in the first classroom sequence, as Stephen Cooper points out, "Penderton's pompous improvement upon Clausewitz [the major extols 'the night attack'] . . . foreshadows Private Williams's nocturnal forays into Leonora's bedroom."[14]

The characters of *Reflections* blend together. The strong parallel between Williams and Weldon is perhaps the most striking example of this tendency, which is the more remarkable because it occurs in a work whose main figures are simultaneously isolated from one another. Leonora and Alison are associated through such details as the fire that Leonora lights and the one burning in Alison's bedroom, the similarly colored clothes they wear, their childlessness (Alison has lost her infant daughter and Leonora treats Firebird as if he were her child), and the man whom they share. The blending of Anacleto with his mistress extends to his disappearance when she dies. Frequent dissolves underscore the interchangeability of the actions and identities of central characters.[15]

At the same time, however, Huston maintains his usual practice of separating the photographic planes of his figures in order to suggest their emotional distance from each other. Almost never are characters in precisely the same optical planes; even Leonora and Morris, as they straighten up following a pastoral tryst, are seated in the front and back seats of Morris's convertible – a bit of filmic choreography that impressed Huston's production manager.[16] Only after the murder, in the hysterical pans among the dead soldier, the officer, and his wife, do the protagonists share the same photographic plane – a technical necessity for this camera movement. But the horizontal distance of the characters from each other largely emphasizes their separation, and the mutuality that may be suggested is grievous, a sharing of bafflement and death.

The paradoxical isolation of characters and the fluid boundaries between their identities create a typically Hustonian irony. The shared humanity of the figures in *Reflections* ought to bring them together and ameliorate their loneliness; but in their obliviousness or shame of what they are and want, they sentence themselves to a sort of solitary confinement. As elsewhere in Huston's work, we can hardly avoid the combination of alienation and bad faith so important in existentialist novels and plays. Huston's psychoanalytic convictions are also very much in evidence, especially his belief about the crucial place in human happiness of the ability to give and receive love and the importance of home, a place of security and esteem among other people.

Although we frequently see them taking care of each other, the central figures of *Reflections* are ineffectual in their efforts to help or heal either their companions or themselves. For all his devotion to Alison, Anacleto is locked away and unable to assist her when her husband has her declared incompetent. Morris's inability to make contact with his wife occasions some sad comedy when he attempts to give her a drunken good-night embrace, kissing the pillow of her empty bed while she sits across the room in darkness. In the sanitarium, the pompously genial director assures her that she "won't be getting up tomorrow morning" – a pleasantry that leads to one of the ruder ironies of the film when Alison dies of a heart attack that night.

Williams bathes and rubs down Firebird after the horse runs away with Weldon; but the reverse shot in this sequence shows the battered major unattended, treating his lacerations himself. Leonora begins to clean him when he arrives home, but abandons her efforts in order to go to Firebird. Weldon is no more gentle as his wife's keeper. He kicks her sharply when she has fallen asleep in front of the fire, then wrestles her upstairs to her bedroom and undresses her without desire or affection.

The extreme version of these failures of concern and healing is found in parodied actions of death and rebirth. As Frye observed, irony can typically be seen as a parody of romance.[17] One of the radical stories of romance, as he also observed, is the story of Proserpine, a narrative of disappearance-death and reappearance-rebirth that expands to include the entire world in its dying winter and reviving spring. Leonora's association with woods and flowers mildly recalls Proserpine; and the name of the horse that she rides, Firebird, translates that of another emblem of rebirth, the Phoenix.[18] Huston also identified Anacleto's picture of the peacock as "a kind of Phoenix bird." But Leonora brings death to Williams and ruin to her husband; and the closest she comes to restoring life to anyone is her petulant wish that Alison come back to life so that she (Leonora) might have the grieving Morris's full attention again. In a small detail that also evokes parodied rebirth, Weldon smears his face with "rejuvenating cream."

Reflections renders as ironic parody the upward movement to truth and love with which romances tend to stage their turning points. The final sequence is notable among these disappointed ascents. As Williams creeps up the stairs, the familiar imagery of bars, shadows, and blinds dominates the scene; and when Weldon switches on the light in his wife's room, he does not come to terms with the truth but instead loses entirely any self-control or understanding and kills the childish soldier who squats harmlessly at the foot of Leonora's bed. Williams suffers death, Weldon in an instant is transformed from a professorial officer into a murderer, and Leonora, a Sleeping Beauty slightly past her girlish prime, awakens not to love but to death.

The simple expository sentence of McCullers's novel that opened the picture reappears on the screen at the end: "There is a fort in the South where a few years ago a murder was committed." But it has been complicated by our understanding of the inadequacy of such statements to incorporate the human meanings or motives that can make sense of such facts. Though we now know the actors and victims of that summary sentence, what we have learned serves to deepen their mystery as much as to explain them. As Morris says about his wife, "the thing that we all overlook, everybody forgets, is that who really knows what happened to her in her mind? Nobody knows that." The concluding pans from Weldon to Leonora to Williams and back again and again and again do not represent a consolidation of knowledge for camera or audience but fragmentation and bewilderment. Such bafflement applies equally to the figures that the camera jumps among: neither Leonora nor Weldon seem able to make sense of the scene that they are part of, and Williams, of course, can no longer make sense of anything. By the end of the film, what the audience understands best is how difficult it is to comprehend the workings of love and loneliness and rage.

Heaven Knows, Mr. Allison, The Maltese Falcon, and *Reflections in a Golden Eye* give particular weight to dilemmas that arise from a human nature at once social and isolate, corporate and single, in which an internalized collective consciousness and morality are inevitably part of every individual psyche. Such dilemmas regularly arise in other Huston films as well. The reconcilability of the communal and personal sides of characters varies with the films in which their stories unfold. The central figures of *The Asphalt Jungle*, mostly criminals and misfits, have lives that alienate them from society and put them in opposition to its public morality. But their largely predatory mode cannot accommodate their needs as human beings. Indeed, they are made vulnerable by the very desires that Huston regards as fundamental to human psychology. The catastrophes after the robbery result in part from incompatible motives within characters who can function effectively only in opposition to society but who at the same time need the human warmth and security of other people. At the center of the film is Dix (Sterling Hayden), the hooligan in desperate quest to recover the home that was taken from him when his family lost their farm. (His situation anticipates that of Perce in *The Misfits*.) The psychological incoherences within characters conceptually extend to the society of which they are part; for the respectable are not terribly different from the bank robbers and other crooks, who are generally the more sympathetic figures. Crime may be a left-handed form of human endeavor in *Asphalt*, but it is not particularly sinister.

Crippled by both the biology and the sociology of his exhausted aristocratic heritage, Henri de Toulouse-Lautrec in *Moulin Rouge* finds a home in the demimonde, then through his art recovers the esteem of his family and a place in society. But he is unable either to give or to receive love when to do so would have meant happiness, and he attains the equivocal triumph of fame and momentary tranquillity only as he dies. His conflict with his heritage is lethal. Similarly, the world in which Claudia and Heron come of age in *A Walk with Love and Death* is fatal to their love and happiness. They achieve both, but like Toulouse-Lautrec, find happiness only in death – a paradox embodied in the posthumous voice-over with which the film ends. (Huston used the unusual device of a dead narrator to comic effect with the Preacher, played by Anthony Perkins, in *The Life and Times of Judge Roy Bean*.) The society that they are unable to escape on earth claims and destroys them, as we gather it does everyone else during the Hundred Years' War in which Huston's tragic romance is set. Yet the lovers are unwilling to flee their world, for it comprises too much of their identity to be abandoned, except with life itself. Hence the curious equanimity with which they await approaching death.

In its unalloyed irony, *The Kremlin Letter* puts its characters into a world, like that of *The Asphalt Jungle*, where people are defined almost exclusively in opposition to each other. More extreme in its portrayal of pervasive alienation than the earlier film, *The Kremlin Letter* has central figures whose identities all but disappear into the mirrors, masquerades, and unstable personae of espionage and national security. If the irrepressible human need to offer and accept love cannot be entirely extirpated, in this movie it results only in making characters vulnerable and miserable; it has no outcomes in happiness or security. The cruelty of the dilemma that Rone (Patrick O'Neal) faces in the last shots sums up the incompatibility of his world with love or cherishing of family. It is a world as cold as the snow-covered streets of Moscow that we see behind the opening credits. The identities of its characters are inexorably preempted by their illusionist profession, which creates a self-contained society in which theatrical weirdness replaces personality. Indeed, the other central character of *The Kremlin Letter*, the spy played by Richard Boone, does not have an ascertainable identity; he may or may not be Sturdevant, a ruthless assassin supposed to have killed himself twenty years earlier.

Prizzi's Honor, from one point of view a variation on *The Maltese Falcon*, can be seen from another as a comic, domestic version of *The Kremlin Letter*. Its protagonists, like spies, lack the freedom to seek either a home of their own choosing or the love in which people are most themselves while being most fully lost in another. Charlie (Jack Nicholson) has the illusion that he exists as an autonomous person who can fall in love and marry outside the Prizzi family into which we see him initiated as a child. But by the end of the film he has had to abandon such ideas in order to stay alive, and in a demonstration of the implacability of closed societies, he practices his profession as hit man upon his own wife, destroying the private family that cannot coexist with the Prizzis.

The Dead, Huston's valedictory cinematic thinking about the conflicts and consonances between social roles and personal emotions, shows us a central figure (Donal McCann) whose life is subtly pervaded by social roles – from his understanding of himself as European, British, or Irish through his place among family and friends, to his marriage. Set against those roles is the grand passion Michael Furey felt for McCann's wife Gretta (Anjelica Huston) in her young womanhood. Such a love represents a self-creation and autonomy that social roles, even intimate ones like marriage, cannot supply. At the same time, Gabriel's idealization of his wife's story has something of the quality of Weldon Penderton's romanticizing of the life of the enlisted man. Gretta's memory becomes Gabriel's dream as much as his wife's, and we cannot forget that the snow falls on Michael Furey's lonely grave along with those of everyone else. His love does not free him from his human destiny. Few of Huston's works, indeed, allow us to forget that mortality, like the snow on the night of the Feast of the Epiphany in Dublin, 1904, effaces "all the living and the dead."

Humans share a destiny at once common and lonely; for we all die, but we die by ourselves. The pervasiveness of that understanding in Huston's tragic or existential sense of life means that his characters must be compounded of conflicting elements, the corporate with the individual, the ordinary and universal with the idiosyncratic. From *Heaven Knows* through *The Maltese Falcon* to the psychological dead ends of *Reflections*, Huston does not lecture on what should be. Indeed, his films rarely prescribe. We overhear his thoughts and observations or overlook them through the window of the movie screen, points of view that distance us, remove us as objects of address. The three films discussed at length in this chapter, and others, register Huston's consciousness of the inescapable strains that we face in living both sides of our natures, or in suppressing one to favor the other.

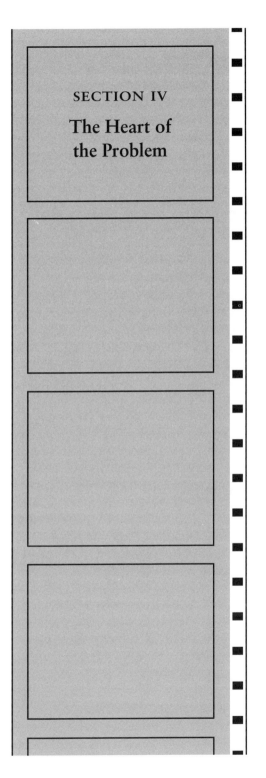

SECTION IV

The Heart of
the Problem

Freud

Fat City

THE films discussed in the previous section, in which personal desire or identity conflicts with social expectations, nonetheless locate the primary responsibility for what happens to individuals in themselves. "*Le ver*," asserted Camus, "*se trouve au coeur de l'homme.*"[1] The worm is to be found in people's hearts. Huston's version is more Freudian: "The sources of bad luck reside in the unconscious. We inflict it on ourselves as a kind of self-punishment."[2] There is plenty of such bad luck in *Fat City* and *Freud*; but there is also the more fundamental bad luck of being born human. The description of *that* original misfortune may be borrowed from Ecclesiastes, one of Huston's favorite books: "It is an unhappy business that God has given to the sons of men to be busy with" (1:13). Our business is unhappy because we are born to die and we know it, a combination that makes inescapable the sense of vanity underlying all human enterprises.

CHAPTER X

Freud (1961)

Wherefore putting away
lying, speak every man
truth with his neighbor:
for we are members
one of another.

Ephesians 4:25
(King James Version)

Perhaps the most intensely verbal of Huston's movies, Freud *is also one of his most systematically designed and graphically expressive.*

From its origins, narrative film has exhibited a fascination with psychology generally, with abnormal psychology in particular, and – perforce – with psychoanalysis. Among the filmmakers who have shown an interest in such matters, none was better informed or more thoughtful than John Huston, who made *Let There Be Light* in an Army psychiatric hospital; *Freud*; and an unremarkable movie, *Phobia* (1980), about a psychotic psychotherapist.[1] As we have seen, moreover, Huston persistently adapted literary works that focus on people in situations that shake the foundations of their personalities and on people at the edges of social and psychological normality. *Freud* represents in distilled form much of Huston's cinematic thinking about human injury and self-betrayal; it is equally concerned with the courage required to achieve self-knowledge and with the renewal that self-understanding makes possible. To the meditation on life and psychological health of *Let There Be Light*, *Freud* adds an insistence that self-knowledge must be the analyst's as well as the patient's, and that it must also be the artist's, who tells the stories of both. It is a detail of great significance that Huston himself supplied the voice-over narration in both films and, in *Freud*, that his is the voice representing the hero's introspective thinking.

The importance of existentialism in *Freud* is unmistakable, particularly since its screenplay is based to a considerable degree upon a scenario that Huston commissioned from Jean-Paul Sartre for $40,000.[2] The story of that collaboration has been repeatedly told.[3] In brief, Huston employed Sartre to write a screenplay about Freud's intellectually formative years. But from the beginning, Huston told Benayoun, "The basic idea, that of Freud as an adventurer, an explorer of his own unconscious, came from me."[4] Sartre's first version would have run about five hours.[5] After conferences with Huston in Ireland, Sartre returned to France only to submit an even longer second version. An annotated copy of the final shooting script assigns chief authorship for approximately 30 percent each to Huston, Wolfgang Reinhardt, and Sartre, and 10 percent to Charles Kaufmann.[6] The final revisions were not acceptable to Sartre, who insisted that his name be withheld from the credits.

Making *Freud* proved a harrowing task. Huston's collaboration both with Sartre and with other writers was frequently contentious. Atypical discord with the principal star, a seriously ill Montgomery Clift, and with some other members of the cast and production crew made filming difficult. More disappointingly, Universal enforced cuts and other alterations, many of which Huston bitterly opposed. During post-production, Huston wrote, "I must admit to being deeply distressed at the direction 'Freud' seems to be going in. . . . 'Freud: The Dark Passion,' like 'Inner Fury,' is of a Twenties vintage. Reviewing the successes of recent years, one's hard put to find such fruity labels." He goes on to argue against cutting the picture, because when they did so "the suspense had gone out of it. It is too long and it can't be cut – but it can be divided [by an intermission]."[7]

Unhappily, Huston lost these and other arguments with the executives of Universal. An important episode involving a patient who had been assaulted by her father and another dealing with the anti-Semitism Freud experienced from the medical establishment in Vienna were omitted.[8] At least one sequence was moved. At a length of about two hours and twenty minutes, *Freud* was given a limited release late in 1962, some cuts having already been made on the basis of preview audience reactions. Later, with twenty more minutes removed and the title changed to *Freud: The Secret Passion*, the film was released for wider distribution. To Benayoun, Huston declared *Freud* "literally mutilated," a statement that must have been especially painful for a director who wrote, "For 18 years I was determined to make this motion picture."[9] Nonetheless, both the longer and the shorter versions of *Freud* remain powerful works. The longer version is the stronger; one hopes that excised footage has been preserved and that the version desired by Huston might eventually be approximated. This discussion will use the initial release version, *Freud*.[10]

Like most of Huston's films, *Freud* traces an adventure, but in this case an unconventional intellectual and psychological one. Although its archetypes of character and action are to a degree constrained by historicity and obscured by changes imposed in post-production, *Freud* has the unmistakable shape of a romance, with the usual descents into an underworld in pursuit of a great prize, followed by reascents – in this film, psychological rebirths or epiphanies. When history conflicted with meaning, the latter prevailed. "We have taken liberties with fact in order to tell the truth."[11] Huston consciously selected the plot shape of a tumultuous quest-descent, writing of "the sheet lightning and sulphur I had in mind," of wanting to make a film "that breathed brimstone."[12] His introductory voice-over at the beginning of the movie is equally explicit: "This is the story of Freud's descent into a region almost as black as hell itself, man's unconscious, and how he let in the light." Within the story, characters use similar language. Meynert tells Freud to "Go to the heart of our darkness and hunt out the dragon. . . . If you lack the strength, make a pact with the devil. What a splendid thing to descend to hell and light your torch from its fires." At discouraging moments in Freud's quest, high camera positions look in long shot on him below, small and thrust down; subjective shots, especially in Freud's dreams, convey a similar sense of his sinking toward an underworld.

Fate in *Freud* is located in the unconscious. It is not the gods that abridge human freedom, that make our tragedies inexorable, but the dark regions of our own spirits. Descending into those regions, we challenge our masters there, seize our fate. Freud's mother, intuitive prophetess of her son's hidden purposes, tells him, "Of course you are going to

Charcot. . . . [I know] by your voice, when you talk about it. I shouldn't wonder if it was all decided before your first disagreement with Professor Meynert." In the next sequence, a train whistle startles Freud as he leaves for Paris, causing him to drop and break the heirloom watch that he reluctantly accepted from his father. An older, paternal man returns it with a sympathetic remark, "Oh, what an unhappy accident." Only later will Freud discover the role that the screams of train whistles played in his childish emotional life. His dropping of the watch was a symptom, not a random mishap. That will be one of a number of insights leading to the discovery of fate in the unconscious, to an understanding of human psychological destiny in which, as Freud says, "There are no accidents." But unlike the logos underlying Sophoclean tragedy, the logic of the unconscious is not inexorable. By looking upon our hidden purposes, we gain a measure of freedom from the energies that lead us to seek our own destruction.

Huston shapes Freud's early research as a detective story, a nineteenth- and twentieth-century romantic genre that has been partly sublimated into realism. His treatment reflects both the heritage of the Warner Bros. biographies of the 1930s and 1940s and Huston's personal conviction that the scientist and the artist alike are well symbolized by the fictional detective. All seek knowledge at once dangerous and remedial, and all pursue their quests through clues that obscure or deceive as well as reveal. Freud himself wrote in the *Introductory Lectures on Psycho-Analysis*, "suppose you are a detective engaged in the investigation of a murder, do you actually expect to find that the murderer will leave his photograph with name and address on the scene of the crime? Are you not perforce content with slighter and less certain traces?"[13] A trace remains in *Freud* of a Universal detective movie, *Murders in the Rue Morgue* (Robert Florey, 1932), on which Huston worked as a writer early in his career. The villain, Dr. Mirakle, says of his captive ape that his "shadow . . . hangs over us all. The darkness before the dawn of man." In Huston's own film thirty years later, the hero, Dr. Freud, declares of Oedipus that "the shadow of this doom lies over us all."

It is to the Warner Bros. biographies that *Freud* owes its profoundest debts, especially to one for which Huston was the scenarist, *Dr. Ehrlich's Magic Bullet* (William Dieterle, 1940). Although Sartre's own screenplay shows the same influences, he complained to Huston that "*Freud* altogether resembles, feature for feature, those heroes, the story of which you Americans tell in your films."[14] In fundamental concept and in some details, *Freud* recycles *Dr. Ehrlich*. Both are what Huston called intellectual thrillers. (Interestingly, an untitled, undated, handwritten espionage story that Huston evidently composed while in Washington, D.C., during World War II suggests the degree to which he had already worked out the concept of an intellectual quest. The autobiographical narrator of the story remarks that his interlocutor "was the only person I ever talked to about 'Ehrlich' too [*sic*] who perceived that its true hero was not the man but the 'side chain theory.'"[15]

The narrative of *Freud* begins with a high shot of institutional buildings in Vienna followed by a dissolve to a hospital corridor, a sequence that practically duplicates the opening of *Dr. Ehrlich*. Similar too are the heroes' challenges to their supervisors, which constitute the first conflicts in both movies. As Freud becomes his own most revealing patient, so Dr. Ehrlich's own case of tuberculosis is the first to be definitively identified by his new method of staining tissues. Other similarities include the crucial part that the spouses of Ehrlich and Freud play in their husbands' intellectual breakthroughs. The language describing therapy in *Dr. Ehrlich* anticipates that in *Freud*. The cure for syphilis is announced as "the magic number by which devils may be cast out of the bodies of men." On his deathbed, his treatment confirmed, Dr. Ehrlich calls for combat with other, equally difficult, human evils: "There can be no final victory over diseases of the body unless the diseases of the soul are also overcome. They feed upon each other . . . epidemics of greed, hatred, ignorance . . . we must never stop fighting."

Perhaps the most intensely verbal of Huston's movies, *Freud* is also one of the most systematically designed and graphically expressive. In the visual organization of *Freud*, Huston, like his hero, will admit "no accidents." The opening image with which we hear Huston's voice seems Rorschach-like and random, but it introduces a significant visual motif that will reappear insistently throughout the film. The nonrepresentational shape is suggestive of an eye, a breaking wave, a fowl, an electronmicroscope photograph, and so on. On the right side of the image, an inverted hooklike curve is succeeded by other shapes, then a very similar one with lighter tonalities appears during Huston's voice-over. An elaborate dissolve returns it to the original darker value and reveals the initial and final image of the credit sequence to be the same.

A design reminiscent of this hook shape recurs on the wall-hanging before which Freud interviews a guilty woman and other patients. Always his own most informative analysand, Freud recounts and ponders his first dream in front of the same tapestry, and there he falls asleep and dreams again while contemplating his mother's bracelet. Given these contexts, the hook shape takes on suggestions of a "?," a question mark. This association predominates at the moment of intellectual climax, as first Freud and then his wife Martha (Susan Kohner) are photographed in front of the tapestry while Freud comes to the difficult conclusion that "There must be sexuality in childhood." Martha's encouragement of her husband recalls her earlier association with the "?"-shape, which appears in the pattern of the carpet at their wedding.

The opening shape carries at least one other important visual association, closely related to psychological inquiry, and insistently threatening. It resembles the scorpions that Meynert uses to illustrate his admonition to Freud to "leave to the night what belongs to the night." As an evocation of the poisonous fantasies of darkness, the hook-scorpion shape appears on the forehead of Freud's mother during the harrowing dream that he suffers after interviewing Carl von Schlosser (David McCallum). In the last dream related by Cecily Kortner (Susannah York), the scorpion shape reappears on the painted woman in the tower, Cecily's mother. Linking the dangers of darkness and nightmares with psychoanalytic explorations, the motif of the "?-scorpion" typifies the resonant visual design of *Freud*. It also typifies the fluidity of the meanings that arise from the unconscious, and the capability for almost infinite metamorphoses of the signs and symbols the unconscious employs both to protect and to reveal its deepest secrets.

The shapes of the credit-title sequence also connect the "?-scorpion" with some of the dominant images and themes of *Freud*: eyes and seeing. The twisting vortex that follows the first abstract shape suggests an eye, as well as a galaxy, swirling water or weather, and so on. The symbolism of the vortex-as-eye will be confirmed in Freud's first dream, when the design on the cave wall behind the woman condenses through a dissolve into eyes on her face.

Such images recall similar eye-vortices that Hitchcock had used a few years earlier to emblematize dissolution in *Vertigo* and, more famously, at the end of the shower sequence in *Psycho*. As a mystery with psychoanalytic configurations, *Vertigo* may have been an important predecessor of *Freud*; in any event, Huston seems to allude directly to the flower in the "portrait of Carlotta" of Hitchcock's film when he photographs the portrait of Cecily's father, then tracks in on the flower in the lapel. As Donald Chankin has noticed, Hitchcock returned the favor two years later in *Marnie*, when the heroine mockingly alludes to *Freud*, promising to be "up on my poor paralyzed little legs by the very next scene."[16]

During the first narrative sequence, Meynert lights a match in front of the eye of the hysterical patient whom Freud, against orders, has admitted to the ward. Her pupil contracts, thereby "proving" that the woman is faking her blindness. A little later, images of eyes are repeated in another hospital, Charcot's, and this time Huston implicates Freud in the patients' illness by repeated cutting between close-ups of Freud's eyes and the hysterical patients.

In the von Schlosser episode, including the dream that forms its middle section, eyes figure centrally. In the first part, when von Schlosser embraces a dressmaker's dummy that he calls "Mother," a revolted Freud covers his eyes. During Freud's subsequent nightmare, he is unable either to fully look upon or to fully turn away from the spectacle of von Schlosser embracing Freud's own mother; he stares in horror from behind a hand that covers one eye. In the third section, when he revisits the von Schlosser house, Freud stands behind a fence that shadows one eye and leaves one in the light – as in the shot of Brigid at the end of *The Maltese Falcon*. Only when he acknowledges the wrong that he has committed do both his eyes appear open and illuminated.

"The eyes shall be closed," reads the famous emblem above the gate in Freud's second dream, which follows his collapse at his father's funeral. Freud's self-interpretation is that sons are commanded to close their eyes to the sins of their fathers, for "Ham was accursed by his father for seeing him naked." But the film as a whole implies that the eyes must be opened, however painful and terrifying that may be. The necessity of confronting painful reality is fundamental in Huston's ethical and psychological thought; throughout his career, he insists on the liberating power of facing the truth, especially when it shames or frightens us.

During her false memory of her father's death, Cecily covers her eyes at "the hospital" when she is compelled to identify her father's body. Like Freud, she cannot bring herself to look upon her father's sins, and she later suffers psychosomatic blindness as a result. After Freud pushes her through the distortions of her memory to the truth, her blindness disappears and she looks out between the bars of her fingers – a gesture that recalls Freud before the von Schlosser house. Her gain, however, costs her the anguish of recalling that her father died in a whorehouse, killed "by lust." Huston does not suppose, nor did Freud, that the truth can be confronted comfortably. The alternative, however, is no less painful, and it precludes the healing made possible by self-understanding and self-forgiveness.

Freud ends by reemphasizing the imagery of eyes, of facing painful truths to achieve self-knowledge. During his lecture on childhood sexuality, Freud's eyeglasses are prominent, and he describes those who cannot resolve juvenile sexual conflicts as doomed to the fate of Oedipus, "condemned to wander through life blind and homeless." His audience's violent rejection of what he is saying replicates his own revulsion when he first confronted evidence of childhood sexuality in Carl von Schlosser's chamber.

But Huston avers that there is no going back to our dangerous innocence. As *Freud* ends and the image on the screen returns to the eye-galaxy, Huston's magisterial voice-over resumes. "Know thyself." This arduous enterprise has been equated through the imagery of the motion picture with "see thyself." The eyes must be opened inwardly if we are to expose to light the infections that make human life so painful and dangerous, if we are to combat "the epidemics of greed, hatred, ignorance" that Huston wrote about in *Dr. Ehrlich* twenty years earlier. *Freud* emphasizes how terrifying such self-knowledge was for its hero and for his colleagues in Vienna. Eighty years after Freud's discoveries, will we find the courage to undertake our own journeys of self-discovery? Huston makes no grand promises: "Let us hope."

Like the abstract shapes that open and close the film, representational images during the narrative figure forth visual meanings that blend together like the self-transforming symbols that Freud discovered to be the language of the unconscious. The light and darkness evoked verbally in Huston's opening voice-over and in Meynert's private encounters with Freud are equally realized in the cinematography. The matches and candles that Meynert and Charcot use in their medical demonstrations form part of this set of images, as do the powerful contrasts of light and dark in Freud's dreams and during his second visit to von Schlosser's house. When Freud opens the door on a dying Meynert, he lets in a shaft of light that illuminates the professor's face; closing the door as he departs, he leaves the dying man in darkness.

Light associated with the quest for truth streams through a variety of windows: in Charcot's lecture hall; later as Freud listens to von Schlosser; and in Cecily's bedroom, especially as Freud and his patient discuss her last symptom, her love for her analyst. When Freud finally accepts the existence of childhood sexuality, light vanquishes darkness: Martha crosses the room, opens the window, and admits the sun of a new day. In doing so she emphasizes her role as one of a series of characters – among them Breuer, Meynert, and Cecily – who like Freud himself shrink from his quest, but who finally urge him to its completion.

While Freud walks through alternating brightness and shadow beneath a series of arches, Huston's voice articulates his hero's inner self-questionings; we will see him in a similar situation as he contemplates (again in Huston's voice) the "unthinkable" possibility that the child Cecily may have desired her father. These shots join the imagery of light and darkness with that of another central complex of imagery in *Freud*: arches, caves, and other yonic shapes – that is, shapes suggestive of female genitals and/or of birth. Such settings frame the coming to terms with repressed feelings and memories that Freud and his patients achieve and the gradual development of Freud's theories.

As with the hook-scorpion shape, arches are frequently associated with emotional danger and darkness, most obviously in the arch that spans the entrance to the Jewish cemetery in front of which Freud collapses. Arches frame Meynert as he declaims against "diabolical ideas and the unconscious" after Freud's first lecture. The cave setting of two of Freud's dreams further suggests connections between the unconscious and the underworld. In Freud's dream following the funeral of his father, the train that leaves him behind exposes a row of arched windows as it draws away.

Less threateningly, arches are also associated with conception and birth, both literal and figurative. Freud and Breuer go upstairs through a hallway of interlinking arches as they rush to the aid of Cecily when she goes into false labor. Repeated shots of the arched and flowered headboard of Cecily's bed prepare for this moment; on one occasion, Huston photographs her in front of the headboard holding a doll that her father gave her as a child and that will become part of her wrongful admission that he sexually assaulted her. The arched openings of the locks on von Schlosser's bed chamber and the hotel room in Cecily's recountings of her father's death are related to other images of the conception and birth of ideas and memories. The insertion of keys into these yonic locks makes an appropriate phallic contribution. (One wonders if censors familiar with notions of Freudian symbolism might have hesitated to pass these images.)

Like the memories and emotions of its characters, the visual motifs of *Freud* flow almost indistinguishably into one another. (Dana Polan observes that such a conception underlies Sartre's original screenplays: "The visual style is itself based to a large degree on strategies of condensation and displacement. . . . ")[17] A blackboard behind Freud during his first lecture displays an arched shape that appears to be a cross-section of a human brain. Behind Cecily when she is hypnotized are partly arched windows, one open and one closed, like Freud's eyes earlier. The association of arches with the windows of illumination and truth occurs again when Freud stands in front of a large arched window while Cecily tells her dream of the red tower, which itself contains an arched opening. Arches are invoked by close-ups of Cecily's eyebrows. They are linked again to eyes and discovery when the openings in the garden wall while Cecily and Freud talk are at first partly obscured, then fully revealed by a slight camera movement as Cecily completes her memory. The arches of windows are also occasionally associated, as similar shapes were in *The Maltese Falcon*, with the proscenium of the stage, arena for make-believe. In front of a large arched window, Cecily histrionically declares, "I'm so tired of being sick!" But her behavior says the opposite, that she cherishes her invalidism as a pledge of her love for Breuer.

Intricate connections and mutable but precisely interrelated meanings occur among other images, many of them familiar from earlier Huston films and destined to return in later ones. Flowers, snakes, trains, lighting fixtures, and – less emphatically than one might expect – various other phallic objects form part of the constellation of imagery that make *Freud* a densely significant movie. Clocks are an ironic motif, for as Freud says and as his father's broken watch dramatizes, "Time does not exist in the unconscious." Diegetic sound operates like imagery in its associative transformations. Aural connections among screams, train whistles, a crying child, and mocking laughter are especially vivid and suggestive.

As usual for Huston, mirrors carry associations of deception, disorder, or illusion. The first shots of von Schlosser's room are dominated by a mirrored vanity. As Cecily creates her fluctuating reconstructions of the past, we see in mirror image the prostitute with whom her father died. We later see Cecily and her father in a dancer's dressing room before an enormous mirror. In the next scene, Cecily paints her own face in a mirror, evidently in response to the woman's remark that "Your father loves dancers." (Cecily's mother was a dancer when she met and married Herr Kortner.) In Cecily's invented memory of a childhood sexual encounter with her parent, we watch in mirror reflections as her father carries her into his room.

We note a subtle touch in Huston's handling of Freud's initial conviction that neuroses result from childhood sexual trauma. Cecily's revelation of her father's supposed molestation occurs after her false pregnancy, during which another physician had examined her and informed Breuer and Freud that she was not pregnant, "nor could she be." In his eagerness to confirm his suspicion, Freud "forgets" this anatomical proof that she could not have been raped by her father. Later he muses that "something is wrong" with Cecily's story, but only because she loves the doll that Freud believes she should hate, since it memorializes her father's presumed assault.

Movement both on the screen (walking or riding in carriages, for example) and into or out of the frame are of considerable symbolic importance in *Freud*. "The film frame itself," as Norman Holland has argued, "becomes an image for consciousness . . . as when Cecily fails to walk and slumps to the floor after Breuer's supposed 'cure,' or when Charcot's male patient collapses, slipping down out of the frame."[18] Huston makes clear that the movement toward full consciousness cannot be easy. Nor is it always wholly voluntary, as is evident in the dream sequences of Freud being pulled into and out of caves, and when Cecily is dragged into the bordello to identify her father's body. *Freud* assigns to the diseases of the soul physical symptoms that impair both the literal and the metaphorical movement of the protagonists. Cecily's blindness and paraplegia and Freud's own breakdown during his father's funeral constitute two vivid instances.

For all the verbal profusion of the script of *Freud*, its words are handled like visual images; they are as fluid, as prone to enigmatic transformations, as apt to mystify or deceive. Both sights and sounds in this film require constant interpretation; both function more as clues that must be construed than as signposts. Both, as Freud says of dreams, "speak in riddles."

Huston's direction and editing are crucial in solving the riddles of words as well as of images. Meynert humiliates Freud by publicly dismissing his first lecture as containing "some ideas that are new and some ideas that are true. But the ideas that are true are not new, and those that are new are not true." Less noticeable than Meynert's contempt is his anxiousness to speak; so eager is he to deliver his attack, indeed, that he rises to interrupt the chairman of the assembly. When he meets Freud in his office, Meynert mocks Charcot's ideas still more savagely, but again with an eagerness that seems inappropriate to the occasion. He concludes by dismissing his onetime protégé: "How would you like your own master to be sick of hysteria, à la Charcot? How well you'd take care of him! No luck. I'm as sound as an apple. Goodbye, Freud. Leave and don't come back." If we begin to think that the professor protests too much, we are right; but we are also a step ahead of Freud. Only later, during Meynert's last scene, will Freud be made privy to the truth behind the earlier outbursts, that Meynert himself has been afflicted all his life with classic symptoms of hysteria. The confirmation of his self-diagnosis, in retrospect, comes from Huston's care that Eric Portman interpret Meynert's lines with some subtle overacting, in his making Meynert a bit too vehement in smashing down the theoretical formulations of the younger physician.

Like Meynert, Breuer refuses to hear words that convey ideas he cannot accept; indeed, he attempts to forbid such words from being spoken. He tries to prevent Freud from publishing or lecturing about childhood sexuality. When Cecily goes into false labor – presumably a symptom of her desire to have Breuer's child, though that idea remains implicit – her physician will not allow her to continue speaking. "I order you," Breuer barks angrily, "to stop thinking these false thoughts." Freud himself has recourse to a similar abuse of authority when his courage fails him with von Schlosser and he awakens his patient with the ultimately lethal instruction that he remember nothing he said under hypnosis. Words that speakers cannot acknowledge often refuse to come. Von Schlosser would like to write poetry, "but I cannot find the rhymes." Later, having fled back to "pure anatomy" and having abandoned his neurotic patients because of his horror at Carl, Freud tells Breuer that the name of that crucial character "escapes me."

Like shapes blending into other shapes, words flow together and combine. In verbal mistakes, riddles hint at their answers. Speaking of her parents' different religions, Cecily says that her mother insisted that she "be brought up a prostitute." Even after she realizes her error, she cannot quite shape the word she meant, "Protestant." As we shall understand more fully later, Cecily as a child came to apprehend her father's affection for prostitutes and, eager to please him, conceived an unconscious ambition for that profession. Later, she fuses the names of her former beloved therapist with that of her current one, "Dr. Freuer." Neither Freud nor Cecily say anything about her slip; but Huston underlines its significance when he dissolves to Martha Freud, evidently a day or two later, looking at a bunch of flowers and reading the card from Cecily that accompanies them.

In no Huston film is the collective aspect of humanity more central to his understanding of what it means to be a person than in *Freud*. Like the words and images of the film, its characters flow into one another. Freud finds himself in virtually everyone around him; at the same time, he helps them struggle toward their own most individual, contingent identities. The film insists on candor not only for self-realization and healing, but because humans define themselves in relation to each other. To know who they are, people must speak and hear the truth about themselves.

Huston's conception of the collective identity of human beings leads in *Freud* to a degree of substitutability among its central figures. Jameson notes that Freud partly exchanges his identity with other characters, and Holland extends Jameson's perception by tracing a pattern of displacements that involves both characters and ideas: "psychoanalysis shows us the unconscious *substitutions* that rule our lives."[19] In Freud's first dream, von Schlosser's mother becomes Freud's, and the dreamer awakes to call his spouse "Mother." "No dear, it's Martha, your wife, Martha," she corrects him gently. He pulls back to look at her, then resumes his embrace. When he replaces Breuer as the object of Cecily's affections, Freud tells Martha that both he and Breuer may be "reflections of someone else's image, an original which for some reason she's repressed." "I thought love was something between a man and a woman who were meant for each other," frets Martha. "What about us? Are we only reflections of others in our past?" Freud does not shrink from the question. Emotional interchangeability extends to the most intimate of relationships. "It may be you bear a likeness to some image in my heart, some forgotten image," he answers. As when he awakened from his nightmare, Freud then moves to Martha and embraces her.

The conclusion that people rediscover the images of others in their spouses does not compromise or diminish Freud's particular love for his wife. Indeed, if the film suggests that loving one person includes love for others, then the romantic ideal of the man-and-woman-made-for-each-other seems limited and meager. The more fluid conception in *Freud* enlarges the scope of love, but at the same time it preserves the uniqueness of individual occurrences. At the end of *The Night of the Iguana*, Shannon switches from proposing to travel with Hannah to partnering Maxine. Huston does not imply inconstancy or opportunism in Shannon's actions, only that he is a human attempting to find the right person with whom to make a home.

As people rediscover and love others in their spouses and friends, they also find themselves. *Freud* posits a common human nature with shared emotional predispositions, paramount among them people's need to verify themselves in each other. The intricate origins of our deepest feelings must be perceived and expressed if we are to know ourselves and to meet life, as Freud says to Cecily, on its terms. For Freud to do that, he must both find himself in other people and find in himself all humanity. So must everyone. Love is perhaps the most intense of such essential connections, but it is not unique. In other relationships also, humans attain their identities by coming to know each other. When Freud resumes Cecily's treatment, Huston repeatedly uses a two-shot composition that puts a sculpture in the frame, gazing at Freud while Freud gazes at his patient. The sculpture connects art with Freud's science and adds another auditor to the scene, humanity in its past as well as its present. At this point in their therapeutic relationship, the chief work of doctor and patient is to attain a mutual trust that will allow them to communicate. Cecily and Freud must undertake their quest together. In order for Cecily to uncover and express the intimacies of her being, Freud must discover along with her the intimacies of his own. As the sculpture suggests, their joint voyage is also the voyage of all humanity toward a self-understanding that has been its aim since classical times.

Freud must also grant full confidence to his wife. When he asks her not to read his manuscripts, he attempts to withhold himself from her. Similarly, Martha must trust her husband, accept what she finds so dismaying, that he must question his patients about "such things." We should notice that Martha never agrees to her husband's request that she stop reading his work in progress, nor does he insist upon it. Later, her familiarity with his writing will prove crucial, as she quotes his student diaries to him and thereby catalyzes his understanding of childhood sexuality.

His trusting intimacy with his mother has a similar importance for his personal and intellectual quests (they are the same). From her he learns that his "memory" of his father doing something to his sister could not be genuine, for his sister had not been born at the time. Thus he eventually comes to understand that he, like Cecily, has invented a memory whose origin is a childhood fantasy, not the reality of an aggression by an adult parent. Huston's voice represents the thoughts of the adult Freud: "She was naked to the waist, I remember." The screen shows Freud as a child, looking at his mother in front of a mirror. We can see only her back, but the child can presumably see the reflection of her face and body. Freud's father arrives and draws his wife with him into the adjoining room. "Souls burn in hell," Freud-Huston muses, "the hell of hatred, of jealousy. I wished him dead." To escape that hell, it is necessary to descend to it again, to liberate the anguish entombed but still alive there. Huston suggests that no one can make that descent alone, or come back alone. For the descent, Freud requires the assistance of his mother. What he finds so appals him that he proposes to quit Vienna and his practice. To reascend, he requires the understanding of his wife.

Most commentators on *Freud* have observed the succession of characters who serve as father figures, sometimes vengeful, sometimes benign: Freud's father, Meynert, Charcot, Breuer, and less individualized colleagues. (Sartre's screenplay emphasizes this emotional arena even more than Huston's movie does; in particular, Sartre assigns great importance to Freud's dependent relationship with Fleiss, who disappears from the film.) Meynert laughs scornfully in Freud's first dream and a looming male figure calls on Freud to "honor me, your father" when he dreams of the cave again. A striking dissolve on the occasion of Meynert's terminal illness juxtaposes his image briefly onto Freud's face. On his deathbed, Freud's father "gives" Breuer his son, assigns him a paternal role that Breuer will later call that of a "spiritual father."

Freud resents answering Meynert's summons to his deathbed, and when he does set off, he makes an acerbic remark that goes a long way toward explaining why father figures have such power over him. "He's dying, Siggie," says Martha. "How amazed he must be at the thought. He always took himself for Jehovah," her husband replies. When Freud later proposes to give up Vienna, he does so because "I dishonored my father." How much more terrible that offense must seem, if he feels that he has also dishonored God.

The Oedipus complex requires specific sexual identities, a mother and a son, but *Freud* does not suggest that different genders lead to fundamental differences in children's psychological development, since their dynamics of desire and jealousy arise analogously. As is the case in Huston's other films, *Freud* does not present men and women as having divergent emotional capacities, needs, or vulnerabilities. On the contrary, within the broad pattern of substitutions, parallels between Cecily and Freud imply the opposite: that being human, not sex, is the crucial factor in identity.

Much of what Cecily and Freud share originates in the residue of their relationships with their fathers. Cecily possesses forbidden knowledge of her father's sins, though in her hysterical blindness she for a time manages to close her eyes. Freud imagines that he witnessed his father assault his sister. Thus he has in common with Cecily the apparent possession of forbidden knowledge created from a false memory about his parent. Freud and Cecily each experience a temporary inability to walk that is connected to anxieties about their fathers. Each projects onto objects associated with their fathers – Freud's pocket watch and Cecily's golden cup – strongly ambivalent emotions. Each dreams of a woman marked with the hook-scorpion shape and associated with snakes. Cecily experienced the happiest days of her life when she was allowed to act her mother's part with her father; Freud reconstructs his own childish wish to replace his father in his mother's life. Faced with their juvenile desires, both recoil in horror. When she begins to comprehend that she hated her father for rejecting her, Cecily "cannot bear to be this person"; when he understands that he has invented a crime to justify his jealousy of his father, Freud wishes to abandon his investigations.

The parallels between Cecily and Freud and the intimate connections between the health of the doctor and of his patient are even more emphatic in the film that Huston planned than in what was finally released. Most obscuring was a change in the sequence of scenes. In the version that Huston intended, the episode of Freud walking in the Jewish cemetery, finally at peace with the memory of his father, immediately follows his last scene with Cecily. That scene ends with Cecily saying, "Would you please tell Mama I'd like to see her?" Cutting to Freud in the cemetery would have emphasized that Cecily's cure follows the same path as Freud's. Because the "Royal Ministry of Communication" that Freud and Cecily have created together is composed of both, Freud cannot obey Breuer when his collaborator pleads, "Do not make this girl the touchstone of your theory." For Freud to remove Cecily from his theory would be to remove himself, so intimate are the connections between his discovery of her emotional injuries and of his own.

Huston urgently wished to keep the ending of *Freud* that was originally filmed, a scene in which Freud forces an anti-Semitic colleague who has knocked off his hat to clean and return it to him.[20] Anti-Semitism was another theme to which Sartre gave an emphasis that is diminished in the realization of the film, but one that Huston retained to a degree and wished to accentuate further – despite the strongly negative reactions of preview audiences.[21] The original ending would have resolved the memory from his childhood that Freud relates to Breuer, of an anti-Semite knocking off his father's hat and calling him "dirty Jew." Freud's father simply picked up his hat and continued on without protest, and from that moment his son saw him "less as a god and more as a man." The son, we infer, sought new gods in new father figures.

The scriptural story of Ham, and Freud's exclamation to Martha, "Tell it not in Gath, my love, and above all hide the good news from the Philistine!" remind us of his religious background. Freud's Jewish identity functions in Huston's film in part to emphasize his nonconformity, and especially his alienation from fellow physicians and scientists. Original and revolutionary, his theories shock a culture that proscribes discussion of sexuality, and that tolerates Jews with ambivalence. His Jewishness also opposes him to the hypocritical moralism of Meynert and other sanctimonious colleagues. Both the pejorative treatment of moralism and its association with institutionalized Christianity are characteristic of Huston. When Meynert denounces a hysterical woman as a faker trying to get attention and escape responsibilities, the framing places a cross on the wall directly above his head. Later Meynert's subordinate self-righteously forbids hypnosis in the hospital. He too stands under a cross.

Though humor in *Freud* is spare and subtle, the righteous indignation of Freud's colleagues attracts Huston's satiric impulses. At the end of Freud's wedding, his father crows that "Martha has here a genius, and soon the whole world will know it." Huston mischievously dissolves to the lecture hall, where Freud is concluding a paper that receives only polite, scattered clapping, followed by the disparagement of the chairman and the vehement attack of Meynert, who is applauded heartily. By comparison with the actions of the enraged audience of his second lecture, however, this reception is enthusiastic. The second lecture, too, follows an ironic transition: Huston cuts from Freud declaring that "The time comes when one must give up all one's fathers and stand alone," to the extreme hostility of his colleagues, his professional fathers. After enduring hooting, laughter, angry thumping, and spitting as he expounds the theory of the Oedipus complex, the speaker sarcastically thanks his audience: "Gentlemen, I am deeply grateful for your kind attention. You have not ceased to display the detachment, the love of truth (a shout from the audience, 'What truth?!') for truth's sake that ennobles our profession."

Other moments of humor arise mostly in the characteristic wit of Huston's direction of actors and in his editing. At the end of one of Cecily's sessions, Freud asks her to describe a man in her dream. Looking evasive, she denies being able to do so; then she hears the welcome chime of a clock. "My precious hour gone, so soon," she says sweetly. The camera then follows Freud into the hall, where he observes the tell-tale carnation in the portrait of Herr Kortner, the answer to his question.

During the last sequence with Cecily, Freud explains, "This makes your dream an allegory. Through love, it says, you'll be able to reveal your secrets. . . . When they're told, and understood, you'll be cured." Huston's movie constructs a similar allegory, an allegory of humanity's journey toward self-understanding and self-forgiveness. "Progress, like walking, is achieved by losing and regaining one's balance," Martha reads from Freud's student diary. "It is a series of mistakes. From error to error, one discovers the entire truth." The original sense of "err," "to wander," is entirely relevant. The end of wandering is self-knowledge, "the single hope of victory," as Huston says in the epilogue, "over man's oldest enemy, his vanity." The mortal alternative to that painful quest is manifest in the dying Meynert, who dismisses his life as "a sham" and is perishing "in a state of pride, ignorance." Searching into the underlying realities of one's life, however excruciating, carries no genuine risk; for, as Freud declares to Breuer and as Meynert confirms, "Whoever the truth can kill is doomed anyway."

Self-knowledge requires that we find the courage to "bear to be this person" and understanding that allows us to dissolve our horror at what we are. To disarm what Huston called "the sometime assassin Freud found deep within each of us," we must expose the unconscious and accept what we see there.[22] Freud's wife forgives him, in effect, both for having invented a theory that dishonored his father and for being "the guilty one." "Through love," Freud can finally understand that no sin has been committed. The next day he will ask Frau Kortner, "Must there be a guilty one?"

Are humans guilty if they cannot help but sin? One of the last exchanges between Freud and Cecily brings us to the bedrock understanding of human nature that informs Huston's *Freud*. "The innocent is born into a world in which it cannot help but lose its innocence. I sinned too; I dreamed of killing my father." "Then you were a monster too," returns Cecily. "No," answers Freud with a new tranquillity, "I was a child." The loss of innocence is human destiny; its recovery is a task of the greatest consequence. In order to return from the hell into which we are all thrust, we must believe in our capacity to redeem sins we could not help but commit. At the end of *The Winter's Tale*, Paulina tells Leontes that to bring his queen back to life, "It is required / You do awake your faith."[23] The requirements of Huston's own romance of rebirth resemble Shakespeare's. To leave the regions of darkness demands not just understanding and forgiveness, but faith. Looking ahead to her future cure, Freud says to Cecily, "Believe me." Newly tranquil in turn, she answers, "I do."

Like Freud, Huston understood the shame and self-betrayal that life enforces upon everyone and with which we must come to terms if we are to experience the joy – or even the "common unhappiness," as Freud once said – of which we are capable. Along with the doctor and his patients, the filmmaker who recounts their stories must also come to know himself, to forgive his own sins, and to believe in other people and himself. In Huston's untitled espionage narrative, the speaker admits that "there are those with a profound consciousness of original sin – such am I."[24] In his film of seventeen years later, the terms for "original sin" have changed. But the speaking of Freud's mind in Huston's voice identifies the writer and director with its errant hero. Like the detective and the scientist, the artist observes, understands, and discovers himself in a humanity that is at once his subject and his fate.

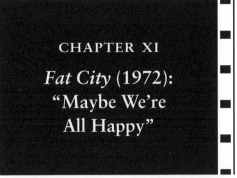

CHAPTER XI

Fat City (1972): "Maybe We're All Happy"

Like *The Misfits*, it is one of those allegorical stories concerning the condition of man which I like so much.

John Huston[1]

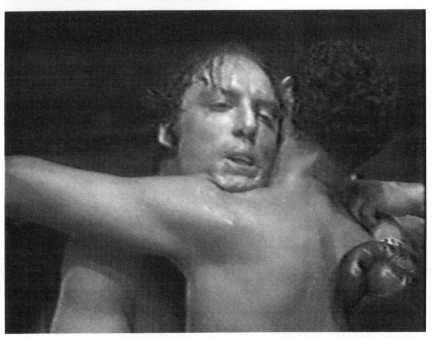

The battered, exhausted fighters depict simultaneous intimacy and isolation, the unbridgeable gulfs that separate people even during their most ardent combative embraces.

Fat City might best be described as an existentialist comedy. Similar to *Reflections in a Golden Eye* in its refusal to pass judgment, but warmer toward its protagonists and more affectionate in its humor, *Fat City* portrays characters living near the margins of a society in which they manage tenuous existence. At the same time, however, their circumscribed world supplies a kind and supportive company. Characters' misfortunes are mostly either self-created or derive from dilemmas inherent in being human; they rarely originate with society. Although no one dies in *Fat*

191

City (one sign that it is a comedy), it is thoroughly imbued with the consciousness of mortality and the simultaneous necessity and vanity of striving.

Fluid pans and tracking shots of Stockton, California precede the credits. They condense and generalize the main point of the stories that will follow: people hang together, sustaining each other. An aerial view dissolves into a string of double exposures that blend persons and places into others, make them equivalent, and suggest that what we are about to see applies to everyone. The first few minutes of *Fat City* play a lyrical variation on conventional opening sequences in which establishing shots are followed by close-ups of a single locale. The most obvious implication of that convention was verbalized in the epigraph that opened the television series, "The Naked City." Each week, an anonymous speaker intoned, as I recall, something like the following: "There are eight million stories in the naked city. This is one of them." Huston himself employed such a standard curtain raiser (without the voice-over) for *The Maltese Falcon* and used versions of it for opening credit sequences of *The Asphalt Jungle* and *The Kremlin Letter*.

Although a decayed Stockton is being redeveloped into expressways and rubble, the people who are the main source of imagery in the first sequence look relaxed, peaceful, and companionable. They enact an urban version of Gay's prescription in *The Misfits* for "just living." Doing so, they make up a community – even when they are occasionally shot singly, as is a white-haired man who takes off his hat to smooth his crew cut and who looks a little like Huston himself. The resemblance is appropriate, for the attitude of the film toward its subjects will be one of sympathy and identification. *Fat City* is an allegory of the human condition and no one – audience, actor, or filmmaker – can be outside or above it.

Amused empathy, along with Huston's characteristic sense of fun, makes *Fat City*, as Hammen suggests, "strangely comic as it is sad," despite the fact that "the lot of these characters is not a happy one."[2] As I argued in the discussion of *The African Queen*, however, the basis of comedy is not its invitation to laughter so much as the movement of its characters from isolation or conflict toward integration and harmony. Laughter is a reflex that such actions facilitate, in part because of the emotional luxury afforded by the other great principle of comic plots, the exclusion of real injury or pain. *Fat City* approaches serious suffering, but the evenness of its tone and the resilience of its protagonists hold most dire consequences at bay. At the same time, the tendency of its characters to help each other through hard times fulfills the condition of social integration. The inclusive sense of common humanity with which the film is imbued represents a wider, equally fundamental, comic assumption. Together we make up humankind, whether as characters in movies or as an audience watching them or as their creators.

The comedy among the characters of *Fat City* is broad as often as it is subtle. Among the performances, the virtuosity of Susan Tyrell's alcoholically volatile, hoarse Oma is especially notable. Like much film comedy, *Fat City* insists on the messiness and intractability of the world, especially the recalcitrant physicality of its characters. Billy (Stacy Keach) flat on his back in his sweaty bed, dirty feet, bulging briefs, disheveled thinning hair and all; Ernie (Jeff Bridges) floundering about in the mud and dark, anticipating his proclivity for being knocked out in the ring; the trunk lid that won't close; the nose that Babe can't breathe through on wet days and his "ruined" throat; Faye's (Candy Clark) pregnancy despite being "pretty careful"; Oma's gaping clothes and the trash cluttering her tiny apartment – such mundane examples of the confrontation between human need and the unwieldy world are viewed through a Bergsonian lens. Despite attempts at control by the characters, the physical machines of their bodies as well as their insensate surroundings do as they do. People collide, drift apart, collide again. The human world, like the molecular one, moves more or less at random, in entertaining, unpredictable Brownian motion.

The director makes other jokes more quietly. Earl admits that he doesn't know much about prizefighting, but he is played by Curtis Cokes, once a top-ranked professional middleweight, who probably knew more about that subject than anyone else on the set, including Huston. (Actors play boxers and a boxer becomes an actor.) Editing is repeatedly playful: Babe holding forth about a fighter's urine specimen, "piss in that bottle . . . just as clear and pure as fresh drinkin' water," then Huston cutting to Ernie's car in a drenching rain, stuck in the mud after he and Faye have first made love; later a dissolve from Ernie being knocked out in the ring to his car, being beaten decisively again, as Faye jabs and feints him toward marriage.

In general, Huston removed from the novel an incipient despair and sense of isolation and replaced those qualities with stubborn optimism and a feeling of community. He also replaced the dreariness of Gardner's setting with sunlight and a chipper, colorful palette. In the novel, "A carload of boxers departed in the rain"; in the film they go excitedly off in sunshine, piling into the car in front of the dazzling white wall of the gym.[3] The first time Billy goes into the fields, Gardner describes him as arriving drunk and in the "agony [of] getting up after three hours sleep." The bus blunders into the wrong field, the laborers curse the driver, and they sit in racial groups, "Negro paired with Negro, white with white, Mexican with Mexican and Filipino beside Filipino."[4] Huston transforms this episode into something like Curtin's idealized description of the peach harvest in *The Treasure of the Sierra Madre*. En route, the workers manage grumpy but amiable banter; there is no sign of racial tension or segregation; and the blue school bus arrives at a golden field where men, women, and children of all hues collect and trim onions under a brilliant sky. A brassy, upbeat instrumental version of "Help Me Make It Through the Night" accompanies the dialogue-free sequence, which ends with a sweaty Billy looking tired but peaceful.

Huston reversed the conventional gritty look of boxing locales as they appear both in the novel and in Hollywood fight films. The portrayal of boxing begins in the novel with a description of the gym as a dank cavern "in the basement of a three-story brick hotel."[5] Huston moves it upstairs to a light, airy room in a white building. Inside the gym, everyone is cheerfully dressed in bright tints that anticipate Ruben's peach shirt and the colorful, enthusiastic crowds at the boxing matches. In the palette of *Fat City*, blue and warm oranges, tans, and purples preponderate. Touches of red suggest emotional intensity, but the relaxed, even tone of the film extends to its colors, and reds rarely dominate. The strongest use of red is reserved to underline the violence of prizefighting: the blood in Lucero's urine and the scarlet coursing down Ernie's face after his nose is broken.

Other alterations of Gardner's book warm the setting and situate the characters more comfortably in the world and among other people. The baffled irony of the novel begins in "the Hotel Coma" and ends in a bus station where "unkempt sleepers slumped upright on the benches." Irony is ameliorated in the film, most incidents of which conclude not in defeat but in a frequently comic anticlimax. The first boxing matches are bracketed by Ruben's ebullient announcement that "we got the winners" and his bewildered complaint afterward as he sits with his defeated fighters, "I don't know what kind of deal we were getting tonight." When we next see Buford after his Ali-like declaration that "I'm gonna kick his [opponent's] ass so bad every time he takes a bite of food tomorrow he's gonna think of me," his face is swollen and lumpy. Ernie's unhappy debut ends in the dressing room as a stablemate dons his bloody trunks. When he tries on a white sequined robe later, Ruben brags to the salesman, "Won his last three fights. They couldn't touch him. Kid's fast." Ernie bounces happily before the mirrors, "The champion of the world!" Cut to his next fight and Ernie toppling after twenty-three seconds of the first round, before Babe can finish folding his new garment. Less comically, Billy's improbable victory over Lucero turns to ashes when he learns that his "blood and sweat" has netted him only a couple of hundred dollars and he finds himself alone in his hotel.

Daily pleasures and irritants, small courtesies extended, assistance supplied – *Fat City* meditates on the common humanity expressed in ordinary people, gestures, and events. Billy Tully looks for a match to light the last cigarette of his pack as the story begins and will again be seeking a light just before it ends. People clumsily cook dinner for each other, drop bottles that break; watery catsup floods a plate; cars get stuck in the mud; couples dress up and go on double dates; singles go to bars; Tully zips the back of Oma's dress as they stagger onto the street; Babe lends Tully two or three dollars for movies, day after day. Mundane and peculiar, "the art of our necessities," as Lear mused after he lost them, "is strange."

The beautifully dreary, sadly hilarious, lonely, congenial, brilliant final sequence sums the human qualities that we see from the opening cinematic collage through the two dozen or so episodes that make up the action. Like the opening sequence, the conclusion is entirely of Huston's creation; there is no source in Gardner's novel. Seated at the counter of a cafe-card room with Ernie, whom he has prevailed upon to keep him company, Billy looks at the stiff old Asian man getting their coffee. "How'd you like to wake up in the morning, an' be him?" (a pause, Ernie mumbles, "God.") "Jesus, the waste! (pause) Before you can get rollin', your life makes a beeline for the drain."

Billy shows the wear of his boxing career and his balding age, and he looks as if he has spent the last week sleeping in a dumpster. His patronizing pity for the old man is risible.[6] Unless we are dozing, however, we should not miss the implication that this scene has for us as well as for Tully. The folly of his supposing himself to be the waiter's better is equally ours if we presume our own superiority. Were we ready to think something like, "How'd you like to wake up and be Billy Tully?" In the battered Tully, Huston drew an emblem of human fate and accorded him, along with amusement, respect and sympathy. If we are no better than he, he is no worse than we.

When the old man brings coffee, Billy and Ernie carefully thank him. Ernie ventures, "Maybe he's happy." It is difficult to read either irony or its absence in Billy's answer: "Maybe we're all happy." (This exchange may allude to – in any event, resembles – the last lines of Camus's "The Myth of Sisyphus": "The struggle itself toward the heights suffices to fill the human heart. One must imagine Sisyphus happy.")[7] Tully brightens, looks at the old man, smiles, and half-mockingly says, "Right?" Comprehending the smile, the man returns it. Ernie smiles too. It may be that we are all happy. Or unhappy. Most likely, both at the same time. What becomes increasingly clear as the sequence continues is that we need the "all."

"Think he was ever young once?" asks Billy, retreating from his speculation. "No," grunts Ernie. Tully, tentatively: "Maybe he wasn't." The Hustonian equilibrium. He was young once, as Billy was and as Ernie is but soon will not be. Or are we all young, as long as we are alive? Do we lose our youth in a moment, assuming with birth itself the fate of aging and dying?

Tully revolves his stool to look at the room. The camera zooms to a very tight close-up of Billy's stunned face. The cafe goes silent; here begins what is for me one of the most powerful short sequences in all cinema. In a view that the zoom assigns to Tully's eyes, all obvious movement at the card table is arrested. But something of life remains. The shot, in fact, is not a freeze-frame but simply shows people holding still.[8] At this instant, the distinction between inside and outside disappears. We cannot separate the subjectivity of Tully, which includes the accumulated brain damage of years of prizefighting, from the reality of the world, which seems to have stopped, but not quite. Tully experiences a little death or an epiphany. Through his consciousness, we witness what Camus identified as the origin of the absurd, the confrontation between human need and the senseless silence of the world.[9]

The camera pans to an adjacent table, also almost motionless, cuts back to Tully's face, then back to the table. A spectator starts to walk away, the babble of voices rises again, the men at the table shift in their seats. Tully sighs as he returns from the isolation he has just experienced. As he does so, Ernie says, "Hey, old buddy, I'm gonna take off." Billy turns to face him: "Hey, stick around. Talk awhile." For five seconds he looks into Ernie's eyes. "Okay." Tully nods and smiles and the two mutely sip their coffee, sitting nearly motionless as the film ends and the song returns over brief closing credits: "Yesterday is dead and gone,/ And tomorrow's out of sight,/ And it's bad to be alone,/ Help me make it through the night."

The silence with which the two men "talk awhile" appears incongruous, but the kindness of Ernie's gesture and the communion to which it leads overwhelm the irony.[10] The camera set-ups at the beginning of the sequence in the cafe are oblique, shooting the two men at angles. In the last shot, the camera faces Billy and Ernie from between them; they are precisely side by side, in the same photographic plane. As we have seen, Huston rarely uses this shot, but when he does, it invariably signifies a "breaking of barriers between people." Despite their ambivalence and reticence, the mutuality of Billy and Ernie at the end of the film is no more ironized than we are allowed to look down on them from a superior position. At the same time, the limit of their mutuality, perhaps of all human intimacy, remains undeniable.

Ethnicity – a side of American life generally more associated with divisiveness than community – is handled in *Fat City* as another aspect of the common humanity of the characters. Everyone in the movie conspicuously has it – including Caucasians, who are no more a majority in this human landscape than anyone else. The subset of Stockton that includes boxing and day labor, bars and seedy hotels, is an unidealized working-class model of integration. The Hispanic Ruben Luna (Nicholas Colosanto) tells his wife about "a white kid [who] came in today." He has "nothing against coloreds, it's just that Anglos don't wanna pay to see two colored guys fight; they want to see a white guy fight." He handles two black fighters, a Hispanic, and Ernie – whom he labels "Irish Ernie Munger." "But I'm not Irish," his fighter protests. "I just sent 'em in that so they'd know you were white," Ruben explains. Elsewhere the same casual melange: diverse ages, sexes, and colors in the onion-topping crew; the same in the bars and boxing audiences.

Oma rails about prejudice, but she is herself at once the most (verbally) and least (in terms of whom she is willing to marry or live with) prejudiced person in the film. The widow of a "full-blooded Cherokee Indian," she is divorced from a white man and living with an African-American when Tully meets her. Although she insists that "White Man is the vermin of the earth," she tearfully tells Billy a few minutes later, "I love you so much!" Her men, like boxers and day laborers, come in all colors. They share human virtues and weaknesses and fates that submerge distinctions of race or background. When Billy assures Oma that "you can count on me," a certain truth overshadows the obvious falsehood of his assertion. If Billy individually can scarcely be relied upon, perhaps human beings in general can. Most of the time, somebody will help you make it through the night.

Noting the substitutability of "human beings or what they desire" in Huston's films, Norman Holland cited in particular the boxers of *Fat*

City.[11] They shuffle age as well as size, race, and social condition. Huston described Ernie as Billy's "younger counterpart who's headed in the same direction despite the living lesson before his eyes."[12] From Tully walking to the Y, the image dissolves to Ernie punching a heavy bag; later it will dissolve from Ernie to Ruben. From Babe, Ruben, and their four fighters in a Monterey bar, Huston cuts back to Tully, entering a bar in Stockton. When Ernie debuts as a boxer, Ruben is as fretful as if he were going into the ring for the first time himself. The three men are replays, shadows of one another. A little younger than Ernie is Buford, modeled on the young Muhammad Ali, a reference that carries the substitutability of boxers beyond Huston-Gardner's fiction.

Ruben hopes that Ernie will "listen to me and let me put everything I know into 'im." But he is fated not to be listened to. His wife falls asleep as he talks to her; he can barely get through his story about Ernie's blood sample; and Tully stands railing at him, ignoring Ruben's pleas to get out of the street. A later conversation between Ruben and Babe suggests why the boxers are doomed to repeat one another's deviations, why they learn so little from each other. "Well, I lost another one. Ernie snuck off and got married," his manager announces unhappily. "All that energy they waste. If they're not getting married, they're getting arrested, or joining the Navy, or killing themselves on motorcycles." Or drinking or smoking or "out gettin' me a little." Interchangeable in time as well as place and person, they do pretty much what young men have always done. Ernie, and Billy before him, and Ruben and Babe before them. Babe asks, "What can you expect?" – a rhetorical question that in this film applies across the board. It applies as well to the filmmaker, former ranked lightweight in California and a young man whose path to age led through the same extravagant, normal expenditures of energy.

Aging and in bad health (Huston was using an oxygen tank on the set because of his emphysema), the ex-fighter directing *Fat City* was not so different from the battered characters in his movie, nor exempt from the metaphor of decaying Stockton. An honest eye for his movie was an honest eye on himself. Jameson judges *Fat City* to be "one of the most eventoned films that Huston, or anyone else, ever made."[13] Studlar writes that its "even anticlimactic tone . . . and the detached camera style extend the stylistic tendencies in many of Huston's other films."[14] Modestly, Huston himself observed that the chief virtue of *Fat City* "is its modesty."[15] Despite its quiet objectivity, the tone of the picture is affectionate. Perhaps the best cue for responding to it is a shot of Tully with hoe and handkerchief – entertained, sweaty, and sympathetic – listening with another worker to a third telling his story.

The substitutability of boxers applies also to lovers. *Fat City* portrays without regret or mockery the ordinary equivocations and maneuvering that arise from the loneliness, distrust, and need of each other that men and women share. The relaxed companionship of Ruben and his wife is not undercut by her falling asleep as he talks to her in bed, nor by his casual observation that a waitress "sure knows how to fill a skirt," a talent that his wife has left with her youth. Billy tells Ernie, "I get the fight, I get the money, I send for my wife." Given that he is living with Oma, his plan is a little surprising. He continues, "You know, Ernie, there are some women that love you for yourself, but that doesn't last long." Despite his melancholy aphorism, he goes on to extol the compensations of marriage.

After assuring Billy, "You're handsome. You are. All you need's a little flair," Oma coaxes him to try on Earl's sports jacket. But as he does so, she loses interest in him and cries while thinking about the absent Earl, "eatin' his heart out in the pokey." After Earl revisits her, Oma is evasive with Billy. When Billy drifts back to her apartment (he left her before his fight, at Ruben's urging), he finds his predecessor reinstalled and wearing one of his tee shirts.

Huston enriches the theme of amorous interchangeability with a set piece inserted into the hoeing sequence. One of the laborers tells of drifting from his wife to a neighbor woman, his philandering lubricated by wine and revealed by roses – a combination that costs him his marriage and provides a "wine and roses" punch line that alludes to Blake Edwards's film of a decade earlier.

The marriage into which Ernie drifts begins as a convincing, glamourless, car-seat courtship. From his startled discovery that Faye "has never done it before" to her maneuvering him into half-agreeing to marry her if she is pregnant, the portrayal of their relationship avoids the romantic aura that movies usually attach to young lovers. At the same time, it indulges in little satire. When Billy tells Ernie that the younger man has "everything goin'" for him, we are not likely to snort, despite our knowledge of how he got his family and the hazards that his marriage surely faces. He does have, after all, a wife, a son, and a good reach. If human life in *Fat City* has little more to offer, the movie at the same time urges that such things are not to be lightly dismissed.

In a burst of bar room philosophizing, Tully tells Oma, "Free depends upon what you mean, free. I mean, if it's not free, can you call it love?" This 1960s cliché pretty well fits *Fat City*. Huston understood both the constraints of human life and its existential freedom. However unhappy and baffled Huston's characters may be, they maintain their freedom and optimism as long as they confront the truth about themselves – or most of it. Their love may not be romantic, but it is part of the acceptance the characters of *Fat City* grant each other and themselves.

For most of the characters, the outcomes of love are as anticlimactic as the fights. Indeed, Tully makes up to Oma in the bar much as he practices his profession in the ring, by "busting [his] head" on a jukebox. He experiences with Oma the same loss of peace of mind that he suffered with his wife. Oma too practices love as if it were a fight, one that she can only lose, especially by winning. She regales Billy with the announcement that Earl "raped me." She then continues, incongruously, "Don't look at me like that. I'm not ashamed to say it. I've never been ashamed of the act of love. I believe it's a part of life." After Faye yields her virginity, she asks, "How was I, compared to the other girls?" Ernie grunts an absent-minded "Okay"; then, trying to make up for his inattentiveness, he further offends her by allowing that "anybody would have thought you had all the practice in the world." (His equivocal compliment recalls Billy's incredulity about Ernie's lack of experience in the ring.)

Anticlimax in *Fat City* turns into self-cancellation. After Billy spends the opening minutes of the film looking for a match, he flicks his unlit cigarette into the gutter. When he goes to the gym to get back in shape, he pulls a muscle after a few minutes, then repairs to a bar. Ruben tells Ernie to pace himself in the ring, reverses his instruction by telling him not to hang back, then tells him again to pace himself. As Jameson remarks, his advice "cancels itself out. There's no advice to give."[16] Compliments can be as self-canceling as advice: "You're the only son-of-a-bitch worth shit in this place," Oma declares to Billy. Having told Ernie at first that "I think you got it, kid," Billy retracts his praise at the start of the last sequence by claiming that "I said to myself then, I said, 'Now there is a guy that is soft in the center.'"

Ernie's softness, his grudging responsiveness to Billy's need (and to Faye's) is rather his strength than his weakness; it is the quality that connects him to other people. The dialogue is deft and resonant in its plainness throughout the last sequence. Words and silence join action and stasis in modeling the contradictions and self-inflicted defeats that lead to Billy's perception that life itself is self-canceling, that it makes a beeline for the drain. At the same time, arriving at this point culminates the discoveries of the film and returns us to the living together without illusion or despair of the opening montage.

"The paths of glory," as Thomas Gray wrote more augustly in the line that gave Kubrick a title, "lead but to the grave."[17] Nonetheless, the washed-up fighter, companioned for the moment by an acquaintance he has just insulted, remains upright despite his vision of the futility of life. In his stubborn instinct to persist – as in the perseverance of a few dozen other Huston protagonists – we see the modest heroism that the director finds plausible and celebrates. The outcomes and ethical centers of films like *Fat City* elevate not defeat, however noble, but survival, however compromised and ignoble.

Boxing serves as the central metaphor of *Fat City*. The brief, limited heroism that it allows, its joy, pain, and capacity to reveal human nature and fate extend beyond the ring to the lives not only of the fighters but also of their companions, wives, managers, and acquaintances. The pleasure and beauty the sport promises its acolytes is evident in the anticipation with which Billy strides to the YMCA, in Ernie's sun-lit approach to the Lido gym, and in the radiance that Ruben brings to his instruction of young boxers. At the same time, Huston does not glide by the pain of prizefighting. The warning associated in Huston's films with mirrors and reflections adds cautionary overtones to the shots of Billy going to the Y, which begin with him reflected in store windows, and those of Ernie arriving at the Lido gym, a mirror on the wall beside the door as he enters. Scarred faces, hemorrhaging kidneys, and mashed noses testify to the inevitable injuries of a sport in which no one can for long avoid opponents' punches and occasional butts. The spectacle of Billy at the end of the picture, for all that his situation exemplifies the human condition, also reflects partly the outcome of his career in the ring. Billy is drifting toward a particular pathos that a young Huston fictionalized thirty years before he made *Fat City*, "that dim hazy heaven, where the boys who liked to take it spend their days."[18]

Billy returns to the ring because he runs out of seasonal day-work and because, as he says, "the job I really like hasn't been invented." In this regard, he resembles the obsolete cowboys of *The Misfits*, with their horror of wages. Although Studlar's view of the film as portraying a symptomatology of what she calls "working-class lives" or "myths of American masculinity" strikes me as excessively specific, her insistence upon an economic dimension has considerable justification.[19] Having been fired or laid off from various jobs, Billy tells Oma, "You know, I guess I'm just going to have to start fighting again." Later he makes the same vow, but Huston immediately cuts to Tully once again in the pre-dawn crowd of agricultural laborers. The rigors of training and fighting are not easy to resume. Nor do they prove lucrative. The economic outcome of his comeback is not much different than that of working in the fields (an activity that Billy assures Ernie is "almost as good as roadwork for gettin' back into shape"). The complaint of one of the onion toppers, "I worked like hell all day yesterday; after they made the deductions, I only had five bucks left!" sounds very much like Billy's complaint about the hundred dollars left him for his bloody fight with Lucero after Ruben's deductions.

The woes and small glories of the fighters represent the constraints and injuries of working with, for, against, and among other people – as we see in fields and cafes as well as in boxing rings. Ruben serves as surrogate father to Billy, giving him advice and forgiveness, and accepting his reproaches. We learn from Ruben that when Billy started losing fights, his marriage broke up; and it is to Ruben that Billy confesses, "Ever since my wife left me, it has just been one mess after another." The festive, noisy crowds in the arenas give the boxers an identity in society, as do the posters that announce Billy's comeback fight. After the matches, Ruben and his fighters and their wives gather with familial warmth. That warmth, however, gradually evaporates when Billy leaves the group to ride back to his room with his manager and then quarrels with him about money and the old grievance of Ruben's having failed to accompany him to Panama for his fight with Fermin Soto.

The most expressive image of boxing as a metaphor of the simultaneous closeness and antagonism between human beings occurs during the fight between Tully and Lucero. The battered, exhausted fighters clinch, their arms wrapped around one another and their faces pressed together. Huston does a quick close-up two-shot: the first over Tully's shoulder of Lucero clutching his opponent with vague, unfocused eyes and mouth slack with pain and fatigue; the second past Lucero's back with Tully's gloves clasping him, blood running from his brow, and his eyes as distant, his face as stoic in exhaustion. Like the last shots of the film, these depict simultaneous intimacy and isolation, people's battles and their needs for intimacy, and the unbridgeable gulfs that separate them even during their most ardent, combative embraces. The combination of ardor and conflict summarizes the paradoxical understanding of human relations that pervades the film.

The heroism of boxing in Fat City is one of tenacity and survival, what André Bazin called the transformation of "life into a stubborn irony at the expense of death."[20] Lucero's pills, blood, acceptance of pain, and dignity as he leaves the arena through darkening halls all display his courage.[21] After his beating, he is showered, composed, striding briskly toward his future. Although Tully is querulous and grubbier, his heroism is no less. When he is smashed to the canvas in the second round, we hear Ruben yelling to him, "stay down, Billy." But he does not stay down, either in the ring or outside it. Nor can he entirely get back on his feet. Against Lucero he fights on, but he is semi-comatose and does not realize that he has won the fight when the referee stops it. "Did I get knocked out?" "No, we won! we won! You won, Billy, you won!" Opposites are both true; Billy was knocked out and he won. Moreover, he is at once "we" and "you." His heroism, Huston suggests with a generosity we may be reluctant to accept, is also ours.

Jameson writes that "characters in *Fat City* achieve a kind of survivalist sublimity," and Huston called them "people who are beaten before they start but who never stop dreaming."[22] As important as their doggedness, however, is their understanding and acceptance of themselves and their situation. Without that, they would be imbeciles or lunatics. They exemplify an existentialist stance that Huston often insisted upon and that Sartre characterized succinctly: "With despair, true optimism begins, the optimism of the man who knows he has no rights and nothing coming to him."[23] Oma, Tully, and the other characters of *Fat City* live such "true optimism."

An unstressed Christian imagery like that in *Let There Be Light* and *The Treasure of the Sierra Madre* also reflects in *Fat City* the optimism of despair. The crosses in the opening montage of Stockton, the crucifix on the wall by Ruben's matrimonial bed, Tully's "Jesus, the waste!," Oma's "Oh Christ, Mary, and Joseph!" directed at Tully – all mildly associate religious faith with human shortcomings. Interestingly, Huston emphatically associated Christianity with boxing in the first story he published in the *American Mercury*. At its conclusion, two young fighters agree that just as they fixed their match, so "Christ and Judas were in cahoots . . . it was all fixed."[24]

Earl declares that Oma's condition as a "juice-head" is "on account of unhappy life an' all that shit. Nothin' I can do about that, so I don't let it worry me none." The blunt acceptance of human injury that he exemplifies, his toleration and decency, are primary ethical values in a film that portrays all people as one way or another afflicted by debilitating pasts and present conditions about which they can do little. As in most Huston films, understanding the truths of our lives, however unpalatable, is prerequisite to good faith and whatever meaningful action may be possible. Characters do what they can for themselves and each other in the hard light of such understanding. In *Fat City* life takes place in the terrible time between yesterday and tomorrow. As Dobbs found in *The Trea-*

sure of the Sierra Madre, what we are alone is not enough; we need each other to make it through the night, the present, with its sorrows and anxieties.

By indirect, inconspicuous gestures as well as more directly, the characters of *Fat City* accommodate each other: the transients of the opening sequences talk peacefully together; wordlessly, a man moves over at the bar so that Oma can sit with Earl; Ruben hesitates, makes sure that Billy can "spare it" before he lets the fighter repay him. Above all, there is the decency of Ernie at the end, his willingness, for all of his desire to get home, "to clap a comradely hand on the shoulder of the man he wishes he could get away from."[25] Huston casts a sympathetic, grateful eye on such kindness, such assent to the truths of ourselves and others, and on the acceptance of mutual human obligations that comprehension brings, almost by default.

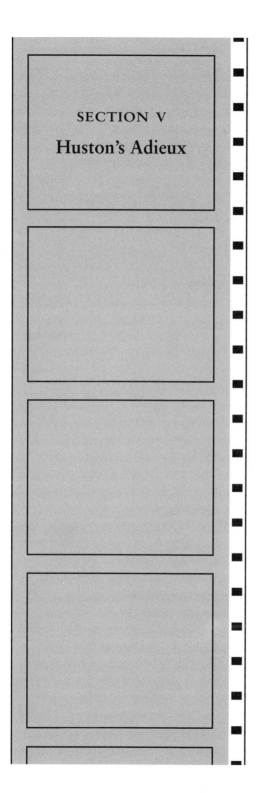

SECTION V

Huston's Adieux

The Dead

An Open Book

The cab carrying Gabriel and Gretta acquires overtones of death.

Commentary on *The Dead* is haunted by scholars of modern literature. As a result, the movie has been little considered except in relation to the revered short story "The Dead" of James Joyce's *Dubliners*. Even Naremore, who elsewhere argues against judging Huston as a straightforward adapter of the fictions of others, takes the lectern as a literary critic claiming his proper territory. "Clearly, *The Dead* wants to be received as a kind of translation, and it solicits the attention of a group of critics (myself included) who are inclined to judge Huston's performance as an interpreter of a known and respected text."[1] The formulation of this statement underscores its implausibility: "Clearly," a word usually signaling that whatever is about to be asserted is anything but self-evident, is followed by a personification of the film. Yet if Naremore is aware of the difficulties of the approach that he takes to this film, few other commentators seem conscious that they may be evading *The Dead* more than engaging it when they consider it primarily as a "translation."[2]

We approach the film with more hope of illuminating it, I think, if we treat it in the same way as the multitude of other movies that adapt literary properties, as a work of art in its own right, to be viewed and interpreted equally by those who know the precedent fiction and those who do not. Striking fidelities to or departures from its literary source offer clues as to what direction one might look, but cannot serve to support interpretations of the movie as do, for example, its cinematography, writing, acting, editing, or design. *The Dead* is not different in this respect from *The Maltese Falcon* or *Reflections in a Golden Eye*.

Indeed, it follows its source scarcely as faithfully as those films do theirs. In terms of divergence from its precedent fiction, *The Dead* resembles pictures like *Moby Dick*, *The Night of the Iguana*, and *Under the Volcano*. Comparison to Joyce's "The Dead" reveals that much of the dialogue of Huston's movie is rewritten and some is added. A crucial character and incident, Mr. Grace and his recitation, are created from whole cloth; also added is the nascent romance between Bartell D'Arcy (Frank Patterson) and Miss O'Callaghan; various existing characters are increased or diminished in importance; significant imagery augments that which already exists in the story.

The Dead stands among Huston's most glorious achievements. Like most of his pictures, it was edited largely in the camera, and nothing is wasted during its immaculately paced hour and a quarter. Its actions and themes are those that dominate Huston's career: hope and disappointment; people facing or avoiding the truths of their lives; vanity, in both senses of the word; passing time; the illuminations of art and ritual; the expressiveness of faces that are at once uniquely themselves and images of all humankind; death; and the communion that human beings share along with the loneliness they cannot escape.

"One is pressed to recall in which of my films the heroes failed, in which they succeeded," Huston said. "Their end doesn't mean much to me. It is the *company* in itself that constitutes an adventure."[3] At the center of the company in *The Dead* is Gabriel Conroy (Donal McCann), next to whom the camera is occasionally placed. He is harried, isolated in the midst of the party, a bit of a snob, and quietly desperate – like the maid, Lily, the first and last person with whom we see him in his aunts' home.

At the end of the film, Gabriel comes face to face with himself. As he gazes at the swirling snow, he understands that he shares with his wife and his community the uneasy present, the motionless past, and the future nonexistence that is the fate of everyone.

Among the images adopted from Joyce's story is that of snow, with which the movie begins and ends. Indeed, the opening shot of *The Dead* quietly sets forth most of the imagery to which the central meanings of the film adhere: snow, horse-drawn cabs, people in groups, and – through the windows – dance. After briefly going into the house, the camera returns to the snowy street, an action that it will repeat during the dinner, again as Gabriel and his wife Gretta (Anjelica Huston) go through snowy roads to their hotel, and finally during Gabriel's internal monologue, the last sequence of *The Dead*.

"Where are the snows of yesteryear?" The traditional association of snow with dissolution intensifies as the film proceeds. The opening subtitle sets the wintry scene in 1904, a time from which none of its characters could have survived to ours. Later the camera goes outside into the snow at the beginning of dinner, then returns through a dissolve that suggests passing time. Snow is visually echoed by a pattern of flecks against a dark background on the dining room walls, and Gretta's story of Michael Furey's death begins, "T'was in the winter, the beginning of winter." In the last sequence, the snow that "is general" over Ireland becomes the central emblem of passing time and death.

Cabs rolling through snowy streets are also associated with time. They usually enter the frame and/or depart before Huston cuts, creating a time-lapse photography effect in which they come and go without leaving much sign of their presence. As the story begins, a cab enters the lower right of the frame just after the date-place title appears; as it exits, the title fades away, disappears like the cab itself. Between the beginning of the feast and dessert, Huston compresses time with a similar shot of another cab entering and leaving the frame. In the first shot of the film, young men and women emerge from cabs. At the end of the party, weary older people mount into one: Mr. Brown, barely awake and unraveling as the hour grows later; the alcoholic Freddy (Donal Donnelly); and Freddy's aging mother, radiant early in the evening but now complaining crossly.

The cab carrying Gabriel and Gretta to their hotel rolls through snow as it acquires overtones of death. In the first shot, it is pulled by a steaming horse that trots obliquely at the camera until it disappears; in the second, we look down on a frame diagonally divided in half: a dark river fills the upper left side of the screen, a snowy road runs along it on the lower right. The cab enters from the right and leaves at the left. Huston then cuts to an arched bridge over the dark water; the cab enters right and leaves from the left once more. The mythological overtones of the dark water and the crossing suggest a journey toward the land of the dead, a suggestion that the final sequence will amply confirm. (A shot tracking the moving cab, which hardly changes position in the frame, expresses the emotional stasis between the husband and wife inside.) Though Gabriel urged his companions not to "brood or stoop to gloomy moralizing," the cab ride from the home of his aunts to the hotel promotes such a shift in his own thoughts and emotions. Metaphorically, it becomes a short journey through time toward death.

Snow falling through the night sounds a visual chord with a set of related images, lights set in various ways against the darkness. The snow and the lights suggest both the passing of time and the brief moments during which people show bright against the background of eternity. Street lights are reflected in the black water of the river. Candles burn down. Three blaze in a candelabra as Mary Jane plays, bracketed by her two aunts at each end of the piano. During her performance, an elaborate camera movement from behind the piano gives the burning candles particular emphasis. At one point, the framing for a close-up of her and Aunt Julia removes one candlestick, so that the remaining two continue the numerical parallel between the two women and the lights. A candle illuminates the lace and cherubs on a bedside table as Aunt Julia sings. Another burns in the hotel room as Gabriel and Gretta undress. Two – one each for her surviving sister and for Mary Jane – occupy the room where Julia lies when Gabriel imagines her death. Later in his soliloquy, Gabriel recalls the images of the candles when he thinks of himself, "transient as they, flickering out. . . ."

The authenticity of set properties and the fashions of costume and hair styles are of particular importance in this film because such details add vividness to its pervasive theme of time passing and past. "Karin, the script supervisor, had never worked with anyone like John, who wanted to know every detail – costume, hair, placement," reports Grobel, writing about work on the set of *The Dead*.[4] Such emblems both recall the past and emphasize its pastness. When the camera leaves the drawing room during Julia's singing and wanders through her memorabilia, traces of her personal history sum up much of the progression of a life and of its hopes, disappointments, and consolations.

Reminders of death are everywhere in *The Dead*, to the extent that a viewer might wonder whether the monks need to sleep in their coffins "to remind them of their last end." "They say you never pass O'Connell Bridge without seeing a white horse," murmurs Gretta. "I see a white man this time," answers her husband, and a subjective shot looks up at a snow-covered statue. Gretta's bit of urban folklore and the white statue invoke another pair of ghosts, Gabriel's "late, lamented grandfather" and his horse Billy, who detoured to walk stubbornly around the statue. A ghostly horse making circles around the statue of a dead king, whether for demented love or from habit, suggests an entropic view of time and events, an emblem of things spending themselves in going around and around until they fall from sight. Gabriel's vision of time in *The Dead* is not regenerative but ironic, leading to "dwindling and dissolving."

The circular movement of dancing in *The Dead* suggests a more ambivalent feeling for time. On the one hand, the dancers express their sociability, grace, and vitality – as they do in a number of Huston's other movies. On the other hand, the rhythmic regularity of their steps, their movement in circles, and the way in which they enter and leave the frame associate them with images of passing time. Dance suggests age approaching death when Gabriel briefly remembers or imagines himself dancing with Aunt Julia just before he pictures her wake. As the camera peers through falling snow at the solitary couple, we hear Gabriel's thoughts: "Soon she'll be a shade too, with the shade of Patrick Morkan and his horse." A few seconds later, the image dissolves to Julia's face in death, laid out "in that same drawing room."

Like dance, music has double associations with life and with mortality. D'Arcy's singing of "The Lass of Aughrim" recalls for Gretta the long dead Michael Furey, who sang the same song; a current production of "Mignon" reminds Mary Jane of a young soprano who died. Her remembrance leads to Mr. Grace's eulogy for the singers of a still earlier generation and to Aunt Kate's affecting recollection of the English tenor Parkinson. But although the remembered singers are gone, they live again in the memories and emotions of those who heard them sing, much as the cafe performers of *fin de siècle* Paris live in the memory and art of Toulouse-Lautrec in *Moulin Rouge*.

When the Clerk leads Gabriel and Gretta up to their hotel room, the camera holds on the staircase for several seconds after they have disappeared and we see three shadows move across the empty stairs, like spirits of the dead moving through spaces they have vacated. Within the hotel room, the shade of Michael Furey is very much present in Gretta's revelation of his love and death. At the same time, the shades of the living couple share the screen through their mirror reflections and as shadows projected on the walls.

The tonalities of the sequences leading to the hotel and within it approach black-and-white. Colors are muted by dim light, by the black and white clothing of Gretta and Gabriel, and by snow, shadow, and night. Within the hotel room, color exists mostly in the couple's skin tones, which contrast with predominantly monochromatic images associated with the hovering past.

Throughout the sequence, Gabriel and Gretta are doubled by their shadows, images that suggest both their own pasts and a future when they, like everyone else, will be shades. In one eloquent shot, Gabriel embraces Gretta and asks her to tell him what is troubling her. She holds him off slightly as she starts to tell him. At the same time, she shifts her head and thereby brings into contact the shadows on the wall behind them. Does this movement suggest that Gretta and Gabriel are coming together in spirit as she begins to reveal her love of long ago? That the married couple had an intimacy in the past that exceeds that of the present? Or does the shadow of Michael Furey replace the husband Gretta holds away? Other interpretations are surely possible, but picking among them is not important. Of significance is the evocation in a single image of past, present, and future, and the remarkable multiplication of meaning and emotional intensity that Huston achieves with the utmost economy of image and word.

A moment later, an equally precise and expressive framing shows Gretta sitting on the bed; as she speaks, her husband's shadow looms behind her on the wall while Gabriel himself, diminished by distance from the camera, stands in front of a mirror in which his image is diminished further. Again, this complex shot suggests a multiplicity of meanings, among which we may include Gabriel's loss of stature because of his faintly threatening behavior, the childish petulance of his body language, and his shrinking presence in his wife's consciousness as she recalls the last weeks of her youthful lover.

Themes of love set against isolation are also expressed throughout *The Dead* by its other figures. The representation of love and conflict between men and women ranges from expressions of sexual cynicism to the matrimonial romanticism in Aunt Julia's rendition of Bellini's "Arrayed for the Bridal"; from the mild antagonism mixed with flirtatiousness that Molly Ivors directs toward Gabriel to the intensity in Mr. Grace's recitation of "Broken Vows" and in D'Arcy's singing. Within all variations, love is to some degree entwined with loss or betrayal. Ultimately, love and loss blend, love drifting toward death and death assuming the voluptuous fascination of love.

The first exchange about love sets a conventional notion of courtship ending in marriage against an equally conventional notion of hypocrisy and sexual predation. To Gabriel's pleasantry about looking ahead to her wedding, Lily retorts, "The men that is now is only palaver, and what they can get out of you!" A less angry but similar characterization of contemporary sexual mores occurs when Mr. Brown observes that the pillows in the cab have doubtless been used "for other purposes, going twice around the park." Not so coarse but hardly more romantic is the joke of one of the young men that "our beds are going to be icy tonight. Be worth getting married just to keep warm."

Somewhere between straightforward sex and idealized amorous passion is the portrayal of the possible start of a romance between D'Arcy and Miss O'Callaghan. When he and she break the wishbone of the goose, her companion significantly says to her, "I hope that we were sharing the same wish." Later they will linger behind the departing guests to talk of birds, in particular the nightingale, which the singer assures Miss O'Callaghan is "not at all" like that drawn in "the ode of Mr. Keats" (presumably a symbol there of "drowsy numbness" or "easeful death"). He sings to her, as he apparently declined to do for the company at large, and the two leave the party together.

Earlier, Aunt Julia performs "Arrayed for the Bridal," which movingly combines its passionate vision of a bride just before her wedding with the reality of the aged singer's decline. "Thirty years ago, I hadn't a bad voice, as voices go," she says in wistful acknowledgment of Mr. Brown's playful condescension and the inebriated praise inflicted on her by Freddy. While Mr. Grace does his recitation, the camera tracks past the faces of four young women, who listen enraptured and will later exclaim, like a chorus, "It was lovely." "I thought it was beautiful!" "Imagine being in love like that." The romantic D'Arcy ventures that "It would make a beautiful song."

But the poem that Mr. Grace reads tells of more than intense love; it is true to the title he gives it, "Broken Vows." It recounts the apparent sexual betrayal of the speaker, to whom a faithless lover has made extravagant promises but from whom he (or she, the sex is ambiguous) has taken everything, including God.[5] Mr. Grace will return to the theme of his poem in a different key when he explodes about "Parnell, betrayed by a woman!" The intensity of love and the devastation of betrayal also constitute the situation of "The Lass of Aughrim," who has arrived at the door of her lover after having been turned out of her home to wander in disgrace with the baby that resulted from "the night . . . we both met together."

The intensity of love and betrayal in Mr. Grace's poem, the aesthetic passion implicitly contrasted with the performer's loss of youth in Aunt Julia's singing, and the sensuality and tragedy of Mr. D'Arcy's song all suggest that love and the anguish of its loss lead to the grave. The sentimental attraction of sorrow as well as amorous joy imply that tragic love is a sublime end; and death itself is enviable, as Gabriel will later assert, when embraced "in the full glory of some passion." Similarly, Miss Furlong describes the loveliness of a current operatic production: "It was so beautiful, I can't describe it. My God, when you hear Rudolpho's aria . . . you hardly want to go on living."

The traditional cast for a story of unhappy love is a threesome, among whom at least one will suffer bereavement. The triad of Gretta, Gabriel, and the memory of Michael Furey becomes visible only at the end of the film. Nonetheless, earlier clusters of three prefigure the cast in the hotel room. Mr. Brown arrives talking of "the three Kings" and their gifts, but presents flowers only to the two sisters, omitting his third hostess. Moreover, he is (banteringly) "quite put out . . . to find out that you've been waiting for somebody other than me to arrive." During Gabriel's speech, he refuses to take "the part that Paris played in ancient times, to choose among them [the three hostesses]." But bringing up the idea is itself labored and odd, as if one must refuse an implicit expectation to choose – an implication reinforced by Gabriel's clichéd "last, but not least" in speaking of Mary Jane. As Gabriel and Freddy escort Mrs. Mallins downstairs, the old woman calls Gabriel "a fine, strong man," then goes on to "wish the same could be said for my Freddy." A little later, the uneasy threesome of Freddy, Mr. Brown, and Mrs. Mallins generates strife when Mrs. Mallins wishes that Freddy "could get away from that man" and Freddy tells their companion to "watch your tongue, Brown, in the presence of my mother." We do not directly see what is perhaps the most significant trio before the final sequence. When Gretta listens with deep emotion to D'Arcy's song, we may recall that he is not performing for her but for Miss O'Callaghan, and that Gretta was earlier unsuccessful in persuading him to sing. In the final sequence, Gabriel will reflectively make another comparison: "To me your face is still beautiful, but it's no longer the one for which Michael Furey braved death."

In addition to groups of three with their traditional power to splinter romantic sexual love, cultural conflicts separate people along broad social lines. England and the Continent are set against Ireland, usually to the disadvantage of the last. Mr. Brown calls Mary Jane's toilet soap "frankincense and myrrh from London's West End," and the galoshes that Gabriel has bought are instantly impressive to Aunt Julia when she learns that they are worn "on the Continent." Gabriel goes bicycling in Europe "for a change and to keep in touch with the languages." In response to Molly Ivors's baiting after he has declined her invitation to tour the Aran Islands, Gabriel declares that "Irish is not my language" and that he is "sick of my own country." Mr. Grace agrees with D'Arcy that the Irish would not have revered Verdi as did the composer's countrymen. Mr. Grace's recitation, a "translation from the Irish by Lady Gregory," is received in startled silence. The first reaction is Aunt Kate's, "It's very strange . . . but beautiful"; followed by Mr. Brown's voice, off camera, "I've never heard anything like it." On the opposite side is Molly Ivors, who not only plans an Irish tour but also accuses Gabriel of being a "West Briton." The separation that her political beliefs creates between her and admirers of English and Continental culture is symbolized by her early departure from the party to attend a "Republican meeting" and by the Irish phrase she offers in parting, "*Beannacht libh!*"

The presence of Mr. Brown raises another distinction among the members of the party, that between majority Catholics and those Mary Jane delicately calls "of the other persuasion." Mr. Brown is bewildered by the rules of the order that Freddy Mallins will be visiting and tries to understand the penance done by the monks for remission of sins of those in the "external, outside world" as "free insurance." It is typical of Huston's dislike of organized religion and its dogmatic differences that he shows the members of the party as clear about little concerning their sects except their power to separate people through labels and antagonisms.

As characters discriminate between Ireland and Britain/Europe so they make a parallel distinction between city and country. Most of the Dubliners look down on the less cosmopolitan people and culture of the western Irish countryside. The first instance of such cultural prejudice arises when Freddy tells Mr. Brown "the latest about old man Gallaher and the young one" whose mother "came up from the farm" with a runt piglet on which her rustic daughter could practice maternal skills before having her own children. D'Arcy characterizes the "brutal" diction of an operatic understudy as being like that of "an auctioneer at a cattle fair." Gabriel's assumption about a disoriented cabbie is not just that he is "not a Dublin man," but that he comes "somewhere from the West of Ireland." In response to Molly Ivors's memory that his wife comes from the

West, Gabriel corrects her defensively, "her people do." City-country comparisons are closely related to class discriminations; when Gabriel wishes to heighten the comic effect of his story about his grandfather, he demotes him from owner of a starch mill to "glue boiler."

Against divisive energies of nationality, city-country antagonisms, personal triangles, or class status are set the unifying influences of social ceremony and art. Most obvious is the dinner party itself, with its dances, its singing of "for they are jolly good fellows," and other congenial rituals. As a subject and a practice, art connects people. Despite some polite disagreements, the discussion of a current opera production and of Dublin's musical past brings the diners together over Mary Jane's memory of "poor Georgina Burns," Mr. Grace's praise of the "old days of Bel Canto," and Aunt Kate's memory of Parkinson's "pure, sweet, mellow English tenor." Even Freddy's claim for "the Negro chieftain" in "the panto at the Gaiety" draws only Mr. Brown's implied dubiety.

The unifying effect of music and recitations derives in part from the pleasure that people share in listening to them, in part from their predisposition to be pleased. For all her technical dexterity, Mary Jane's performance has only modest expressive appeal. Nonetheless, it is applauded enthusiastically, even by the young men who withdraw for a drink during her playing. Great applause greets the flaming pudding, declared by Freddy to be "a work of art." But he praises the ceremony of presentation, not the prospect of eating dessert; a minute later we hear him tell his mother in an undertone that he needs celery to eat with the pudding "to deaden the taste."

Aunt Julia's singing is received with an enthusiasm that becomes painful. Much of the audience's responsiveness, again, comes from its generous predisposition. But this sequence is not the simple spectacle of pathos that most reviewers have described. Although the aged singer's voice no longer has the steadiness or range that the song requires, her remaining technique and the feeling she conveys are considerable. The sentimental irony of an old spinster singing about a young woman's beauty on her bridal day works upon the audience within the film as upon the audience in the movie theater. Her listeners need not wholly manufacture their appreciation. Gabriel's elaborate toast to the three hostesses, similarly, has an effectiveness that is partly attributable to the receptiveness of his audience, partly to the craft of his own performance – despite its often hollow quality – and partly to an inherently moving situation.

Mr. Grace's recitation begins with Aunt Kate's request that he "beguile us yet again," but his performance requires no predetermined responsiveness. The sincerity of Mr. Grace's own enthusiasm is signaled by his taking off his glasses and putting aside his written script a third of the way through the poem. Camera work emphasizes the rapt attention that his audience shares. Shots of the listeners suggest a series of group portraits, and the initial silence and diffident comment that greet the end of the poem testify to its effect. Mr. Grace is the sole major character that Huston and his son Tony, the credited screenwriter, added to Joyce's story; his name underscores the emotional abundance of the poem he introduces.

The developing romance between Bartell D'Arcy and Miss O'Callaghan that the Hustons also added begins during the dancing, gathers impetus during dinner, then leads to the growing intimacy represented by the tenor's private performance. His singing needs no special pleading; Frank Patterson's interpretation is perfectly controlled and expressive. It concludes the party with a marker of the power of art to bring people together and to express their common emotional capacities and needs.

The audience of the film, united in the darkness of a movie theater, becomes an extension of the audiences within the film. Like most titles, those of *The Dead* make self-conscious the experience of the audience as an audience. The opening titles and the closing credits also contribute to the main themes and images of the film that they enclose. In the simplicity of white lettering on a black background, they hardly draw attention to themselves. But the fading in and fading out of the names at the beginning, the Irish harp of the opening titles and the harp and fiddle of the closing ones, and the white words against the dark background anticipate and recall the snow, the subdued lighting and color of sets and costumes, the importance of music to the development of the film, and the theme of human transience with which the story ends – the inevitable fading of all people from "the world itself which they reared and lived in." The final credits extend the imagery and implications of the film into the existential time that follows it.

Although he is a guest and not a host, Gabriel is at the center of the small society that comes together for the party. He bears the burdens of its leading figure. Some social responsibilities come his way by assignment, others through his assuming them. All weigh on him. He is generally regarded as the solution to the problem of Freddy, who is likely to arrive "stewed" and hard to manage. Gabriel makes the speech that is the summation of the festivities. As the evening ends, he takes on the job of getting the drunken Freddy, his cranky mother, and the somnolent Brown into a cab. His responsibilities, moreover, will continue beyond the evening; Mrs. Mallins requests Gabriel to keep an eye on her son when she returns to Scotland.

A faint air of ambiguity attaches to some of his role as presiding male. First, his conversation with Lily brings forth her oddly intimate complaint about men. More notably, his offer to see Molly Ivors home resonates with her earlier wink and flirtatiousness. Does he hope to be alone with her? These mild hints scarcely suggest even fantasies of impropriety, however, let alone acts. We are likely to concur with Gretta's assessment of her husband, that he is "far too responsible" to deviate from the path of duty.

The high spirits that Gabriel briefly displays outside by the cab as he finishes the last of his social chores reflect the degree to which he has been oppressed by his tasks as adult-in-charge. His after-dinner speech – ironically the occasion for giving voice to the group's "true spirit of camaraderie" – especially arouses his anxiety. He repeatedly turns away from the company to consult his notes worriedly, and Huston often photographs him standing alone, the dancing and conversation behind him. His aunts describe him as "lurking in the corridor like a little boy sent out of class."

Feeling more like an outsider than a central member of the party, Gabriel does not much respond to its pleasures. He stands alone looking bored and irritated during Mary Jane's "academy piece" (Joyce's phrase), in contrast to his wife, who listens appreciatively with Mr. Grace. He is untouched by Mr. Grace's recitation, though he leads the audience in polite applause. Again, he is contrasted with Gretta, who is so affected by the end of the poem that she does not join in the clapping; indeed, she appears violated by its conventionality. Bored by the chat of Freddy Mallins and his mother, Gabriel walks away from each of them before they can finish their anecdotes. He seems as weary of the people at the party as he declared himself to be of his country.

Gabriel's self-doubt reappears in his insecurity about his wife. A series of shots of Gretta from her husband's point of view builds toward the revelation of profound loneliness in Gabriel's concluding internal monologue. We typically see Gretta in congenial association with other people, often men. When the camera is not associated with Gabriel's perspective, it views these associations sympathetically; but Gabriel's apprehension of his wife is ambiguous. He admires her beauty and grace; at the same time, he seems uncertain of his importance to her. Gabriel does not see her dancing with D'Arcy (who kisses her hand with some ardor), but he sees her sitting with Mr. Grace and Mr. Brown and dancing with a number of young men. She is also particularly close to the three hostesses, with whom she sometimes joins in female bantering about Gabriel's masculinity. "A fine pair of bellows he has," says Aunt Kate. "Oh, he's a man alright," replies Gretta with amusement.

But Gabriel himself exhibits little confidence about his masculine appeal. When Gretta says that she is thinking "about a person I used to know in Galway," her husband quickly convinces himself that it must be "someone you were in love with," a conviction that expands to the assumption that she is still in love with the unknown someone. Gretta hardly notices Gabriel's jealousy and never confirms his suspicion beyond saying "I was great with him then" – "then" being her late girlhood and "great," one assumes, meaning something like "very close" (almost surely not "pregnant"). Only her revelation that Michael Furey died long ago cancels Gabriel's jealous fantasy about her wanting to go to Galway to see her old lover.

The most important character in *The Dead*, Gabriel may be thought of as a more complex, sympathetic version of Pilot in *The Misfits*. Like Pilot, he is better educated than most of the people around him, more articulate, but self-absorbed and isolated. The clichéd sonorities of Gabriel's speech resemble Pilot's poetic posturings, but Gabriel's rhetoric is less self-serving and less self-revelatory. Although Gabriel's social polish keeps him from appearing antipathetic, he seems to have little esteem either for himself or for his companions. Both he and Pilot look to a woman for self-validation, but neither offers much emotional support in return. Gabriel's self-knowledge and desire to be in good faith, partial as those qualities may be, nonetheless redeem him from the nearly unalloyed egocentricity and anger of Pilot.

Gabriel belongs to a class, of which he is the most sympathetic member, of self-absorbed, emotionally starved figures who crop up repeatedly in Huston's films. The Bette Davis character of *In This Our Life* is the first and perhaps the most exaggerated; we may also include, among others, Rose's brother in *The African Queen*, Marie Charlet in *Moulin Rouge*, the Mother (Lillian Gish) in *The Unforgiven*, several characters in *The Kremlin Letter*, and Albert Finney's Geoffrey Firman in *Under the Volcano*. Huston's regard for Gabriel is greater than for analogous characters in earlier works (with the possible exception of Geoffrey Firman), but the defects and shortcomings of the protagonist of *The Dead* are clear, and we should not mistake Gabriel's consciousness as receiving Huston's endorsement or controlling the dominant meanings of the film. We are encouraged to empathize with his sense of mortality and isolation, but not uncritically.

From the perspective of a camera that is only intermittently identified with Gabriel, the marital estrangement that he admits to at the end is of his own creating and imagining. Indeed, much of the time that we see Gretta and her husband together, they share an amused concord about how to regard the people around them. Gretta is good natured about her husband's officiousness, twitting him affectionately about his worrying over his speech, his well-meaning bossiness with their children, and his insistence that she wear galoshes. While Gretta dances and her husband listens to the chatter of Mrs. Mallins, the spouses exchange understanding smiles, as they do later while Aunt Kate holds forth about what is obviously a hobbyhorse of long riding for her, the ingratitude of the church toward her sister.

The most painful moment between husband and wife occurs when Gretta urges Gabriel to accept Molly Ivors's invitation: "Oh, Gabriel, do go! I'd love to see Galway again!" Gabriel's response is startlingly cold. The framing that follows his chilling reply puts Gabriel on the left edge of the frame and Gretta on the right, and we may remember that he goes every summer on a bicycling tour of the Continent with "some fellows." His yearly vacations evidently do not include his wife. The only other moment of marital discord is mild and stereotypical. Gabriel blames their late arrival on the "three mortal hours" that Gretta spent dressing. If this banter is not as good-natured as hers, it does not seem hostile.

As Gabriel waits to leave, he notices Gretta listening to D'Arcy's song. Alternating shots of him and his wife make clear that those of Gretta are at least partly subjective. Obviously moved, she stands like a Madonna in front of the stained glass on the stair-turning. He looks at her; she looks inside herself. Gabriel's attitude suggests a worshiper, a slightly possessive one, not a partner in mutual intimacy. The song ends and Gretta startles, coming back into the present much as she did at the end of Mr. Grace's recitation or when Lily broke the reverie about old Parkinson by telling her that the pudding was ready to be served. On all three occasions, she is absorbed in thoughts of her own that she must put aside to take up present occupations.

When Gabriel kisses her hand in the carriage on the way to the hotel, she hardly responds. Gabriel looks vexed and releases her hand. Then he tries to break his wife's mood with the story of his grandfather's horse, but his courtship still meets no success, and Gabriel once again looks frustrated. In the hotel room, we see Gretta's reflection in the mirror before Gabriel, a shot that emphasizes the distance between them. Gretta's friendly remark about her husband's responsibility suggests, however, that her distance reflects no anger toward him, as Gabriel seems to assume. "Tell me what you're thinking," he urges her. "Tell me; I think I know what the matter is. Do I know?" The film leaves us to guess what Gabriel supposes "the matter" to be – his abrupt rejection of her desire to go with him to Galway, perhaps? In any event, his approaches to Gretta in the cab (already identified as an erotic venue by Mr. Brown) and in the room suggest an ordinary amorous purpose not hard to imagine given that the couple are without their children and staying in a hotel for the first time in four years.

Gabriel is clearly not expecting Gretta's response, nor does he know how to react to her story, at least after his jealousy becomes irrelevant. He is unable to say anything beyond asking – the question is itself tinged with sexual suspicion – whether Michael Furey went home from the garden (or, by implication, to young Gretta's room). Gabriel does not complete his gesture of stroking his wife's hair as she falls asleep. The source of his restraint is ambiguous: a unwillingness to disturb her or to impinge on her sorrow? A sense of his own inadequacy? His conviction that he is insignificant to her?

However that may be, the end of his evening has not arrived as he hoped or expected; there will be no lovemaking or other intimate celebration of their marriage. As his monologue begins, Gabriel turns his disappointment against himself: "How poor a part I've played in your life. It's almost as though I'm not your husband and we'd never lived together as man and wife." Gabriel's self-deprecation then expands to his sense of insignificance and transience in the universe itself.

This is a complex ending. Gabriel has the last words and the last images of the movie as he looks out the window at the frozen street and the snow, and as he imagines Aunt Julia's death, Michael Furey's grave, and the desolate winter countryside. He becomes at the end of the film a more attractive figure – no longer insisting on his superiority, but sympathetically thinking of his wife and Aunt Julia and facing his mortality. Alone, he appears to acknowledge more deeply his connections to his wife, his aunts, the people of Dublin, his country, and the universe of space and time. If we are thinking of *The Dead* as Huston's meditation on his own approaching death, we will be moved by Gabriel's humility and his solemn eloquence – uncluttered by the rhetorical flourishes of his earlier speech.

But John Huston remained himself to the creative end, and the solemnity of the close of his last film is more skeptical, richer and more delicately balanced, than it at first seems. For Gabriel's isolation and mortality, his loneliness in the face of death that he shares with all humankind, are partly extensions of the stiffness and self-absorption that we have seen throughout the film. His sadness originates not so much in any indifference of his wife toward him as in his own inability to understand a gesture of intimacy that does not have him as its direct object. Indeed, Gretta's narrative extends a gift of self-revelation and trust exceeding what her husband anticipated. "Oh, the day I heard that! That he was dead!" Gretta sobs and casts herself into Gabriel's arms. Her story ends there. Gabriel leaves her asleep on the bed and stands looking out at the snow, finding within himself a desolation to equal the scene before him, despite his "riot of emotions." His most painful thought comes near the end of his meditation, "I've never felt that way myself toward any woman, but I know that such a feeling must be love." From that moment, his reflections all turn to his last end.

Most members of the audience will find within themselves echoes of his resignation. Yet Gabriel's tragedy is not simply the fate of humanity-born-to-die. It is also the tragedy of someone who has lost or never found the comfort of truly embracing other people, among them his wife. The images of the Irish wasteland that he imagines are images of his spirit. Gabriel's memento mori invokes not just a bittersweet melancholy but fear as well for those who waste or turn away from the warmth that people offer each other.

The most frequent object of Huston's camera, Gabriel sometimes establishes its point of view, and occasionally serves as the source of subjective shots – as when he first enters the parlor full of dancers, for example, and when he rises to speak after dinner, and during his closing meditation. But the camera remains mostly independent of both his implied point of view and his direct subjectivity. Generally, indeed, it maintains its independence from any of the characters. With its mobility, energy, and initiative, the camera in effect functions as the central character in the film.

Like the guests, the camera arrives on the street and only gradually enters the house to join the festivities. It goes into the hall, then briefly returns outside. It enters the house a little more fully when it looks down the stairs from behind the two aunts. All the early shots are static and the transitions between them simple cuts; the dollying and panning that will become frequent later in the film begin when the Conroys arrive and the camera tracks Gretta up the stairs. As the film continues, the camera is increasingly immersed in the festivities and the frame progressively fills with partygoers.

Like a character, the camera is frequently blocked by guests who cross in front of it; at one point, it threads its way through dancers, following

Freddy as he goes to his mother. When Mary Jane plays, the camera moves discreetly behind the piano and assumes a closer position from which it photographs the performer and Aunt Julia. Its movement accentuates its presence; a simple cut to a new camera position could equally well have established the shot. When Aunt Julia sings, the camera leaves the room; with it we approach stairs that wind upward, then muse over the memorabilia in what is apparently the singer's bedroom. During Gabriel's speech, the camera passes down the table by means of a crane shot that cannot be identified with any of the characters. It returns with a low-angle dolly that balances the crane shot and that again reflects only its perspective. During the closing monologue, as we have seen, the camera is partly identified with Gabriel; but even then it retains a separate identity, looking at him from outside the window and later tilting up to the snowy sky over the sea. We are likely to apprehend this last shot as coming equally from Gabriel's imagination and from the independent intelligence that has guided the camera throughout the film.

During a televised interview, Huston told Bill Moyers that "the things the camera does are what the eye does also."[6] In *The Dead*, the camera acts more as an eye than as a window. It serves as surrogate for characters and for the audience; but it is also a character in its own right, thinking to look at certain people or things at certain times, implying by choices and juxtapositions its expectations, its way of engaging the world, its personality. We recall Huston remarking that he did not generally wish his audiences to identify with particular characters but "with the picture itself . . . , feeling a fascination for the whole material rather than being emotionally involved with the hero or heroine."[7] For *The Dead*, this formulation needs modification. The "whole material" is presented to us by a camera with which we will identify from its (and our) diffident entrance at the beginning of the evening, through its increasingly frank scrutiny of the people who have gathered and the places they occupy, to its penetration of the mind of the film's central character.

The techniques with which Huston thinks as a camera are at once exquisitely accomplished and inconspicuous. According to Tony Huston, "Dad himself has said about his camera work, 'It's what I do best, yet no critic has ever remarked on it. That's exactly as it should be. If they noticed it, it wouldn't have been any good.'"[8] Like many of Huston's films, *The Dead* depends equally upon sharp montage and the long takes and deep focus of *mis en scène*. It is a motion picture full of motion. When the camera is still and the editing leisurely, the frame is full of moving figures; when the figures are still, the camera moves and the pace of the editing is likely to increase.

The four-hundred-odd shots of the narrative average about eleven seconds, but very few individual shots are of average length. Huston's sense of rhythm is evident in the lively, varied pacing of the narrative and in the cinematography and editing. The greater part of running time is occupied by long takes, often sustained through multiple camera movements. Occasional sequences, usually associated with moments of narrative excitement, are constructed of many images and rapid cutting. The first flurry of quick cuts occurs when the aunts mistakenly think that Freddy has arrived; the excited pace of the editing imitates the excitement of the characters. During Mary Jane's *molto allegro* piano piece the editing is also rapid. During Mr. Grace's recitation, cutting rhythms are varied, reflecting his performance. Aunt Kate's diatribe against the ingratitude of the church is accompanied by a multiplicity of images rapidly succeeding one another, like her words. The sequence in the hotel room begins with a long take of three and a quarter minutes and five camera movements. It gives a transparency to Anjelica Huston's account of Michael Furey, conveying a sense that we are observing the scene without rhetorical mediation. The last shot of *The Dead*, a tilting of the camera up from snow-covered rose vines, past hills to the sea beyond, and finally to a heaven full of clouds and snow, recalls the posthumous vision of clouds over the ocean that concludes *A Walk with Love and Death*.

The importance of "the *company*," of humans finding their identities in relation to other people and to society as a whole, is reinforced by Huston's camera work. *The Dead* often looks like a photo essay, with compositions that not only frame people, but in which people frame each other. His camera creates as well as records the community of the film. The depth of characterization in *The Dead* comes largely from visual data, from group and individual cinematographic portraiture and from the frequent tracking and cutting that rearranges figures into different clusters and shows them from different angles. These constant reframings are achieved both by the sort of camera movement that accompanies Gabriel's speech and by cutting among different angles, as during earlier conversation at the table.

The company of *The Dead* is united in part, as Gabriel says, by "thoughts of the past, of youth, of changes, of absent friends that we miss here tonight." At the thematic center of the film is a series of meditations upon loss and the passing of time. Lap-dissolves, conventionally, signify movement in time; they occur infrequently but to powerful effect. Huston dissolves from the table to the snowy street, then back to the table to compress the progress of the dinner. The shot to which he returns, the stripped skeleton of what we earlier saw as a fat roast goose, has characteristic Hustonian aptness and wit. After Gabriel's speech, another dissolve winds the party down to the departure of the guests.

The first dissolves of the film occur after the camera has left the room in which Julia is performing. While her singing continues on the sound track, seven successive dissolves among Julia's personal mementos serve to compendiate her life in lyrical synecdoche. From porcelain angels, a vase, and a candlestick on a lace-covered table (which we may take as the present), the image gives way to a slow pan down a needlework sampler dated 1865. The first dissolve of the film thus carries us not forward in time but thirty-nine years backward. From that point, the images progress forward through objects that emblematize Julia's lifetime. The sampler is succeeded by an old-fashioned framed photo of a man in a uniform (Julia's father?) with two metals on ribbons neatly before it. A precise match-dissolve to another photo showing three young women (Julia and sisters?) gives way to a third photograph of a young married couple with a baby (Mary Jane and her parents?). Then back to another piece of needlework, embroidered with a verse that reflects what may be the desire of middle age to cope with impatience and disappointment: "Teach me to feel another's woe, / To hide the fault I see; / That mercy I to others show, / That mercy show to me." Next appears a collection of porcelain and glass slippers, traces of Cinderella that resonate sadly with the singer and her song. The camera finally dissolves to a crucifix with beads resting on what is evidently a prayer book or volume of Scripture, a suitable emblem for Julia's present old age. Since no more time remains to travel, Huston simply cuts back to Aunt Julia finishing her song.

Similar camera work and editing are also of great importance at the conclusion. Huston's visual art at once reveals the interior of Gabriel's mind and heart (as do Gabriel's words) and maintains a point of view outside him. (The camera thus imitates the double perspective of Joyce's prose.) The dissolve that begins the final sequence in the hotel room has the conventional signification that time has passed. Those during Gabriel's internal soliloquy, however, first move him imaginatively back in time to his memory of dancing with Aunt Julia; then to the future with images of her wake; and finally back to the present in which he contemplates his own transience.

"Snow is falling. Falling faintly in that lonely churchyard where Michael Furey lies buried. Falling faintly through the universe and faintly falling, like the descent of their last end, upon all the living and the dead." As Gabriel thinks, the camera shows a leafless, twisted tree, then cuts to an extreme close-up of twined, ice-covered rose vines. From the snowy ground it slowly tilts up past a hilltop to reveal the sea beyond, then the horizon. Finally ground and sea disappear and the camera fixes on the sky, from which random snowflakes fall toward and past the lens. A few seconds later, the film ends with a rapid dimming of the screen to black, its first fade.

The image of falling snow replicates a subjective shot earlier in Gabriel's meditation, but the shots of tree, rose thorns, hill, sea, and sky are at once true to his thought and specific to themselves – unimaginable but for the camera that renders them visible. The sense of a filmmaker both within and outside his subject typifies the emotional and formal balance that Huston consciously sought in most of his films. It also typifies an artist fully involved with the humanity that provides his themes. Huston's last images as a filmmaker recall those that mark his career almost from the beginning: faces that maintain their mystery as much as they reveal emotions; a lovely countryside, inscribed by people but finally offering them no favoritism among living things; the sea; the sky; and flecks of light against a darkness that will finally assume dominion, both at the end of the film and at the end of life.

Huston wrote of motion pictures: "all those shots, cut together, . . . the past on the winding reel; the present on the screen; the future on the unwinding reel. . . ."[9] The last reel of *The Dead* is John Huston's last last reel. No footage remains to unwind. The artistic and intellectual adventure of his forty-six years of directing films concludes with darkness and with a conventional tribute to the community that every film memorializes, from stars through gaffers and assistant cameramen to accountants, interns, and caterers. "The actors, crew, technicians – all are caught up in the little planetary system, which one day simply comes to an end. Suddenly it's over, and you can never go back to it."[10]

If we see Gabriel as a surrogate for Huston, we must also see as an emblem for the director the camera soaring outward from his mind into the universe. Another emblem is the community of Dublin, of Ireland, and of the world that is both within and beyond the isolate Gabriel. Wonderfully independent in both his life and his creations, Huston was also in the abundance of his gifts and energy a genius in an art that is the joint creation of a multitude of collaborators, of production companies, of literary and cinematic traditions, and of audiences. Like the understanding of humanity that his films embody, Huston was at once himself alone, "nobody's man," and humankind in its incarnation of past, present, and future.

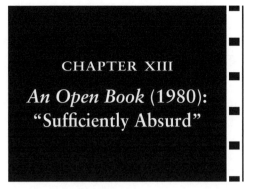

CHAPTER XIII

An Open Book (1980): "Sufficiently Absurd"

Writing to the publisher Simon and Schuster in 1972, Huston proposed an autobiography, "a book with a unique approach. . . . The closest I know would be Gertrude Stein's autobiography of Alice B."[1] Eight years later, *An Open Book* appeared from Alfred A. Knopf under its prestigious Borzoi imprint. In the meantime, in 1977 Gerald Pratley had published *The Cinema of John Huston*, a brief survey of Huston's life and films through *The Man Who Would Be King* and *Independence* ('75), incorporating reminiscences and introductory remarks about the pictures by their director. Pratley's book may possibly have stimulated the completion of Huston's, but *An Open Book* shows almost no trace of the earlier work. On one occasion, speaking of Humphrey Bogart's determination to make *Beat the Devil*, Huston told Pratley, "That stiffened my back," a phrase that he repeats in the same context in *An Open Book*.[2] Such echoes occur with extreme rarity, however, probably no more than half a dozen times in the autobiography. *An Open Book* represents a far more carefully crafted and complete work than the casual remarks Huston made for Pratley. Heavily reworked early chapters and revisions of late drafts and galley proofs in the Herrick Library collection testify to the consideration Huston devoted to his memoirs.

A detailed index identifies one audience to which *An Open Book* is directed: readers seeking factual detail about the circumstances of Huston's life and filmmaking or about the myriad luminaries with whom he worked and socialized. On the other hand, the publishing agreement between Huston and Knopf suggests that we should exercise caution about regarding *An Open Book* as an entirely reliable source of information. The standard contract has one phrase provocatively lined out: "that all statements contained therein purporting to be facts are true."[3] Nonetheless, much of what Huston relates in *An Open Book* can be confirmed by other accounts, and I believe that the overwhelming majority of its "facts are true." If Huston sometimes seems larger or livelier than life, that impression comes from the extraordinary places and people he was associated with and the extraordinary energies and talents he possessed. He probably was, indeed, an unusually concentrated, energized version of a human being.

In discussions of Huston's films I have cited much of the information that his autobiography provides about specific pictures and Huston's picture-making in general, so I will not be repeating that material here. Nor does *An Open Book* provide a basis to suppose that one can fully understand "John Huston the man." Too much is missing – most of what we would call Huston's private life, for example. But *An Open Book* offers the opportunity for another view of John Huston the creator. It supplements and enriches what we see in his films and confirms their main thematic and aesthetic tendencies. Like his movies, *An Open Book* rotates and recombines clusters of fundamental images and ideas: death and its (partial) antidote, love; community; the animals and landscapes of the natural world; the homes that people find or make; the entertainments, glories, and ironies of striving when the inevitable end of any enterprise is not "forever after" but "nevermore."

Not counting the index, *An Open Book* consists of 371 pages of text illustrated by several groups of photographs and divided into thirty-seven chapters. The succession of chapters recalls the succession of episodes in Huston's films. A very short opening, three pages, is followed by a series of evenly paced chapters that establish a sort of basal rhythm. Chapters 2 through 14 average fourteen pages, and only two diverge from that length by more than three pages. The tempo established, the remainder of the book varies it: of the next twenty-three chapters, only a few have close to fourteen pages. As *An Open Book* moves to its conclusion, its scenes, like those of a film, shorten, with a single exception that emphasizes by contrast the quick pace of the remaining chapters. The last seven chapters have six, five, four, sixteen, six, four, and four pages – fast cutting at the end.

The chapters themselves unfold like acts in a play. Most are composed of a number of episodes – or occasionally a single one – that build to a resolution or summarizing irony. The unity of the chapters is thematic, narrative, or both. Chronology has an important role, but it is often secondary within chapters, while it organizes the broad sequence of the chapters themselves. Though Huston did not do so, it is easy to assign descriptive titles to many of his divisions. Doing that for chapters 22 through 25 gives some sense of how they are organized: 22, "*Beat the Devil* and Bogie"; 23, "Making *Moby Dick, Heaven Knows, Mr. Alli-*

son, and *The Barbarian and the Geisha*"; 24, "David O. Selznick"; 25, "Going to Africa for *The Roots of Heaven*."

The eye and ear of the painter, dramatist, and filmmaker shape Huston's prose. Dialogue is crisp and telling. Huston's recollections often take the form of verbal sketches. Two Army experiences, for example, are rendered in striking visual imagery. The first describes the funeral of a pilot.

The coffin with the pallbearers materialized out of the fog, and the ghostly ceremony began. The chaplain commenced the service with: "In my Father's house are many mansions . . ." and with those words the fog lifted. In the background I could see a smoking volcano, widely scattered thunderstorms and, finally, a half-dozen rainbows. (p. 94)

The second occurs outside of San Pietro, during the Italian campaign.

We moved up through the area of attacks and counterattacks, and I have never seen so many dead as on that day. It had rained during the night. We saw machine-gun emplacements, guns and equipment clean and glistening, with ammunition shining in the early-morning sunlight, while all around were the dead. (p. 111)

The dominant motifs of *An Open Book*, like many of Huston's films, consist of variations on themes of what might be called "equivocal success" or "fulfilling failure." Concluding chapter 1, Huston observes that he has but a single recurrent dream, one in which he is "ashamed of being broke and having to go to my father for money." It doesn't make much sense, he suggests: "Why, then, should I have that dream in which I feel weak, dissolute, and shiftless? It doesn't match up with anything, symbolically or otherwise. It's a random dream" (p. 5). At the beginning of chapter 37, the last, Huston tells a joke on himself in which he naively handles a deadly sea snake to show a man and his young son that it is harmless. A few days later, he learns that "The snake I picked up is related to the cobra, only more venomous. . . . Although I am well pleased it [being bitten] didn't happen, I cannot conceive of a more appropriate end for yours truly – sufficiently absurd in both the existential and purely comic senses." (p. 371)

Despite Huston's playful denial that the dream has any significance, these bracketing anecdotes summarize much of *An Open Book*. The dream matches up with a great deal, actually. Not only does Huston acknowledge having been broke and improvident more than a few times, but the most common stories in *An Open Book* are of ironic failures, episodes of reversed or thwarted expectations, and death. Huston knows that we remain childishly helpless and culpable at some psychic level. In an early draft, he wrote, "not all that deeply below the surface we are very similar one to another."[4] Everyone feels "weak, dissolute, and shiftless."

The anecdote of the snake is equally revealing. The absurd in a "purely comic" sense permeates *An Open Book*. We misread Huston's autobiography, just as we misconstrue his movies, if we are oblivious to his pervasive playfulness, irony, and sense of comedy. Existential absurdity is also of pervasive importance; the universe lacks transcendent meaning, coherence, or value. Huston's insistence on the absence of pattern in his life and art exemplifies his existentialist cast of mind. "My life is composed of random, tangential, disparate episodes," he writes just before telling about his "random dream." "I fail to see any continuity in my work . . . nor can I find a thread of consistency in my marriages" (p. 5).

But the episodic, frequently repeated, generates its own consistency, its own patterns. "The picture-maker's life is subdivided into many lives," the director observes (p. 263). Huston's childhood was also subdivided into many childhoods: a home first with both parents, then his mother and grandmother, then his mother and her second husband, then increasingly with his father. He also traveled back and forth between his divorced parents, setting a pattern for the nomadic personal and professional life that he would follow as an adult.

An existentialist sense of the absurd can lead either to despair and spiritual surrender or to the affirmative "leap of faith" espoused in Sartre's ethics or Camus's fiction. Huston's autobiography has closer affinities with the affirmative response. Its ironies are illuminating and even reassuring. The shadow that hung over Huston's childhood for two years – when he was misdiagnosed as condemned to early death by Bright's disease – led him to a *carpe diem* in the face of the void that would define his posture toward life and art. "I had overheard enough of Mother's conversations with the specialists to know that I was doomed. I said to myself, 'Well, if that's so, I'm going to swim in the canal before I die!'" (p. 20) The diagnosis and treatment were in error, but Huston grew up to know that the final diagnosis is the same for everyone: we shall die. His existentialist art responds as did the child, "Well, if that's so, I'm going to . . ."

Such an orientation toward life, however affirmative, carries within it the knowledge that all existences end with what Wallace Stevens called "death's ironic scraping." Huston's high spirits are a form of bravery. Although the tone of *An Open Book* is rarely tragic or even sad, the majority of its chapters nonetheless end on notes of irony, failure (usually Huston's), or death.

Misfortunes and mistakes with his movies figure prominently. Huston recounts ill-judged interventions by studio executives after he had made his final cut of *The Red Badge of Courage* and complains of the disastrous reworking by John Wayne of *The Barbarian and the Geisha* after the director had left what he thought was the final version with the producer. Losing battles with studio executives after the filming of *Freud* and its failure at the box office are especially dismaying. Huston faults his own bad judgment in going ahead with *The Roots of Heaven* and *The Mackintosh Man* ('73) when he lacked strong screenplays, and in making a film that he did not finally believe in, *The Unforgiven*. He persuaded Ray Stark, the producer of *The Night of the Iguana*, to let him make the picture in black and white, but "Looking back now, I think I was probably wrong" (p. 309).

Huston had many close and durable relationships with women during his life, but he also acknowledges and takes responsibility for those that withered: the break-up of his first marriage because of his affairs and Dorothy's alcoholism; and the dissolution of the next one when he "was not sufficient to the occasion" of Lesley's depression following her loss of a premature infant (p. 85). Nor can he protect his mother from death; when she goes to surgery for a brain tumor, he assures her that "They can fix it." But "They gave her an injection and took her up to surgery. She never regained consciousness" (p. 77). Unable to wait for Marietta Tree to sort out her feelings for her husband, Huston impulsively marries Evelyn Keyes only to learn a few weeks later that Marietta, with whom he was deeply in love, had decided to get a divorce. Other missteps with women are less painful: a severe case of diarrhea turns an assignation with "a minute red-head named Lennie" into "another of life's darkest moments" (pp. 105–6), and Huston compounds the "financial disaster" of his divorce from Evelyn with a losing coin flip that costs him his half of his collection of pre-Columbian art.

But failure need not be regrettable. Accepted with good humor, it may be a salutary reminder of the limited power that one has over life. "The best men," writes Huston, "tend to think of themselves as failures" (p. 336). And Huston tends to think of the people he admires, everyone who strives, as failures of a sort. For the sake of the painter who "furnished the foundation of whatever education I have," Stanton MacDon-

ald-Wright, Huston writes, "I wish I had done better because of him"
(p. 29). MacDonald-Wright himself apparently had only modest success
as a painter during his lifetime and in his old age "felt like a nuisance"
and occasionally contemplated suicide (p. 29). As to Huston, his one re-
curring dream is of weakness and inadequacy.

The exemplar of comic irony in *An Open Book*, as for many other aspects of his son's life, is Huston's father Walter. As an inexperienced
young engineer of the power and water company of Nevada, Missouri,
he made a mistake that apparently led to a catastrophic failure of water
pressure and the destruction by fire of half the town. One of his first attempts at acting ended with forgotten lines and his dismissal as an "id-
iot." Only temporarily daunted, Walter Huston went on to a distinguished professional career and "later became a close friend of people
like Bernard Baruch, George C. Marshall, Arturo Toscanini and Franklin
D. Roosevelt. If ever there was a caterpillar who became a butterfly, it
was my old man" (p. 13).

Another comically hapless relative was Walter's brother, Huston's Uncle Alec. After getting drunk and disgracing himself at a costume party,
he loses the claim check for his overcoat and has to walk from 43rd to
14th Street dressed as Louis XVI and followed by jeering urchins. Back
at his apartment, he discovers that a running tap has ruined the property of his downstairs neighbor. All he can offer as compensation is an overhead projector that he designed. Huston imagines him demonstrating his
invention, undaunted by recent misfortunes, "animated by the same enthusiasm and faith he has shown from the beginning. Infinitely sad and
funny" (p. 40).

Most stories of comic failure cast Huston himself as the antihero. At
the beginning of his career as a maker of documentary films for the Army,
he "supervised the operation [himself] so there would be no slip-ups."
The first attack and its recording is "a marvelous success" – except that
the film sent to the lab proves to be blank. Huston forgot to run out the
leader in any of the cameras (p. 92). From that start, however, he goes
on to make *San Pietro* and *Let There Be Light*, as well as *Report from
the Aleutians*.

When his wife fails to place the huge bet he instructed her to make on
a horse that wins at long odds, an enormously expensive exercise of her
initiative, Huston is determined to "show a little class." He tries to take
the loss graciously. "What is there to say, Evelyn? These things happen."
But she persists in trying to explain her error and finally Huston, having
lost "so damned much money that it made me sick to think about it,"

explodes. "And there went my whole image of myself. There went Gentleman John" (pp. 138–9).

He is extravagantly praised as a writer by H. L. Mencken; but the only witness to this triumphant moment is a "beautiful but distractingly innocent and simple" young woman who has no idea who Mencken is. Another unappreciated moment of glory is enshrined in *The Bible . . . In the Beginning*, when Huston as Noah leads the animals onto the Ark. "No one, including the Italian animal trainer, believed it possible." But the director persists, trains the animals himself, and the shot comes off perfectly. Nonetheless, like Mencken's encomium, this triumph passes unregarded: "I never heard a regular theater audience applaud this scene. . . . After all, everybody knows that animals always walk into an Ark two by two" (p. 319).

The grandfatherly advice with which Huston ends *An Open Book* amounts to a catalogue of his most egregious mistakes. His attitude toward these and most of his errors and omissions is probably best emblematized by another story about his father. "It had been his dream all of his life . . . to perform Shakespeare on the stage." Finally, Walter stars in a production of *Othello* that is an enormous success in Central City, Colorado. Robert Edmund Jones agrees to direct and produce it in New York, but there the reviews are bad. Full of trepidation, Huston takes the papers to his father's hotel.

[J]ust as I was about to knock, I heard laughter from inside. "Well," I thought, "he won't be laughing when he sees these! I was glad that at least I would be on hand when he read them. As I entered, I saw the papers strewn all over the floor. He was laughing at the reviews! He was laughing at himself! All those years of work and planning that had gone into his *Othello* . . . down the drain! This was to have been his definitive performance. The joke was on him. Pretty soon he had me laughing too. (p. 184)

One can see where at least part of the inspiration for the end of *The Treasure of the Sierra Madre* originated – and why Walter Huston was precisely the right actor to deliver Howard's Olympian laughter.

Death, everyone's ultimate and inevitable failure, is treated in *An Open Book* like other important events, as a triumph or defeat chiefly in relation to how it affects the human community of those who die and those whom they leave behind. The saddest deaths, for Huston, make estrangement permanent. John Gore, Huston's maternal grandfather, angered Huston's mother by entertaining her former husband and his new wife. Instead of her usual Christmas gift of fine neckwear, Huston's mother, "full of spite, . . . purchased six cheap, vulgar neckties and sent them to him with the price tags attached" (p. 15). After she remarried, "Mother lost track of her father." Later she learned of his death and went to arrange his burial. An alcoholic, he died in a cheap hotel, leaving only an empty whiskey bottle and "two telescope cases full of raincoats, which he had been selling door to door. In a corner of one of the cases Mother found six cheap neckties, with the price tags still on them" (p. 16).

Huston was supposed to direct *A Farewell to Arms* for David O. Selznick, but the collaboration ended in a series of disagreements. A year or so later Huston declined to attend a party at Selznick's house, telling Selznick's wife, Jennifer Jones, that he was still angry but that he would "'get over it one of these days. Then if you still want me, I'll come.' Not long after that, David was dead" (p. 273). For Darryl Zanuck, Huston made what he regarded as a rather vacuous film, *The Roots of Heaven*, a failure he felt to be his own fault. He wishes that he could make up an injury to a friend by remaking the movie, "with Darryl. But that's impossible because he died the other day" (p. 282). When the choice is between doing an injury that death might make irremediable and accepting a wrong, Huston chooses the latter unhesitatingly. After Buddy Adler, the producer of *The Barbarian and the Geisha*, allowed John Wayne to spoil the picture in post-production, Huston "would have taken legal steps to have my name removed from the picture, but learned that Adler was terminally ill with a brain tumor. Bringing suit under such circumstances was unthinkable" (p. 267).

If death can make of rifts permanent estrangements, it can also bring people together. Dying, after all, is what we all must do, and sharing that fate with grace and affection fastens the bonds of our common humanity. When Humphrey Bogart was near death from throat cancer, he continued to entertain his closest friends every evening, although doing so meant having himself hauled downstairs and back up in a dumbwaiter. After getting over the initial shock of Bogie's emaciation, Huston writes, "one quickened to the grandeur of it, expanded and felt strangely elated, proud to be there, proud to be his friend, the friend of such a brave man" (p. 250).

Huston's Aunt Margaret spent her last months with her second husband, Bobby, in a beloved place where she could watch the fall leaves turn. "It was an enchanted period. . . . 'It was Margaret at her best,' Bobby said. And it was also a wonderful and enlightening period for him" (p. 41). On his deathbed, Huston's Uncle Alec feigns expiration by holding his breath in order to avoid talking with a boring second cousin.

"Phoeme came back in and Alec opened his eyes and grinned. He died a few days later" (p. 149). Carson McCullers's visit to Ireland, like Margaret Carrington's last months on the East Coast, may have shortened her life, but Huston does "not regret arranging it. It was a fulfillment for her. She saw it as a liberation" (p. 335).

The deaths of the soldiers whom Huston saw in World War II are tempered by their valiant esprit de corps and by well-tested words of consolation, such as these from one commander: "'Keep going in a straight line. And if someone plucks your sleeve and you look around and he's got a long white beard . . . why you'll know you haven't another care in this sad world'" (p. 93).

Finally there are the consolations of art and ceremony, the profoundest assertions of human community at the end of life. Among such consolations in *An Open Book* are several renderings of funeral tributes and a remarkable account of an American Indian ritual.

The sand painting was for a young girl. Before sunset she was brought in, and the shaman indicated she was to sit beside the painting. Her velvet top was removed. She was about eleven or twelve and her little breasts were just budding, while her ribs showed in stark outline. The shaman and his helpers began to sing. Then, using two fingers, the shaman daubed her torso with the various earth colors. You could see that she was dying of tuberculosis, against which the Indians had little or no resistance, but her great eyes were shining and she smiled happily as the "sing" went on. When the sun was down, the sand painting was destroyed. (p. 59)

Art does not transcend death or transform it into immortality. Rather, it draws people together in the communion of beauty. Furthermore, although the sun goes down and the painting is effaced, Huston also writes that "Every morning is a new creation – something now and forever" (p. 320). As one of the director's favorite books preaches, "To everything there is a season, and a time to every purpose under the heaven/ A time to be born and a time to die. . . ." (Ecclesiastes 3:1–2).

Huston's understanding of the power of death, the melioration of art, and the warmth of human bonds partly accounts for his fondness for practical jokes. Half a dozen of the chapters of *An Open Book* end with stories of jokes, of which Huston is usually the last butt. Like more lasting and formal art, jokes imitate the ironies of life, but they reduce the consequences and shift power from "the Lord or fate or nature" to a human agency. The end of a joke, moreover, typically implies recognition of the shared weakness that unites all people. Most of the jokes involve a degree of pain or threat: the substitution of thrushes for doves in Huston's game bag to make him think that he is losing his sight; Huston's unforgiven laughter after the mud-bath inflicted on his fourth wife Ricki by a rolling horse; the mob enforcer outside his father's dressing room who proves to be Jack Dempsey. Huston's account of a hoax perpetrated on Eliot Elisofon ends with the director's understanding that it has occasioned too much anguish: "Suddenly Eliot smiled. It was like the sun coming up. He said, 'It's a joke! It's a joke!' . . . I wished he had punched me instead" (p. 217).

Evading catastrophe must be assigned to good fortune, since such escapes are finally beyond human capacity. A jealous neighbor of Huston's lifelong friend Suzanne Flon points a revolver at him and pulls the trigger, but the cartridge mysteriously fails to explode when the firing pin hits it. Filming *Moby Dick* at sea, Huston heeds the advice of his script girl Angela Allen to call three extras down from the masts of the *Pequod*. "Just as the last man hit the deck, the three masts went. . . . if I'd called the men down a moment later, they would have fallen to the deck some ninety feet below or been thrown overboard. Either way, we would have lost them" (p. 256). Such narrow escapes are not uncommon in *An Open Book*. They reflect a sense that life itself is a close call, a lucky abundance that one can neither take for granted nor control. Huston would have endorsed the view of another famous filmmaker, Stan Brakhage, who remarked, "It's all a gift – a gift of life and a gift of light, which are really one and the same."[5]

"The sources of bad luck," on the other hand, "reside in the unconscious. We inflict it on ourselves as a kind of self-punishment" (p. 68). This understanding runs through Huston's account of his life. The motivation of the "steps going down" for Huston in England after he loses his job and sends Dorothy back to the United States originated earlier. At the beginning of the 1930s in Hollywood, his marriage broke up, his (now lost) screenplay on P. T. Barnum was rejected, and he suffered an auto accident in which a pedestrian was killed and Huston became fodder for the press. "I felt like a fighter who has been tagged . . . going deeper into that darkness" (p. 63). Huston does not tell us that his youthful Hollywood mistakes and misfortunes led to the collapse of his life in England, he simply shows it happening. Like other deft story-tellers, he leaves many inferences about causality to his readers.

As the disintegration of Dobbs in *The Treasure of the Sierra Madre* shows, an evil fate originates not in our stars but in ourselves. Such fates, when they plague Huston in his filmmaking, as often as not stem from some error of his own – or even from presumption like Danny's in *The Man Who Would Be King*. Record-breaking storms off England made *Moby Dick* terribly difficult, dangerous, and expensive to film. Eventually Huston realizes that the source of the foul weather "was only God. . . . The picture, like the book, is a blasphemy, so I suppose we can just lay it to God's defending Himself when He sent those awful winds and waves against us" (p. 231). Huston explains a series of misfortunes during the making of *The Unforgiven* as the result of bad faith. After he agrees to "stick it out, thus violating my conviction that a picture-maker should undertake nothing but what he believes in . . . everything went to hell. It was as if some celestial vengeance had been loosed upon me for infidelity to my principles" (p. 283).

Fidelity to principles and fidelity to persons are much the same. Huston's famous fistfight with Errol Flynn comes about when the actor says "something wretched about someone – a woman in whom I'd once been very interested and still regarded with deep affection."[6] Indeed, Huston's personal and professional history in *An Open Book* is chiefly an account of relationships. Some flower then decay, like that with Gregory Peck, or that with his childhood companion in pyrotechnics, whom he joins in a series of explosive pranks that end with Huston's being sent off to military school. Back in public school, Huston attends a play at another high school and "became enamored of the heroine"; several years later, she was to be Huston's first wife. The eventual unraveling of that marriage in no way embitters him or reduces the memory of his happiness: "As a result of that euphoric experience, I recommend young marriages to everyone" (p. 48).

About painting Huston writes, "Nothing has played a more important role in my life" (p. 26). Painting too, reveals a world of people to Huston, who still recalls the names of the members of the Art Students League, which took him in as a "seventeen-year-old kid." In particular Val Costello, MacDonald-Wright, and Morgan Russell loom large in Huston's memory. They remain in his life and consciousness for the next fifty-seven years.

Theater exists as another world of people. When his father is cast in *Desire Under the Elms*, Huston spends weeks watching O'Neill and Robert Edmund Jones at rehearsals. "What I learned there . . . would serve me for the rest of my life" (p. 33). As a young director, Huston very much wanted to bring to the stage O'Neill's *A Moon for the Misbegot-*

ten for the New York Theatre Guild, but Warner Bros. refused to release him for the required time. Decades later, Robert Edmund Jones was to become Huston's uncle when he married Walter's sister Margaret.

"I read without discipline," reports Huston, "averaging three to four books a week, and have since I was a kid" (p. 361). He cultivated friends with the same promiscuous enthusiasm he had for books. His autobiography is predictably full of the names of famous movie stars, directors, screenwriters, and executives, and the names of the famous in other fields also glitter like sequins through *An Open Book*: George Gershwin, heavyweight champions Jack Johnson and Jack Dempsey, Frank Lloyd Wright, Diego Rivera, Billy Pearson, Ernest Hemingway, Aly Kahn, Paul de Kruif, E. E. Cummings, Flannery O'Connor, Frank Sinatra, Baron Philippe de Rothschild and his wife Pauline, John Steinbeck.

But Huston's most important companions generally have less well known names. Gladys Hill remained with him as his professional and personal assistant and his collaborator on screenplays from 1960. After her arrival at St. Clerans, Ms. Hill "took over my life, including the parts that don't bear scrutiny" (p. 228). By 1980 Huston's life was also in the hands of "a Mexican girl in her twenties, Maricela . . . [who] runs everything, including me. There would be no Las Caletas [Huston's last home] without her" (p. 4). The opening credits for *The Dead*, the only film Huston ever dedicated, end with "for Maricela."

A person of steadfast independence both personally and professionally, Huston trusts himself and therefore trusts other people. The filmmaker who said, "I court accident" is congruent with the person who entrusts his personal and professional affairs to Gladys Hill and Maricela; and with the director who declares that actors, "given time and freedom . . . will fall naturally into their places, discover when and where to move, and you will have your shot" (p. 366). Even as horseman and fox hunter, Huston extends the confidence he felt in himself to his equine collaborators. "When things are desperate with you and your horse," he counsels, "throw your reins away and take a handful of mane. Leave it up to the horse. Give him as much freedom as you possibly can, and there's a good likelihood of him getting you out of trouble" (p. 234).

Huston is particularly conscious of his family, and of the tradition of adventure he inherited from his forebears. After a few introductory pages, the story of Huston's life begins: "He left a few things: an ivory-handled .44 Colt revolver; a gold watch and a pair of straight-edged razors." And a grandson. "I was named after him: John Marcellus Gore. He was my Grandpa" (p. 6). His other maternal grandparent was the only one of three sisters in whose choice of a husband "security played no part." On Huston's father's side "the family can be traced back to the thirteenth century and a soldier of fortune whose arms and exploits aided the King of Scotland" (p. 9). (Of shopkeepers or farmers, if they existed, the autobiographer declines to tell.) Huston's restless mother "worked for various newspapers: The Saint Louis *Star*, the Cincinnati *Enquirer*, the Niagara Falls *Gazette* and the Minneapolis *Tribune*. . . . I never tired of traveling from town to town with Mother" (p. 15).

Of all family members – very likely of all people – Huston loved and was influenced most profoundly by his father. "My father and I were as close as a father and son can be" (p. 181). As Huston presents himself, so he presents his father – at once a failure and a buffoon, an Academy Award-winning actor and an advisor to the great: "People often turned to my father for advice and instruction. They knew that whatever he told them would be without self-interest. He had an inborn politeness and respect for others." Like his son, Walter seems to have been conscious that our ends are in our beginnings. Dawn foretells darkness, birth promises death. The last image of his father that Huston leaves us is vivid and a little disturbing. Picnicking in a field of wildflowers,

Suddenly Dad leaned over and pounded a flower into the ground with his fist. There were millions of them, but it seemed a terrible act of desecration. Dad pounded some more flowers with his fist, then jumped up and went at them with his feet, prancing about, stamping on flowers. It was shocking! Panic, in a real sense, was in the air. Dad – the Great God Pan! – was at it again. Appalled, Nan asked what he was doing.

"I'm stopping the spring!" Dad said. (p. 186).

An Open Book begins and ends on a recurrent theme in Huston's films, home. "Las Caletas is my third home. The first was in the San Fernando Valley outside Los Angeles. The second was St. Clerans, in county Galway, Ireland. I dare say Las Caletas will be my last" (p. 3). Huston designed and built the first and third and restored the second. They were scattered across the world, as were his childhood residences and the films he made. It is significant, perhaps, that Huston finds his homes only as an adult; the child of itinerant parents, he did not regard any place that he lived with them as home. Finally, Huston settles at Las Caletas, between sea and jungle, living with Gladys Hill and Maricela and Hank Hankins, a pilot he met in Africa. He is among people who secure him a place in the universe. But "the *company*," in which Huston was always more interested than anything else, includes other creatures. *An Open*

Book is full of beloved snakes, monkeys, mongooses, hippos, and, especially, horses. With him at Las Caletas are the beginnings of another Ark: a Rottweiler, two pet deer, a squirrel, a macaw, a boa, a coatimundi, an ocelot, two cats, a pet pig. "I hope to add to this collection – perhaps some otters from the Quimixto River, a puma, a jaguar. . . . So there you are, for what it's worth."

Like "the world's oldest living and practicing poet" in *The Night of the Iguana*, Huston returned to the sea. From a home among esteemed people, animals, and landscapes he looked back at seventy-four years of life and forty years of directing moving pictures. In the five films he made after the publication of his autobiography, familiar themes and images recur: the importance of the ability to give and receive love; the need to make or recover a home; nature and its creatures; and a consciousness of humanity's "last end." The contemplation of death that he began in childhood led Huston to a wry understanding of mortality and, at the same time, to an affirmation of human community and individual identity that precariously balanced the worlds of his life and his movies.

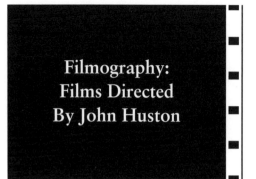

Filmography:
Films Directed
By John Huston

Feature Films	Principal Actors
1941 *The Maltese Falcon*	Humphrey Bogart, Mary Astor, Sidney Greenstreet, Peter Lorre
1942 *In This Our Life*	Bette Davis, Olivia de Havilland, Charles Coburn, George Brent, Dennis Morgan
1942 *Across the Pacific*[1]	Humphrey Bogart, Mary Astor, Sidney Greenstreet
1948 *The Treasure of the Sierra Madre*	Humphrey Bogart, Walter Huston, Tim Holt, Bruce Bennett, Alfonso Bedoya
1948 *Key Largo*	Humphrey Bogart, Lauren Bacall, Lionel Barrymore, Edward G. Robinson, Claire Trevor
1949 *We Were Strangers*	John Garfield, Jennifer Jones, Pedro Armendariz, Gilbert Roland
1950 *The Asphalt Jungle*	Sterling Hayden, Louis Calhern, Jean Hagen, Sam Jaffe, James Whitmore, Marilyn Monroe
1951 *The Red Badge of Courage*[2]	Audie Murphy, Bill Mauldin, John Dierkes, Royal Dano, Arthur Hunnicutt, Tim Durant
1951 *The African Queen*	Humphrey Bogart, Katharine Hepburn, Robert Morley
1953 *Moulin Rouge*	José Ferrer, Collette Marchand, Suzanne Flon, Zsa Zsa Gabor

1954	*Beat the Devil	Humphrey Bogart, Gina Lollo-brigida, Jennifer Jones, Robert Morley, Peter Lorre, Edward Underdown, Ivor Bernard
1956	*Moby Dick	Gregory Peck, Richard Basehart, Orson Welles, Leo Genn, Harry Andrews, Friedrich Ledebur
1957	Heaven Knows, Mr. Allison	Robert Mitchum, Deborah Kerr
1958	*The Barbarian and the Geisha[2]	John Wayne, Eiko Ando, Sam Jaffe
1958	The Roots of Heaven	Errol Flynn, Trevor Howard, Juli-ette Greco, Eddie Albert, Orson Welles, Paul Lukas
1960	*The Unforgiven	Burt Lancaster, Audrey Hepburn, Lillian Gish, John Saxon, Charles Bickford, Audie Murphy
1961	*The Misfits	Marilyn Monroe, Clark Gable, Montgomery Clift, Eli Wallach, Thelma Ritter
1962	Freud: The Secret Passion[3]	Montgomery Clift, Susannah York, Larry Parks, Susan Kohner, Eric Portman
1963	*The List of Adrian Messenger	Kirk Douglas, George C. Scott, Clive Brook, Dana Wynter, Mar-cel Dalio, Walter Anthony Huston
1964	*The Night of the Iguana	Richard Burton, Ava Gardner, Deborah Kerr, Sue Lyon, James Ward, Grayson Hall
1966	*The Bible . . . In the Beginning	Richard Harris, Stephen Boyd, John Huston, George C. Scott, Ava Gardner, Peter O'Toole
1967	*Casino Royale (first sequence)	Peter Sellers, Ursula Andress, David Niven, etc.
1967	*Reflections in a Golden Eye[4]	Elizabeth Taylor, Marlon Brando, Brian Keith, Julie Harris, Robert Forster, Zorro David

1969 *Sinful Davey*   John Hurt, Pamela Franklin,
                                        Robert Morley

1969 *A Walk with Love and   Anjelica Huston, Assaf Dayan,
      Death*   Anthony Corlan

1970 *The Kremlin Letter*   Patrick O'Neal, Richard Boone,
                                        Bibi Andersson, Barbara Parkins,
                                        George Sanders, Orson Welles,
                                        Max Von Sydow, Dean Jagger,
                                        Nigel Green

1972 *Fat City*   Stacy Keach, Jeff Bridges, Candy
                                        Clark, Susan Tyrell, Nicholas
                                        Colosanto, Art Aragon

1972 *The Life and Times of   Paul Newman, Ava Gardner,
      Judge Roy Bean*   Victoria Principal, Roddy
                                        McDowell, Jacqueline Bisset,
                                        Ned Beatty

1973 *The Mackintosh Man*   Paul Newman, Dominique Sanda,
                                        James Mason

1975 *The Man Who Would Be   Sean Connery, Michael Caine,
      King*   Christopher Plummer, Saeed
                                        Joffrey

1979 *Wise Blood*   Brad Dourif, Ned Beatty, Harry
                                        Dean Stanton, Amy Wright,
                                        Daniel Shor

1980 *Phobia*[5]   Paul Michael Glasner, John Coli-
                                        cos, Susan Hogan

1981 *Victory*   Sylvester Stallone, Michael Caine,
                                        Pélé, Max Von Sydow

1982 *Annie*   Aileen Quinn, Carol Burnett,
                                        Albert Finney, Ann Reinking,
                                        Bernadette Peters, Geoffrey
                                        Holder

1984 *Under the Volcano*   Albert Finney, Jacqueline Bisset,
                                        Anthony Andrews

1985 *Prizzi's Honor*   Jack Nicholson, Kathleen Turner,
                                        Anjelica Huston, Robert Loggia

1987   *_The Dead_   Donal McCann, Anjelica Huston,
                                      Helena Carroll, Cathleen Delaney,
                                      Frank Patterson

Films Directed for the U.S. Government

1943   _Report from the Aleutians_   Narrated by Walter and John
                                      Huston
1944   _San Pietro_ (released 1945) Narrated by John Huston
1946   _Let There Be Light_   Narrated by Walter Huston
       (released 1980)
1975   *_Independence_[6]   Ken Howard, Patrick O'Neal,
                                      Eli Wallach

Films marked with an asterisk (*) are currently available on videotape
(in some cases on laserdisk also).

Notes

Introduction

1 Peter S. Greenberg, "Saints and Stinkers: Director John Huston," *Rolling Stone,* no. 337 (19 February 1981), p. 61.
2 Huston writes this in his autobiography, *An Open Book* (New York: Alfred A. Knopf, 1980), p. 336. Later in the same work, he remarks, "I'm not aware of myself as a director having a style" (p. 361).
3 Huston, *An Open Book*, p. 368.
4 Richard T. Jameson, "John Huston," in Stephen Cooper, ed., *Perspectives on John Huston* (New York: G. K. Hall, 1994); originally published in *Film Comment*, vol. 16, no. 3 (May–June, 1980). Robert Benayoun, *John Huston, La grande ombre de l'aventure*, Nouvelle édition mise à jour (Paris: Éditions Pierre Lherminier, 1985), p. 6. Quotations from the Benayoun work will be in English (my translations).
5 Jameson, "John Huston," p. 37.
6 *Proteus*, vol. 7, no. 2 (Fall 1990); Gaylyn Studlar and David Desser, eds., *Reflections in a Male Eye: John Huston and the American Experience* (Washington, D.C., and London: Smithsonian Institution Press, 1993); and Cooper, *Perspectives on John Huston.*
7 Studlar and Desser, *Reflections in a Male Eye*, p. 9.
8 Molly Haskell, "John Huston's Heart of Light and Darkness," *Proteus*, vol. 7, no. 2 (Fall 1990), p. 2.
9 "Huston never claimed the status of an artist, nor even that of an intellectual." Benayoun, *John Huston*, p. 6.
10 Gideon Bachmann, "How I Make Films: An Interview with John Huston," in Cooper, *Perspectives on John Huston*, p. 102; originally published in *Film Quarterly* vol. 19, no. 1 (Fall 1965).
11 Greenberg, "Saints and Stinkers," p. 24.
12 Reprinted in *Agee On Film*, vol. 1 (New York: Grosset & Dunlap, 1969), p. 327.
13 Scott Hammen, *John Huston* (Boston: Twayne Publishers, 1985), p. 3.
14 James Naremore, "John Huston and *The Maltese Falcon*," in Studlar and Desser, *Reflections in a Male Eye*, pp. 121–2; originally published in *Literature/Film Quarterly*, vol. 1, no. 3 (1973).
15 Naremore, "John Huston and *The Maltese Falcon*," p. 124.
16 Jameson, "John Huston," p. 56.

17 Jameson, "John Huston," p. 59.
18 Earlier versions were Roy del Ruth's *The Maltese Falcon* (Warner Bros., 1931) and William Dieterle's *Satan Met a Lady* (Warner Bros., 1936).
19 Quoted in Gerald Pratley, *The Cinema of John Huston* (South Brunswick and New York: A. S. Barnes, 1977), pp. 208–9.
20 Benayoun, *John Huston*, p. 6.
21 Huston, *An Open Book*, p. 303.
22 The quotation is from *Huston, An Open Book*, p. 125.
23 Hayden White, "Keynote Address" at "Humanities Center Fellows Conference," Wayne State University, Detroit, 27 January 1995.
24 Huston, *An Open Book*, p. 334.
25 Robert Benayoun, Interview, "Huston avant le déluge," *Positif*, no. 70 (June 1965), p. 11 (my translation).
26 For Huston's remarks on "the idea" in his films and his desire to make all elements contribute to it, see Bachmann, "How I Make Films," p. 107.
27 Manny Farber, "John Huston, 1950," in Cooper, *Perspectives on John Huston*, pp. 30–4. Also reprinted in Manny Farber, *Negative Space* (New York: Praeger, 1971).
28 David Bordwell, *The Classical Hollywood Cinema: Film Style and Mode of Production to 1960* (New York: Columbia University Press, 1985).
29 Quoted in Thomas Schatz, *The Genius of the System: Hollywood Filmmaking in the Studio Era* (New York: Pantheon, 1988), p. 305.
30 Andrew Sarris, "John Huston," in Cooper, *Perspectives on John Huston*, p. 35. Also reprinted in Andrew Sarris, *The American Cinema* (New York: Penguin Books, 1968).

I. "What We Are Alone Is Not Enough"

1 The quotation is from Paul Petrie's poem "Actæon": " . . . through a veil of blood he saw, too late,/ this world has many names, masks, shifting forms,/and what we are alone is not enough." *Light from the Furnace Rising* (Copper Beech Press: Providence, R.I., 1978), p. 27.

I. 1 *The Treasure of the Sierra Madre* (1948)

1 *The Treasure of the Sierra Madre* (New York: Hill and Wang, 1963; first published by Alfred A. Knopf in 1935).
2 Traven's letter, dated 2 September 1946, is reproduced in Rudy Behlmer, ed., *Inside Warner Bros. (1935–1951)* (New York: Simon & Schuster, 1987), p. 283.
3 Letter from B. Traven to John Huston, 4 January, 1947. Behlmer, *Inside Warner Bros.*, p. 285. John Engell identifies the added scene as Huston's and, evidently unaware of the existence of the correspondence between Traven and Huston, argues that it shows character development "of a kind impossible in Traven's fiction." While Traven's approval of Huston's screenplay and his suggestions do not definitively prove that Huston was writing within the spirit and main themes of the novel, they cast some doubt on Engell's assertion that "Traven's tale of Germanic 'individualistic anarchism' and primitive agrarian communalism becomes, in Huston's hands, a sentimental representation of American Jefferson-

ian individualism." John Engell, "The Textual Treasures of the Sierra Madre," in Studlar and Desser, *Reflections in a Male Eye*, p. 90.

4 Huston speaks of both the importance and the eccentricity of using so much Spanish dialogue in *The Treasure of the Sierra Madre*: "The studio didn't ask for any changes. The only anecdote connected with the picture, except for the things that happened in Mexico, is that I shot a lot of it in Spanish and there is a good deal of Spanish spoken throughout the film. I didn't want the Mexicans speaking Hollywood English. Jack Warner saw the rushes as they came up and said, 'Christ, what's Huston doing? Has he lost his mind entirely? He's making a Spanish version!' Having been in Mexico during my youth increased my determination to make the film there, to capture the true colour that was required for the story." Pratley, *Cinema of John Huston*, p. 63. Interestingly, Walter Huston spoke no Spanish at all, but memorized his lines in that language from a recording made by a Mexican speaker. Huston, *An Open Book*, pp. 147–8.

5 30 December 1946, Behlmer, *Inside Warner Bros.*, pp. 284–5.

6 James Naremore, "Introduction," in Naremore, ed., *The Treasure of the Sierra Madre* (screenplay) (Madison: University of Wisconsin Press, 1979), p. 13.

7 Huston provides indirect substantiating evidence for the importance of the forked cacti when he describes the work of the location crew in the making of *Treasure*. "The Mexican crew was wonderful, attacking their work with a wild energy. They moved large cacti around as though they were potted palms." *An Open Book*, p. 144.

8 John Milton, *Complete Poems and Major Prose*, ed. Merritt Y. Hughes (New York: Odyssey Press, 1957), p. 277.

9 Naremore, *Treasure* screenplay, p. 86. Thirty-six years later, Huston used shots very much like this one at important junctures in *Under the Volcano*.

10 "Letter to Hal Wallis," Belhmer, *Inside Warner Bros.*, p. 126.

11 Belhmer, *Inside Warner Bros.*, p. 284.

12 *Aristotle's Poetics*, trans. Kenneth A. Telford (Lanham, Md.: University Press of America, 1985), pp. 20–1, 30–1.

13 Naremore, *Treasure* screenplay, p. 194.

14 Jameson, "John Huston," p. 55.

15 Ecclesiastes 3:20, 5:16 (King James Version).

16 Lawrence Grobel, *The Hustons* (New York: Scribner's, 1989), p. 458.

17 Northrop Frye, *Anatomy of Criticism* (New York: Atheneum, 1967; first published by Princeton University Press, 1957), p. 193.

I. 2 *The Man Who Would Be King*

1 In an otherwise illuminating essay on *The Man Who Would Be King* ("Taking Us Along on *The Man Who Would Be King*," in Cooper, *Perspectives on John Huston*, pp. 184–96), Sarah Kozloff assumes just such credulity in Huston's audience – though not in herself. Professor Kozloff denounces "the film's racism" (p. 190) and excoriates it and Huston. She sums up much of her indignation in a cluster of rhetorical questions: "Isn't this throwing-up-of-hands-in-disgust-at-the-ungrateful-savages-who-will-not-be-civilized a mirror of the American retreat from Vietnam in 1973? Isn't one of the satisfactions of this film the extent to which it justifies that pull-out? And/or more broadly, the extent to which it jus-

tifies all racism? (*These inner city black youths are savages – let's leave them to their gangs and drugs and retreat with our loot to the suburbs.*)" (p. 191). If one takes these questions seriously, the answer to all of them is a straightforward "no." I am equally doubtful that the casting of Shakira Caine injects "outrage over *miscegenation*" (pp. 190–1) into the film or "emphasizes the connotation of Woman as the Ultimate Savage," (p. 192) "even if" – as Professor Kozloff graciously allows – "this wasn't Huston's conscious intention" (pp. 190–1).

2   Rudyard Kipling, *Complete Verse* (New York: Anchor Books Doubleday, 1989). The following couplet is fairly typical of the tone of the poem: "He crucified noble, he scarified mean,/ He filled old ladies with kerosene" (p. 253).

3   Quoted in Pratley, *Cinema of John Huston*, p. 191.

4   In some respects *The Man Who Would Be King*, as Kozloff argues, qualifies as a "'buddy film,' a love story between two men." "Taking Us Along," p. 192.

5   Pratley, *Cinema of John Huston*, p. 193.

6   Quoted in Stuart Kaminsky, *John Huston, Maker of Magic* (Boston: Houghton Mifflin, 1978), p. 197.

7   Randall Jarrell, ed., *The Best Short Stories of Rudyard Kipling* (Garden City, N.Y.: Hanover House, 1961), p. 128.

8   Kaminsky, *John Huston, Maker of Magic*, p. 200.

9   Pratley, *Cinema of John Huston*, p. 193.

10 Pratley, *Cinema of John Huston*, p. 192.

11 Hammen, *John Huston*, p. 131.

12 Huston, *An Open Book*, p. 205.

13 Pratley, *Cinema of John Huston*, p. 193.

14 Huston, *An Open Book*, p. 360.

I. 3 Hustonian Themes in an Atypical Genre: *The African Queen* (1951)

1   Huston himself felt that *The African Queen* was atypical of his work. "I have a particular tenderness for *African*, even though it is a work which is foreign to me. I don't feel like it is one of *my* films. It is in another vein." Rui Nogueira and Bertrand Tavernier, "Encounter with Rui Nogueira and Bertrand Tavernier," in Studlar and Desser, *Reflections in a Male Eye*, p. 229.

2   The report of Huston's most recent biographer on the filming of *The African Queen* confirms the importance that Huston attached to this shot: "When they returned to work Huston decided that he wanted a steeple with a cross built onto the missionary church. Hepburn told him that since they were supposed to be Methodists, a steeple would be inappropriate. 'Well,' John said, '*this* Methodist is going to have a steeple.' 'He wanted it because he wanted to pan from the tops of the trees down to a cross,' Hepburn said. 'So we had to sit and wait while they built a steeple.'" Grobel, *The Hustons*, p. 374.

3   The similar dialogue in *The Treasure of the Sierra Madre* comes just before Dobbs proposes that he and Curtin take "the Old Man's goods." Dobbs: "How far away do you suppose the railroad is?" Curtin: "Oh, not so far away as the crow flies." Dobbs: "We ain't crows."

4   Quoted in Grobel, *The Hustons*, p. 620.

5   Harold Schechter, *The Bosom Serpent: Folklore and Popular Art* (Iowa City: University of Iowa Press, 1988).

6   Frye, *Anatomy of Criticism*, p. 183.

7   "Comedy, as we have mentioned, is an imitation of the more base, not, however, in respect of every kind of badness, but in respect of that part of the ugly which is ludicrous. For the ludicrous is that sort of mistake or ugliness which is painless and not destructive, e.g. the ludicrous mask is something ugly and distorted but without pain." *Aristotle's Poetics*, p. 10.

8   Northrop Frye, *English Institute Essays* (New York: Columbia University Press, 1949).

9   Katharine Hepburn, *The Making of the African Queen or How I Went to Africa with Bogart, Bacall and Huston and Almost Lost My Mind* (New York: Alfred A. Knopf, 1987), pp. 80–3.

10 The novel is both more explicit and somewhat more limited in its implications: "And – although Rose never suspected it – there was within her a lust for adventure, patiently suppressed during her brother's life, and during the monotonous years at the mission. Rose did not realize that she was gratified by the freedom which her brother's death had brought her. She would have been all contrition if she had realized it, but she never did." C. S. Forester, *The African Queen* (Boston and Toronto: Little, Brown, 1968; first published 1935), pp. 46–7. Citations in my text are to the 1968 edition.

11 John McCarty, *The Films of John Huston* (Secaucus, N. J.: Citadel Press, 1987), p. 91.

12 Speaking to Lawrence Grobel about his work with Huston on *Heaven Knows, Mr. Allison*, Robert Mitchum made much the same point: "He had probably the greatest sense of rhythm and punctuation in dramatic flow of any director I've known." Quoted in Grobel, *The Hustons*, p. 439.

13 The articles were gathered and published as *Picture* (New York: Avon Books, 1969; first published 1952). The quotation is from p. 128 of the 1969 edition.

14 Forester, *The African Queen*, p. 139.

15 Forester, *The African Queen*, p. 141.

16 Forester, *The African Queen*, pp. 307–8.

17 Huston, *An Open Book*, p. 190.

18 "The 1935 novel [American edition] ends with the sinking of the *African Queen* and the apparent drowning of Rose and Charlie on the stormy night they sail out to torpedo the *Louisa*. But in the second edition, published in 1940 by Random House, Forester restored the ending he had originally intended; it had been lopped off by his first editors at Little, Brown, and Company." James R. Fultz, "A Classic Case of Collaboration: *The African Queen*," *Literature/Film Quarterly* vol. 10, no. 1 (1982), pp. 15–16.

19 It may be that the striking underwater shots of Charlie and Rose as they struggle to free the twisted drive shaft suggested to Agee four years later the even more striking underwater shots in *Night of the Hunter*, in which the murdered mother is discovered in a submerged car among gently moving water-grasses and fish.

II. 4 *The Misfits* (1961) and the Idea of John Huston's Films

1   Miller himself reports having taken a similar view. In his autobiography, *Timebends, A Life* (New York: Grove Press, 1987), he writes, "surely we [he and Monroe] still had a future, and the work on this film would somehow help

to make it happen. It was far from accidental that by the end of the film Roslyn does find it possible to believe in a man and in her own survival" (p. 464). Twenty years after the making of the movie, Huston expressed a similar opinion: "He [Arthur Miller] wrote the movie for her trying to save her and, I think, the picture was made in an attempt to save their marriage." Greenberg, "Saints and Stinkers," p. 25.

2   For details see Huston, *An Open Book*; Miller, *Timebends*; and Patricia Bosworth, *Montgomery Clift, A Biography* (New York and London: Harcourt Brace Jovanovich, 1978).

3   Pratley, *Cinema of John Huston*, p. 129.

4   Maurice Yacowar, *Tennessee Williams and Film* (New York: Frederick Ungar, 1977), p. 109.

5   James Naremore identifies such use of characterization as an identifying stylistic tendency in Huston's work: "Most of his good films . . . depend on simple visual symbolism and sharp contrasts of character." "John Huston and *The Maltese Falcon*," p. 122.

6   *Aristotle's Poetics*, p. 14.

7   Bachmann, "How I Make Films," p. 107.

8   James Goode, *The Making of the Misfits* (New York: Limelight Editions, 1986; reprint of *The Story of the Making of the Misfits*, 1963), p. 46.

II. 5 "No Betrayal of Despair": *The Night of the Iguana* (1964)

1   Tennessee Williams, *The Night of the Iguana* (New York: New Directions, 1962), p. 127. According to Huston, Williams disagreed with his changing the end of the play. Years later, indeed, when Williams ran into Huston at a luncheon party, his last words as they left the occasion were "'I still don't like the finish, John.'" This conversation is reported in Huston, *An Open Book*, p. 311.

2   Yacowar, *Tennessee Williams and Film*, p. 106. Scott Hammen, however, takes a very different view from Yacowar's (and from mine). He writes, "*The Night of the Iguana* is little more than a Tennessee Williams play photographically recorded. The modifications Huston and Veiller made in the script are, except for a comic opening sequence that is the liveliest part of the film, inconsequential and very little effort is made to exploit the fact that the action was not restricted to a stage. . . . Huston's presence is largely invisible." *John Huston*, p. 107.

3   McCarty, *Films of John Huston*, p. 144.

4   Yacowar takes a similar view: "The film seems to occupy a central position in Huston's film canon. This is not because he changed Williams's play radically, but because the play basically suited his spirit." *Tennessee Williams and Film*, p. 111.

5   Sarris is quoted in Naremore, "John Huston and *The Maltese Falcon*," pp. 119–20.

6   Yacowar, *Tennessee Williams and Film*, pp. 107–8.

7   Pratley, *Cinema of John Huston*, p. 143.

8   Richard W. Nason, *New York Times*, 28 September 1958, p. 9X.

9   Kaminsky, *John Huston, Maker of Magic*, p. 168; Martin Rubin, "Heroic, An-

tiheroic, Aheroic: John Huston and the Problematical Protagonist," in Studlar and Desser, *Reflections in a Male Eye*, p. 152.

10   Naremore, "John Huston and *The Maltese Falcon*," p. 134.

11   For an informative discussion of Sartre's thinking about film, see Dana Polan, "Sartre and Cinema," *Post-Script*, vol. 7, no. 1 (Fall 1987) pp. 66–88.

12   Perhaps coincidentally, Grayson Hall later had important roles in two vampire horror movies, Dan Curtis's *House of Dark Shadows* (1970) and *Night of Dark Shadows* (1971).

13   Huston, *An Open Book*, p. 329.

14   Huston, *An Open Book*, p. 33.

15   Jameson, "John Huston," p. 63.

16   Kaminsky writes that Huston sees religion "as a part of the fantasy world, a dangerous fantasy that his characters must overcome if they are not to be destroyed or absorbed by it." *John Huston, Maker of Magic*, p. 160.

II. 6 *Let There Be Light* (1946)

1   Huston, *An Open Book*, p. 125.

2   Grobel, *The Hustons*, p. 273.

3   Huston, *An Open Book*, p. 125.

4   Quoted in, respectively, Hammen, *John Huston*, p. 23; and Kaminsky, *John Huston, Maker of Magic*, p. 43.

5   Jameson, "John Huston," p. 33.

6   David Desser, "The Wartime Films of John Huston: *Film Noir* and the Emergence of the Therapeutic," in Studlar and Desser, *Reflections in a Male Eye*, p. 24.

7   Gary Edgerton, "Revisiting the Recordings of Wars Past: Remembering the Documentary Trilogy of John Huston," in Studlar and Desser, *Reflections in a Male Eye*, p. 34.

8   Scott Hammen, "At War with the Army," *Film Comment*, vol. 16, no. 2 (March–April 1980), p. 22.

9   Desser, "Wartime Films of John Huston," p. 20.

10   Desser, "Wartime Films of John Huston," p. 20.

11   Jameson, "John Huston," p. 33.

12   Hammen, "At War with the Army," p. 22.

13   Edgerton, "Revisiting the Recordings of Wars Past," p. 49.

14   Huston, *An Open Book*, p. 123.

15   Huston, *An Open Book*, p. 120.

16   Huston, *An Open Book*, p. 123.

17   Huston, *An Open Book*, p. 125.

III. 7 *Heaven Knows, Mr. Allison* (1957)

1   Huston, *An Open Book*, p. 263.

2   Raymond Chandler, *The Big Sleep* (New York: Vintage Books, 1976; first published 1939), p. 140.

3   Frye, *Anatomy of Criticism*, p. 200.

4   Frye, *Anatomy of Criticism*, p. 200.
5   Frye, *Anatomy of Criticism*, p. 182.
6   Frye, *Anatomy of Criticism*, p. 184.
7   André Bazin, "On the *politique des auteurs*," in Jim Hillier, ed., *Cahiers du Cinema* (in English), *vol. 1: the 1950s* (no. 70, April 1957), p. 251.
8   Twentieth Century Fox was aware of the potential for trouble with this film, and the studio went so far as to have a censor from the Legion of Decency on location. Huston was evidently unable to resist the opportunity that his presence offered. "'Jack Vizzard used to see salacious things in things that nobody else did,' recalled Jilda Smith, who worked as a production secretary on the film. . . . 'So they decided to play a joke on Jack Vizzard. Mitchum came over to Deborah and put one hand down the front of her dress and the other up her skirt. She kneed him and Jack said, "You can't do that!" And Huston said, "I don't see why not." . . . John told him this was the revised scene, that the one before was unusable. Vizzard was absolutely speechless.'" Grobel, *The Hustons*, p. 440.
9   Stanley Cavell, *The World Viewed: Reflections on the Ontology of Film,* enlarged edition (Cambridge, Mass., and London: Harvard University Press, 1979), p. 117.
10 Sir Philip Sidney, *The Defense of Poesie, 1595* (STC 22535, microfilm).

III. 8 Theater, Identity, and Reality in *The Maltese Falcon (1941)*

1   John Huston, *Frankie and Johnny* (New York and London: Benjamin Blom, 1968; first published 1930), p. 85.
2   For extended discussion of the relation of this omitted episode to the theme of retelling stories with strategic deletions in both novel and film, see Stephen Cooper, "Flitcraft, Spade, and *The Maltese Falcon*: John Huston's Adaptation," in Cooper, *Perspectives on John Huston*, pp. 117–32.
3   Recent commentators on the relation between Huston's film and the novel on which it is based emphasize that both proceed by the telling of stories and exhibit considerable self-consciousness about their own status as fictions. John Anderson notes the constant acting of the characters in both film and novel: "Through film, the theatre of the novel is translated directly into theatre itself. The frantic and very self-conscious acting of Hammett's characters is framed by the camera." "The World of *The Maltese Falcon*," *Southwest Review*, vol. 73, no. 3 (Summer 1988), p. 382. According to Leslie H. Abramson, both "probe the methods and values of storytelling" and "Sam's success as a detective is dependent upon his superior talents as a reader of plots and a story teller." Moreover, "Huston's version of *The Maltese Falcon* is a highly self-reflexive work, preoccupied with its origins in print." "Two Birds of a Feather: Hammett's and Huston's *The Maltese Falcon*," *Literature/Film Quarterly*, vol. 16, no. 2 (1988), pp. 112, 115. Stephen Cooper writes of "the novel's plastic ideology of storytelling" and argues that Huston adopts and extends this strategy of the novel. "Flitcraft, Spade, and *The Maltese Falcon*," p. 121. With these essays I am in general agreement, as will be evident. The heavily emphasized particularization of story-telling as *theater* is not to be found explicitly in the novel but is crucial to understanding how in the film Huston presents issues of fiction and of what we now call textuality. Anderson, Abramson, and Cooper all tend to discuss

novel and film together as if they were halves of a composite work of art. As illuminating as that approach can sometimes be, it has two obvious disadvantages. First, it requires an assumption of the identity of the two works that is untrue from most perspectives; the film and the novel are separate works and we should not presume that either one is comprehensible only in the context of the other. Second, such an assumption can occlude some sharp differences between novel and film and obscure the Hustonian particularities of the movie. For an illuminating discussion of differences between Huston's film and Hammett's novel, see Naremore, "John Huston and *The Maltese Falcon*," pp. 119–35.

4   This is the aspect of the film emphasized by most commentators. Colin McArthur describes the world of the film as follows: "Spade replies, 'Everyone has something to conceal.' This remark could stand as a text for *The Maltese Falcon*, in which nothing is as it seems: personal identities are shifting and uncertain, relationships are characterized by duplicity and even objects prove false." *Underworld U.S.A.* (London: Secker & Warburg, 1972), p. 85.

5   Grobel, *The Hustons*, p. 219 (quoting a "Huston interview with Joe Persico, August, 1981"; Grobel gives no further reference for this interview).

6   Considering that *The Maltese Falcon* has done service for a number of scholars as a textbook example of movie construction in the "Classic Hollywood Cinema," one may doubt the assertion of Robert Ray that "a consistent pattern of internal self-criticism and self-consciousness foregrounding cinematic mechanisms . . . has never existed systematically in any body of cinema other than the avant-garde. Certainly, Classic Hollywood's films contained few 'Godardian' foregroundings of conventions." *A Certain Tendency of the Hollywood Cinema, 1930–1980* (Princeton, N.J.: Princeton University Press, 1985), p. 37. Huston's first effort as a director insistently draws attention to its cinematic and theatrical conventions. So will other films across his career in diverse ways and decades, prominent among them *Moulin Rouge* ('53), *The List of Adrian Messenger* ('63), *The Life and Times of Judge Roy Bean* ('72), and *The Dead* ('87).

7   Naremore also notices a staginess about the concluding shots of the opening sequence: "as if we were looking through a proscenium onto a stage." "John Huston and *The Maltese Falcon*," p. 128.

8   Naremore and Anderson emphasize a different aspect of the ending, an aspect that exists alongside the one I stress here and that is consonant with the further understanding of the conclusion that I will present later in this chapter. Naremore describes Bogart as "descending to his own kind of sorrow" in the last shot of the film. "John Huston and *The Maltese Falcon*," p. 127. Anderson writes, "He [Spade] walks down barred stairs and into a world of shadows, descending out of view and into his own hell." "The World of *The Maltese Falcon*," p. 394.

9   Anderson, "The World of *The Maltese Falcon*," p. 385.

10 William Luhr observes, "That window [in Spade's apartment] and curtain become visual motifs increasingly associated with sinister events in and influences upon Spade's life." "Tracking *The Maltese Falcon*: Classical Hollywood Narration and Sam Spade," in William Luhr, ed., *The Maltese Falcon John Huston Director* (New Brunswick, N.J.: Rutgers University Press, 1995), p. 164.

11 The novel is explicit. Spade "laughed and lounged back on the sofa, crossing his legs. 'A cheap enough price to pay for winning.'" Dashiell Hammett, *The Maltese Falcon* (New York: Vintage Books, 1992; first published 1930), pp. 82–3.

12 James Maxfield asserts that Spade must have realized Brigid's guilt "long before he reveals it to us. Probably he was reasonably certain Brigid had to be the killer when he tried to call her at her hotel just after he talked to Tom Polhaus at the scene of the murder." "*La Belle Dame Sans Merci* and the Neurotic Knight: Characterization in *The Maltese Falcon*," *Literature/Film Quarterly*, vol. 17, no. 4 (1989), p. 255. I do not believe that the film encourages its audience to trace Spade's strong suspicions back that far. Spade does ask Brigid if she was involved in his partner's death in an early sequence, but he seems to accept her denial. Moreover, his affair with her argues against his being "reasonably certain" that she killed Archer – unless we take Spade to be more cynical than even the commentators least sympathetic to him have done. Maxwell's point that Spade would have been skeptical from the beginning about his partner's going up an unlighted, blind street with his gun under a buttoned overcoat, however, has considerable force. On the other hand, Spade's scanty knowledge of Brigid or her involvement in the quest for the falcon and his openly expressed contempt for his partner's limited brain power would lessen his suspicion of his new client, as would his attraction to her.

13 This is essentially the conclusion at which a recent commentator on the film arrives. "*The Maltese Falcon*, then, is a powerful statement about crass materialism and personal betrayal. Far from an anomaly in the *film noir* canon, it convincingly establishes through both the character of Sam Spade and the style in which his story is presented, a moral counterweight to the craven world of private gain and double-dealings represented by Gutman, Cairo, and O'Shaughnessy." Keith Cohen, "John Huston and *Film Noir*," in Cooper, *Perspectives on John Huston*, p. 136. Thomas Schatz offers a similar view of Spade's character and moral function: "Spade, whose hardboiled exterior hides a vulnerable moralist and a man of uncompromising integrity . . . is the thematic 'answer' to this world of avarice and superficial elegance." *Hollywood Genres: Formulas, Filmmaking, and the Studio System* (Philadelphia: Temple University Press, 1981), p. 128. At the opposite pole are commentators like Virginia Wright Wexman, who finds Spade to be "a cynically defensive lover. The world continually threatens him, and he must gain dominance over it in order to establish control over his own life." "Kinesics and Film Acting: Humphrey Bogart in *The Maltese Falcon* and *The Big Sleep*," *Journal of Popular Film and Television*, vol. 7 (1978), p. 47. Similarly Maxfield, "He is a prototype of Karen Horney's 'arrogant-vindictive' neurotic, who in response to being treated harshly in childhood 'has a need to retaliate for all injuries and to prove his superiority to all rivals'" ("*La Belle Dame* and the Neurotic Knight," p. 254); and Grobel, "Sam Spade is a cold-hearted, selfish, cynical manipulator" (*The Hustons*, p. 219). More neutrally, Stanley Cavell identifies Spade as a dandy, indeed, "the greatest instance of the type" (*The World Viewed*, p. 57). McArthur observes that "His most conspicuous quality [is] his capacity for survival" (*Underworld U.S.A.*, p. 87). Such widely diverse critical assessments are the usual consequences of the complex ambiguity of characterization in intensely ironic fictions, which typically have equivocal central figures who inspire various and ambivalent responses among audiences.

14 Ilsa J. Bick makes a similar observation: "Spade teeters, however, on the brink

between calculated performance and loss of control – his hand shakes as he waits for the elevator." "The Beam That Fell and Other Crises in *The Maltese Falcon*," in Luhr, *The Maltese Falcon John Huston Director*, p. 193.

15 Hammett, *The Maltese Falcon*, p. 55.

16 Bachmann, "How I Make Films," p. 8.

17 In "'The Stuff That Dreams Are Made Of,'" Rudy Behlmer writes that "'Jack Warner requested a few changes after the film was edited. . . . In the revised ending, the latter part of the scene in Spade's apartment was reshot . . . including a new non-Hammett line in reference to the Falcon – 'the stuff that dreams are made of.'" In Luhr, *The Maltese Falcon John Huston Director*, pp. 119–20.

18 Act IV, scene 1, lines 148–158. Sylvan Barnett, ed., *The Complete Classic Signet Shakespeare* (New York: Harcourt Brace Jovanovich, 1972), pp. 1562–3. A quotation from *A Midsummer Night's Dream* in Hammett's novel disappears in the movie, but it may have suggested the idea of the Shakespearean allusion from *The Tempest*: "Cairo's cry had brought Brigid O'Shaughnessy to the door. Spade, grinning, jerked a thumb at the sofa and told her, 'The course of true love. How's the food coming along?'" *The Maltese Falcon*, p. 199.

III. 9 *Reflections in a Golden Eye* (1967)

1 Eric Sherman, *Directing the Film: Film Directors on Their Art* (Boston and Toronto: Little, Brown, 1976), p. 318.

2 Grobel, *The Hustons*, p. 533.

3 Jameson, "John Huston," p. 82.

4 François Ramasse, "Le regard et la peau" (Gaze and Skin), in Gilles Ciment, ed., *John Huston Dossier Positif-Rivages* (Paris: Éditions Rivages, 1988), pp. 131–3.

5 Nogueira and Tavernier, "Encounter," p. 210.

6 Nogueira and Tavernier, "Encounter," p. 210.

7 Nogueira and Tavernier, "Encounter," p. 210. Stephen Cooper adds a useful distinction to Huston's formulation: a "gap is being constructed between the on-screen voyeur and the spectator in the theater, even as the spectator is being turned toward the voyeuristic. . . . the gigantic close-up of his [Williams's] gaze . . . has alerted us to the self-consciousness built into the film and in turn imposed upon us." "Political *Reflections in a Golden Eye*," in Studlar and Desser, *Reflections in a Male Eye*, pp. 105–6.

8 Nogueira and Tavernier, "Encounter," p. 236.

9 Carson McCullers, *Reflections in a Golden Eye*, in *The Shorter Novels and Stories of Carson McCullers* (London: Barrie & Jenkins, 1972), p. 167. Hereafter, references will be to this edition of *Reflections in a Golden Eye*, cited in the text by page number.

10 Herb A. Lightman, "*Reflections in a Golden Eye* Viewed through a Glass Darkly," *American Cinematographer*, vol. 48, no. 12, p. 900. According to Stuart Kaminsky, the "desaturation is constant until the murder at the end of the film when full Technicolor comes on with a jolt." *John Huston*, p. 175. So far as I know, no one else has reported this effect.

11 Grobel, *The Hustons*, pp. 579–80.

12 In some versions of the videotape of this film, white also associates Leonora with

white-on-white credits that precede the film and that perhaps signify in their absence of color something like simplicity or the proverbial *tabula rasa* of the untaught, uninjured child. The origin of these credits is unclear, however; they do not exist in all versions of the videotape, nor do they occur on the 35-millimeter Technicolor release print that I have seen. In that print, and in other videotapes, the opening credits appear as block letters of nearly the same color as the tannish-gold plain background behind them.

13   John Huston, letter to Eliot Hyman, 15 September 1967, Margaret Herrick Library of the Academy of Motion Picture Arts and Sciences, Beverly Hills, California, John Huston Collection.

14   Cooper, "Political *Reflections in a Golden Eye*" in Studlar and Desser, p. 104.

15   Norman Holland identifies a similar tendency, what he calls substitutability, as being widespread in Huston's work as a whole: "in episode after episode of his films, we see that human beings or what they desire are endlessly substitutable." "How to See *Freud*," in Cooper, *Perspectives on John Huston*, p. 179.

16   Grobel, *The Hustons*, p. 579.

17   "As structure, the central principle of ironic myth is best approached as a parody of romance." Frye, *Anatomy of Criticism*, p. 223.

18   Pratley, *Cinema of John Huston*, p. 163.

IV. The Heart of the Problem

1   Albert Camus, *Le Mythe de Sisyphe* (Librairie Gallimard, 1942), p. 17.

2   Huston, *An Open Book*, p. 68.

IV. 10 *Freud* (1961)

1   *Phobia* (1980) was released for theatrical viewing only in Canada but is available on videotape in the United States.

2   Huston and others assert that Sartre was retained for $25,000; correspondence in the *Freud* files of the Huston papers, however, makes clear that Sartre contracted for a considerably larger sum, $40,000. A letter of 19 January 1960 from Mark M. Cohen, Attorney, to John Huston summarizes the history to that date of the writing of the screenplay. Correspondence between Sartre's agent and Universal also repeatedly indicates that the sum for which Sartre contracted was $40,000. Herrick Library, Huston Collection.

3   For relatively full accounts, see Huston, *An Open Book*; Grobel, *The Hustons*; and the Introduction to Jean-Paul Sartre, *The Freud Scenario*, ed. J.-B. Pontalis, trans. Quintin Hoare (London: Verso, 1985; first published in Paris: Éditions Gallimard, 1984).

4   Robert Benayoun, "Huston avant le déluge," p. 18 (my translation).

5   Huston, *An Open Book*, p. 294.

6   "FREUD/ SCREENPLAY by/ JOHN HUSTON–WOLFGANG REINHARDT/ Final Shooting Script/ February 10, 1962/ Copy 2 – JOHN HUSTON," Herrick Library, Huston Collection. I cannot tell from the printed initials next to the lines of the script who made the attributions, but I suspect that it was Huston himself.

7   John Huston, letter to Mel Tucker, 28 August 1962. Herrick Library, Huston Collection.

8   Janet Walker and Diane Waldman make the omitted sequence of the assaulted woman patient the point of entry for their essay, "John Huston's *Freud* and Textual Repression: A Psychoanalytic Feminist Reading," in Peter Lehman, ed., *Close Viewings: An Anthology of New Film Criticism* (Tallahassee: Florida State University Press, 1990), pp. 282–99.

9   Benayoun, *John Huston*, p. 79; signed program for initial release of "John Huston's Production of Freud," Herrick Library, Huston Collection.

10   The major parts cut from *Freud* to make *Freud: The Secret Passion* are as follows. (1) After the first sequence with Cecily, Freud and Breuer discuss repression in a carriage; Freud is interrupted during a hypnotism session in the hospital; he confronts Meynert who mocks him and Charcot, shows Freud a box full of scorpions (a metaphor, he explains, for meddling with the unconscious), and dismisses him from the hospital. (2) After Freud's first cave dream, Breuer (having been sent for by Martha Freud) visits Freud to discover that he has abandoned hypnosis and his neurotic patients and has returned to neurology; Breuer tells Freud of Meynert's heart attack; a messenger arrives from Meynert, summoning Freud; when Freud arrives, Meynert admits to his own hysteria and urges Freud to return to his earlier researches. (3) After Cecily's last session, Freud is speaking with Breuer, who rejects his "new theory," and refuses to be associated with it; Breuer invokes his authority as Freud's surrogate father to forbid him from addressing the Medical Society, but Freud replies that "one must give up all one's fathers and stand alone."

11   Signed program for initial release of "John Huston's Production of Freud," Herrick Library, Huston Collection.

12   Huston, *An Open Book*, pp. 279, 294.

13   Quoted in Donald Chankin, "The Representation of Psychoanalysis in Film," *Persistence of Vision*, no. 10 (1993), p. 139. The passage occurs in Freud's *Introductory Lectures on Psycho-Analysis* (Standard Edition), p. 27.

14   This comes from a typed, single-spaced letter of seven pages from Sartre to Huston, dated 26 August 1961, that has evidently been translated. Apparently provoked by having been shown a cablegram that Huston sent to Wolfgang Reinhardt on 24 August 1961, complaining about Sartre's behavior, Sartre defends his own conduct and directs a fulsome condemnation against Huston's good faith. He also details his complaints about the ways in which Huston and his collaborators altered his script. In addition to assertions about Sartre's professional irresponsibility and "unconscionable words," Huston's cablegram closed on an especially provocative remark about Sartre having gotten more money for his screenplay than had ever before been offered to "a Frenchman." Herrick Library, Huston Collection.

15   Herrick Library, Huston Collection, p. 15 of untitled manuscript.

16   Chankin, "The Representation of Psychoanalysis in Film," p. 138.

17   Dana Polan, "Sartre and Cinema," pp. 81–2.

18   Norman Holland, "How to See Freud," in Cooper, *Perspectives on John Huston*, p. 171.

19 For his full discussion, see Holland, "How to See Freud," pp. 171–6. The quotation is from p. 175.

20 In a letter of 28 August 1962 to Mel Tucker, Huston wrote about this ending, "I'm prepared to write profound letters on the importance of the scene." Herrick Library, Huston Collection. In other correspondence about *Freud*, he wrote that he regarded ending the film with an emphasis on Freud's overcoming anti-Semitism as keeping faith with the history of the Jewish people.

21 Preview comments are preserved in the Herrick Library, Huston Collection.

22 Signed program for initial release of "John Huston's Production of Freud," Herrick Library, Huston Collection.

23 Act V, scene 3, lines 94–5.

24 Herrick Library, Huston Collection, pp. 4–5 of untitled manuscript.

IV. 11 *Fat City* (1972): "Maybe We're All Happy"

1 Quoted in Pratley, *Cinema of John Huston*, p. 177.

2 Hammen, *John Huston*, p. 123.

3 Leonard Gardner, *Fat City* (New York: Farrar, Straus & Giroux, 1969), p. 38.

4 Gardner, *Fat City*, p. 55.

5 Gardner, *Fat City*, p. 14.

6 In Gardner's novel, Billy's downward spiral after his fight with Lucero is traced in detail, and Huston apparently shot corresponding footage that was omitted from the final version of the film. "After the film was cut Stacy Keach was disappointed that two key scenes were missing. 'What's been cut was when Billy was at the top, when he was the champ. It was a flashback. And there's a whole twenty minutes of film of the downward spiral of Tully after he wins the fight and doesn't get the money that's missing. He goes back to the boarding house, they throw him out, he almost gets knifed in the rain by a guy in the city; he ends up having to sleep in an incinerator, where he's kicked out by this old Chinese guy. You see him just go down, down, down. I was devastated when all that was taken out. That was a decision that Ray Stark and editor Maggie Booth made. Ray said, "It's a downer picture as it is, if it goes any farther down, it's going to make it worse."' Keach didn't agree. 'The movie would have *really* been a great film if you had a chance to see him hit the real bottom. But John thought it was a decision that was made for the best.'" Grobel, *The Hustons*, p. 638.

7 Camus, *Le Mythe de Sisyphe*, p. 168.

8 Jeff Bridges's account of its creation is remarkable: "'It was one of those calls, report to the set at two A.M.,' Bridges said. 'It was an actual location. John was there with his oxygen tank [for emphysema] – he looked like he was asleep or dead. Nobody had the balls to go to him and say, "We're ready, Mr. Huston." All of a sudden his eyes bolted open and he said, "I've got it. Have you ever been at a party when for no reason everybody just stops? When all of a sudden it's all a tableau; you're alone in eternity for a moment? When Stacy turns around, I want everybody to just stop what they're doing." "Why, John?" Keach asked. "I have no idea," Huston answered. "Sometimes the devil just gets into me."'" Grobel, *The Hustons*, pp. 637–8.

9   *"L'absurde naît de cette confrontation entre l'appel humain et le silence déraisonnable du monde."* Camus, *Le Mythe de Sisyphe*, p. 45.

10 Gaylyn Studlar views this scene (and the film as a whole) as being more uniformly ironic: "he and Ernie remain in what amounts to little more than a parody of intimacy." *"Fat City* and the Malaise of Masculinity," in Studlar and Desser, *Reflections in a Male Eye*, p. 195.

11 Holland, "How to See Huston's *Freud*," p. 179.

12 Huston, *An Open Book*, p. 328.

13 Jameson, "John Huston," p. 83.

14 Studlar, *"Fat City* and the Malaise of Masculinity," p. 187.

15 Quoted in Charles Champlin's review in the *Los Angeles Times* of 12 November 1972.

16 Jameson, "John Huston," p. 84.

17 Thomas Gray, "Elegy Written in a Country Churchyard," line 36.

18 This is the last sentence of "Figures of Fighting Men," six sketches that Huston published in the *American Mercury* (May 1931), reprinted in Studlar and Desser, *Reflections in a Male Eye*, pp. 249–53.

19 Studlar, *"Fat City* and the Malaise of Masculinity," p. 196.

20 André Bazin, "The Death of Humphrey Bogart," in Jim Hillier, ed., *Cahiers du Cinema* (in English), vol. 1: *the 1950s* (no. 68, February 1957), p. 101.

21 Martin Rubin writes, "the most heroic character in Huston's *Fat City* is the defeated Mexican boxer, Armando Lucero . . . who incarnates most fully the ideal of existential, Hemingwayesque stoicism." "Heroic, Antiheroic, Aheroic: John Huston and the Problematical Protagonist," in Studlar and Desser, *Reflections in a Male Eye*, p. 155.

22 Jameson, "John Huston," p. 84; Huston, *An Open Book*, p. 338.

23 Jean-Paul Sartre, *"A propos de l'existentialisme: Mise au point,"* Action 29 (December 1944), reprinted and translated into English by Richard McCleary in *The Writings of Jean-Paul Sartre*, vol. 2: *Selected Prose*, p. 159.

24 John Huston, "Fool," *American Mercury* (March 1929), reprinted in Studlar and Desser, *Reflections in a Male Eye*, pp. 246–7.

25 Jameson, "John Huston," p. 83.

V. 12 *The Dead* (1987)

1   James Naremore, "Return of the Dead," in Cooper, *Perspectives on John Huston*, p. 200.

2   The most self-conscious consideration of *The Dead* as an adaptation of Joyce's story that I know is in Stephen Cooper's unpublished doctoral dissertation. Cooper explicitly limits his reading of Huston's film to a consideration of theories of adaptation informed by Freud and Vico. He thus enriches our understanding of the context of the film without any reductive implication that the context somehow more or less completely "explains" Huston's simultaneously original and source-indebted work. Cooper discusses Huston`s *The Dead*, like Mr. Grace's recitation, as "a veritable staged metaphor for the process of adaptation. . . . for adaptation distorts as it reflects, bringing its own mind to bear

upon the mind of the text which provokes and enables – and constrains – it."
Stephen Cooper, *Toward a Theory of Adaptation: John Huston and the Inter-locutive*, unpublished Ph.D. dissertation (1991), University of Southern California, ch. 9, p. 7.

3 Benayoun, *John Huston*, p. 28.
4 Grobel, *The Hustons*, p. 16.
5 The poem is not complete as he reads it, and is retitled (its original title is "Donall Oge: Grief of a Girl's Heart"). The complete text is available in Kathleen Hoagland, ed., *1000 Years of Irish Poetry* (New York: Devin-Adair, 1947), pp. 238–40.
6 "Creativity with Bill Moyers, John Huston," Corporation for Entertainment & Learning, 1982.
7 Eric Sherman, *Directing the Film*, p. 318.
8 Tony Huston, "Family Ties," *American Film*, vol. 12, no. 10 (September 1987), p. 16.
9 Huston, *An Open Book*, p. 366.
10 Huston, *An Open Book*, p. 263.

V. 13 *An Open Book* (1980): "Sufficiently Absurd"

1 John Huston letter of 14 August 1972 to "Mr. Weatherby" of Simon and Schuster. Herrick Library, Huston Collection.
2 Huston, *An Open Book*, p. 246. Hereafter, references to *An Open Book* will be cited in the text by page number.
3 "Agreement" of 22 January 1981 between Huston and Knopf. The only other alteration to what appears to be a standard contract changes "Author" to "Proprietor." Herrick Library, Huston Collection.
4 Herrick Library, Huston Collection.
5 Quoted in Suranjan Ganguly, "Stan Brakhage – The 60th Birthday Interview," *Film Culture*, no. 78 (Summer 1994), p. 21.
6 In an interview with Peter S. Greenberg ("Saints and Stinkers"), Huston identified the woman as Olivia de Havilland.

Filmography: Films Directed By John Huston

1 Completed by Vincent Sherman after Huston joined the Army.
2 Significantly altered in post-production without Huston's participation.
3 Original limited release as *Freud* in a longer (c. twenty minutes) version.
4 Original limited release in desaturated version; general release in standard color.
5 Theatrical release in Canada only.
6 Film shown and videotape available at Independence Hall Visitors Center, Philadelphia.

Selected Bibliography of
Writings on John Huston

Abramson, Leslie H. "Two Birds of a Feather: Hammett's and Huston's *The Maltese Falcon.*" *Literature/Film Quarterly*, vol. 16, no. 2 (1988).

Agee, James. *Agee On Film*, vol. 1. New York: Grosset & Dunlap, 1969. The essay on Huston is reprinted in Studlar and Desser, *Reflections in a Male Eye.*

Anderson, John. "The World of *The Maltese Falcon.*" *Southwest Review*, vol. 73, no. 3 (Summer 1988).

Bachmann, Gideon. "How I Make Films: An Interview with John Huston." *Film Quarterly*, vol. 19, no. 1 (Fall 1965). Reprinted in Cooper, *Perspectives on John Huston.*

Behlmer, Rudy. "'The Stuff That Dreams Are Made Of.'" In Luhr, *The Maltese Falcon John Huston Director.*

Behlmer, Rudy, ed. *Inside Warner Bros. (1935–1951)*. New York: Simon & Schuster, 1987.

Benayoun, Robert. "Huston avant le déluge." *Positif*, no. 70 (June 1965).

John Huston, La grande ombre de l'aventure. Nouvelle édition mise à jour. Paris: Éditions Pierre Lherminier, 1985.

Bick, Ilsa J. "The Beam That Fell and Other Crises in *The Maltese Falcon.*" In Luhr, *The Maltese Falcon John Huston Director.*

Chankin, Donald. "The Representation of Psychoanalysis in Film." *Persistence of Vision*, no. 10 (1993).

Cohen, Keith. "John Huston and *Film Noir.*" In Cooper, *Perspectives on John Huston.*

Cooper, Stephen. "Flitcraft, Spade, and *The Maltese Falcon*: John Huston's Adaptation." In Cooper, *Perspectives on John Huston.*

Perspectives on John Huston. New York: G. K. Hall, 1994.

Cooper, Stephen, ed. "Political Reflections in a Golden Eye," in Studlar and Desser, *Reflections in a Male Eye.*

Desser, David. "The Wartime Films of John Huston: *Film Noir* and the Emergence of the Therapeutic." In Studlar and Desser, *Reflections in a Male Eye.*

Edgerton, Gary. "Revisiting the Recordings of Wars Past: Remembering the Documentary Trilogy of John Huston." In Studlar and Desser, *Reflections in a Male Eye.*

Engell, John. "The Textual Treasures of the Sierra Madre." In Studlar and Desser, *Reflections in a Male Eye.*

Farber, Manny. *Negative Space*. New York: Praeger, 1971. The essay on Huston is reprinted in Cooper, *Perspectives on John Huston*.

Fultz, James R. "A Classic Case of Collaboration: *The African Queen*." *Literature/Film Quarterly*, vol. 10, no. 1 (1982).

Goode, James. *The Making of the Misfits*. New York: Limelight Editions, 1986. Reprint of *The Story of the Making of the Misfits*, 1963.

Greenberg, Peter S. "Saints and Stinkers: Director John Huston." *Rolling Stone*, no. 337 (19 February 1981).

Grobel, Lawrence. *The Hustons*. New York: Scribner's, 1989.

Hammen, Scott. "At War with the Army." *Film Comment*, vol. 16, no. 2 (March–April 1980).

John Huston. Boston: Twayne Publishers, 1985.

Haskell, Molly. "John Huston's Heart of Light and Darkness." *Proteus*, vol. 7, no. 2 (Fall 1990).

Hepburn, Katharine. *The Making of the African Queen or How I Went to Africa with Bogart, Bacall and Huston and Almost Lost My Mind*. New York: Alfred A. Knopf, 1987.

Holland, Norman. "How to See *Freud*." In Cooper, *Perspectives on John Huston*.

Huston, John. *An Open Book*. New York: Alfred A. Knopf, 1980.

Huston, Tony. "Family Ties." *American Film*, vol. 12, no. 10 (September 1987).

Jameson, Richard T. "John Huston." *Film Comment*, vol. 16, no. 3 (May–June 1980). Reprinted in Cooper, *Perspectives on John Huston*.

Kaminsky, Stuart. *John Huston, Maker of Magic*. Boston: Houghton Mifflin, 1978.

Kozloff, Sarah. "Taking Us Along on *The Man Who Would Be King*." In Cooper, *Perspectives on John Huston*.

Lightman, Herb A. "*Reflections in a Golden Eye* Viewed through a Glass Darkly." *American Cinematographer*, vol. 48, no. 12.

Luhr, William. "Tracking *The Maltese Falcon*: Classical Hollywood Narration and Sam Spade." In Luhr, *The Maltese Falcon John Huston Director*.

Luhr, William, ed. *The Maltese Falcon John Huston Director*. New Brunswick, N.J.: Rutgers University Press, 1995.

Maxfield, James. "*La Belle Dame Sans Merci* and the Neurotic Knight: Characterization in *The Maltese Falcon*." *Literature/Film Quarterly*, vol. 17, no. 4 (1989).

McArthur, Colin. *Underworld U.S.A.* London: Secker & Warburg, 1972.

McCarty, John. *The Films of John Huston*. Secaucus, N.J.: Citadel Press, 1987.

Naremore, James. "John Huston and *The Maltese Falcon*." *Literature/Film Quarterly*, vol. 1, no. 3 (1973). Reprinted in Studlar and Desser, *Reflections in a Male Eye*.

"Return of the Dead." In Cooper, *Perspectives on John Huston*.

Naremore, James, ed. *The Treasure of the Sierra Madre*. With an introduction by James Naremore. Madison: University of Wisconsin Press, 1979.

Nason, Richard W. Interview with John Huston. *New York Times*, 28 September 1958, p. 9X.

Nogueira, Rui, and Bertrand Tavernier. "Encounter with Rui Nogueira and Bertrand Tavernier." Reprinted in Studlar and Desser, *Reflections in a Male Eye*.

Pratley, Gerald. *The Cinema of John Huston*. South Brunswick and New York: A. S. Barnes, 1977.

Proteus, vol. 7, no. 2 (Fall 1990). Issue devoted to John Huston.

Ramasse, François. "Le regard et la peau" (Gaze and Skin). In Gilles Ciment, ed., *John Huston Dossier Positif-Rivages*. Paris: Éditions Rivages, 1988.

Ross, Lillian. *Picture*. New York: Avon Books, 1969. First published 1952.

Rubin, Martin. "Heroic, Antiheroic, Aheroic: John Huston and the Problematical Protagonist." In Studlar and Desser, *Reflections in a Male Eye*.

Sarris, Andrew. *The American Cinema*. New York: Penguin Books, 1968. The essay on Huston is reprinted in Cooper, *Perspectives on John Huston*.

Schatz, Thomas. *Hollywood Genres: Formulas, Filmmaking, and the Studio System*. Philadelphia: Temple University Press, 1981.

Sherman, Eric. *Directing the Film: Film Directors on Their Art*. Boston and Toronto: Little, Brown, 1976.

Studlar, Gaylyn. "*Fat City* and the Malaise of Masculinity." In Studlar and Desser, *Reflections in a Male Eye*.

Studlar, Gaylyn, and David Desser, eds. *Reflections in a Male Eye: John Huston and the American Experience*. Washington and London: Smithsonian Institution Press, 1993.

Walker, Janet, and Diane Waldman. "John Huston's *Freud* and Textual Repression: A Psychoanalytic Feminist Reading." In Peter Lehman, ed., *Close Viewings: An Anthology of New Film Criticism*. Tallahassee: Florida State University Press, 1990.

Wexman, Virginia Wright. "Kinesics and Film Acting: Humphrey Bogart in *The Maltese Falcon* and *The Big Sleep*." *Journal of Popular Film and Television*, vol. 7 (1978).

Yacowar, Maurice. *Tennessee Williams and Film*. New York: Frederick Ungar, 1977.

Index